Royal College of Physicians, Edingb.

Historical Sketch and Laws

Of the Royal College of Physicians of Edinburgh from Its Institution to August 1891 -

Vol. 2

Royal College of Physicians, Edingb.

Historical Sketch and Laws
Of the Royal College of Physicians of Edinburgh from Its Institution to August 1891 - Vol. 2

ISBN/EAN: 9783337163129

Printed in Europe, USA, Canada, Australia, Japan

Cover: Foto ©Andreas Hilbeck / pixelio.de

More available books at **www.hansebooks.com**

HISTORICAL SKETCH

AND

LAWS

OF THE

ROYAL COLLEGE OF PHYSICIANS.

HISTORICAL SKETCH

AND

LAWS

OF THE

ROYAL COLLEGE OF PHYSICIANS

OF

EDINBURGH,

FROM ITS INSTITUTION TO AUGUST 1891.

EDINBURGH:

PRINTED FOR THE ROYAL COLLEGE OF PHYSICIANS.

1891.

MORRISON AND GIBB, PRINTERS, EDINBURGH.

CONTENTS.

LIST

OF

The Fellows of the Royal College of Physicians

AT EDINBURGH,

FROM THE FIRST ERECTION OF THE COLLEGE, ON THE 29th NOVEMBER 1681.

— ◆◆◆ —

LIST OF THOSE IN THE ORIGINAL PATENT.

DAVID HAY.	ALEXANDER CRANSTONE.
THOMAS BURNET.	JOHN HUTTON.
MATTHEW BRISBAINE.	JOHN M'GILL.
ARCHIBALD STEVENSONE.	JOHN LERMONTH.
ROBERT SIBBALD.	WILLIAM STEVENSONE.
JAMES LIVINGSTONE.	JAMES HALKET.
ANDREW BALFOURE.	WILLIAM WRIGHT.
ROBERT CRAWFURD.	PATRICK HALYBURTON.
ROBERT TROTTER.	WILLIAM LAUDER.
MATTHEW SINCLARE.	ARCHIBALD PITCAIRNE.
JAMES STEWART.	

LIST OF FELLOWS ADMITTED.

Names of Fellows.	Dates of their Diplomas.	Places where they received their Degrees.	Dates of their Licences to Practise.	Dates of their admission as Fellows.
PETER KELLO . . .	....	..	....	Dec. 11, 1682
JOHN ABERNETHY . .	June 9, 1683	Orange	Aug. 12, 1684	Dec. 4, 1684

From this to the year 1693, the Record is wanting; but, from subsequent sederunts, it appears that during this period there were admitted—

WILLIAM STEVENSON.
WILLIAM ECCLES.
WILLIAM DOUGLAS.
THOMAS SPENCE.
ROBERT HAY.

List of Fellows.

Names of Fellows.	Dates of their Diplomas.	Places where they received their Degrees.	Dates of their Licences to Practise.	Dates of their admission as Fellows.
CHARLES OLIPHANT	....	....	May 15, 1693	Nov. 9, 1693
ANDREW MELVILLE	1683	{ Caen, in } { Normandy, }	July 5, 1694	July 5, 1694
JOSEPH DALRYMPLE	....	....	....	July 30, 1694
JAMES ROBERTSON	....	....	....	Sept. 27, 1694
DAVID DICKSON	Feb. 21, 1690	Harderwick	Oct. 8, 1694	Oct. 8, 1694
GEORGE STIRLING	....	....	Oct. 16, 1694	Oct. 16, 1694
JOHN SMELLOME	....	....	Oct. 23, 1694	Oct. 23, 1694
GEORGE HEPBURN	....	....	Nov. 15, 1694	Nov. 15, 1694
ROBERT CARMICHAEL	July 1, 1694	Leyden	Dec. 3, 1694	Dec. 3, 1694
DAVID MITCHELL	....	....	....	Sept. 14, 1695
Sir EDWARD EIZAT	....	....	....	Sept. 14, 1695
WILL. BLACKADDER	....	....	....	Sept. 16, 1695
GILBERT RULE	....	....	....	Oct. 2, 1695
ADAM FREER	....	Leyden	Oct. 7, 1695	Oct. 7, 1695
ALEXANDER DUNDAS	....	....	Nov. 4, 1695	Nov. 4, 1695
JAMES FORREST	June 12, 1691	Leyden	Nov. 20, 1696	Nov. 20, 1696
WILLIAM JARDINE	March 25, 1697	Harderwick	April 27, 1698	April 28, 1698
JOHN HAY	Jan. 21, 1701	Aberdeen	Nov. 16, 1702	Nov. 19, 1702
JOHN RIDDELL	....	....	Nov. 26, 1702	Nov. 26, 1702
JOHN ST. CLAIR	....	....	Nov. 26, 1702	Nov. 26, 1702
JOHN MONRO	....	Aberdeen	Jan. 7, 1704	Jan. 7, 1704
JOHN DRUMMOND	....	Aberdeen	Jan. 7, 1704	Jan. 7, 1704
JAMES LUITFOOT	....	Orange	Feb. 9, 1704	Feb. 9, 1704
WILLIAM LERMONT	....	Rheims	Feb. 9, 1704	Feb. 9, 1704
WILLIAM STEWART	July 24, 1704	St. Andrews	July 28, 1704	Aug. 15, 1704
FRANCIS PRINGLE	July 14, 1702	Leyden	Nov. 21, 1704	Dec. 1, 1704
CHARLES PRESTON	....	....	Nov. 21, 1704	Dec. 1, 1704
GEORGE MACKENZIE	....	....	Nov. 21, 1704	Dec. 1, 1704
DAVID COCKBURN	May 14, 1705	Edinburgh	June 29, 1705	Aug. 30, 1705
JAMES BROWN	April 12, 1704	Rheims	Feb. 25, 1706	Aug. 12, 1707
WILL. ALEXANDER	July 23, 1699	Rheims	June 18, 1706	Aug. 12, 1707
PATRICK SINCLAIR	Oct. 24, 1703	Utrecht	Nov. 14, 1706	Aug. 12, 1707
THOMAS YOUNG	June 18, 1694	Utrecht	Sept. 23, 1707	Dec. 12, 1707
ROBERT LOWIS	Oct. 29, 1707	Leyden	Sept. 7, 1708	Nov. 9, 1708
JAMES CRAWFORD	July 6, 1707	Leyden	Dec. 12, 1710	Feb. 13, 1711
NIC. MONTGOMERIE	July 30, 1708	Rheims	Dec. 29, 1709	Aug. 5, 1712
JOHN MENZIES	July 8, 1709	Utrecht	May 6, 1712	Dec. 10, 1712
WILLIAM ARTHUR	March 12, 1707	Utrecht	Feb. 9, 1714	June 1, 1714
GEORGE PATULLO	April 23, 1710	Rheims	March 23, 1714	June 15, 1714
JOHN CLERK	July 5, 1711	St. Andrews	June 15, 1714	Dec. 14, 1714
WILLIAM HAMILTON	Aug. 15, 1711	Harderwick	June 15, 1714	Dec. 14, 1714
WILLIAM COCHRAN	Aug. 4, 1712	Rheims	Jan. 7, 1715	Aug. 2, 1715
ROBERT THOMSON	July 15, 1713	Rheims	June 5, 1716	Aug. 1, 1716
JOHN BURNET	Aug. 7, 1719	Edinburgh	Aug. 10, 1719	Aug. 10, 1719
JAMES ECCLES	Nov. 10, 1718	Edinburgh	March 24, 1719	Sept. 29, 1719
JOHN LERMONT	Sept. 17, 1713	Rheims	Nov. 10, 1719	Nov. 1, 1720
JOHN MARSHALL	Oct. 22, 1719	Aberdeen	March 21, 1721	Aug. 1, 1721

Names of Fellows.	*Dates of their Diplomas.*	*Places where they received their Degrees.*	*Dates of their Licences to Practise.*	*Dates of their Admission as Fellows.*
CHARLES ALSTON	Dec. 2, 1719	Glasgow	April 13, 1721	Aug. 1, 1721
WILL. PORTERFIELD	Aug. 24, 1717	Rheims	June 8, 1721	Nov. 14, 1721
DAVID KINNEIR	June 12, 1714	St. Andrews	Aug. 23, 1723	Feb. 4, 1724
GEORGE OSWALD	Aug. 11, 1696 / Nov. 16, 1723	Rheims / Edinburgh	Nov. 21, 1723	Feb. 4, 1724
JOHN RUTHERFORD	July 21, 1719	Rheims	March 24, 1724	Nov. 3, 1724
ANDREW SINCLAIR	July 10, 1720	Angers	Feb. 25, 1724	Nov. 3, 1724
ANDREW PLUMBER	July 23, 1722	Leyden	Feb. 25, 1724	Nov. 3, 1724
JOHN INNES	Nov. 21, 1722	Padua	March 24, 1724	Nov. 3, 1724
ALEXANDER SCOTT	July 22, 1713 / Oct. 2, 1724	Rheims / St. Andrews	Feb. 9, 1725	Feb. 9, 1725
JAMES DUNDAS	Aug. 22, 1722	Rheims	March 2, 1725	Nov. 2, 1725
SIR ALEX. DICK	Aug. 31, 1725 / Jan. 23, 1727	Leyden / St. Andrews	Feb. 7, 1727	Nov. 7, 1727
JOHN STEVENSON	Jan. 1710	Harderwick	May 6, 1729	Aug. 5, 1729
JOHN TAYLOR	March 21, 1727 / July 4, 1727	Glasgow / St. Andrews	Aug. 5, 1729	Aug. 4, 1730
CHARLES NISBET	Oct. 2, 1733	St. Andrews	Jan. 3, 1734	Feb. 4, 1735
JOHN PRINGLE	July 20, 1739	Leyden	Aug. 27, 1734	Feb. 4, 1735
DAVID FOULIS	Oct. 10, 1735	Rheims	Jan. 18, 1737	Aug. 2, 1737
JAMES BAIRD	Aug. 21, 1733 / June 3, 1737	Rheims / St. Andrews	June 21, 1737	May 2, 1738
ROBERT WHYTT	April 2, 1736 / Oct. 31, 1737	Rheims / St. Andrews	Dec. 13, 1737	Nov. 7, 1738
BERNARD ALLAN	May 11, 1742	St. Andrews	Nov. 2, 1742	Nov. 2, 1742
ADAM MURRAY	Dec. 19, 1726	St. Andrews	Aug. 13, 1743	Aug. 13, 1743
SIR STUART THREIPLAND	Aug. 9, 1742	Edinburgh	May 3, 1743	Feb. 7, 1744
JOHN COCHRANE	May 5, 1744	St. Andrews	May 15, 1744	May 15, 1744
ALEX. CAMPBELL	April 30, 1746	St. Andrews	May 6, 1746	May 6, 1746
THOMAS LIDDERDALE	Oct. 20, 1747	St. Andrews	Feb. 2, 1748	Feb. 2, 1748
JOHN BOSWELL	Nov. 1, 1736	Leyden	Sept. 13, 1737	Aug. 2, 1748
DAVID CLERK	Aug. 15, 1746	Edinburgh	Nov. 1, 1748	Nov. 7, 1749
JOHN STEUART	March 12, 1740	Rheims	Aug. 5, 1746	May 1, 1750
JAMES LIND	May 3, 1748	Edinburgh	Aug. 2, 1748	May 1, 1750
THOMAS ELLIOT	Aug. 15, 1746	Edinburgh	Nov. 7, 1749	Feb. 5, 1751
COLIN DRUMMOND	Aug. 22, 1750	Edinburgh	Feb. 5, 1751	May 5, 1752
FRANCIS HOME	March 7, 1750	Edinburgh	May 7, 1751	Aug. 4, 1752
WILLIAM CUMMING	April 6, 1750 / July 9, 1752	Rheims / Edinburgh	Aug. 4, 1752	Aug. 4, 1752
ALEX. STEVENSON	July 12, 1749	Glasgow	Nov. 5, 1751	Feb. 6, 1753
JAMES GRIEVE	1733	Edinburgh	Feb. 6, 1753	Feb. 6, 1753
JOHN FOTHERGILL	Aug. 13, 1736	Edinburgh	Aug. 6, 1754	Aug. 6, 1754
WILLIAM CULLEN	Sept. 14, 1740	Glasgow	Feb. 3, 1756	March 5, 1756
ALEXANDER MUNRO	Jan. 1, 1756	Edinburgh	Feb. 3, 1756	March 5, 1756
PATRICK HALDANE	Aug. 3, 1758	St. Andrews	Aug. 10, 1758	Aug. 10, 1758
NORTH VIGOR	June 12, 1747	Edinburgh	Nov. 7, 1758	Nov. 7, 1758
GREGORY GRANT	May 4, 1753 / May 4, 1754	Rheims / Aberdeen	Nov. 1, 1757	Nov. 7, 1758

List of Fellows.

Names of Fellows.	Dates of their Diplomas.	Places where they received their Degrees.	Dates of their Licences to Practise.	Dates of their admission as Fellows.
ALEX. MUNRO, Jun.	Oct. 15, 1755	Edinburgh	May 2, 1738	May 1, 1759
WILLIAM BAYLIES	Dec. 18, 1758	Aberdeen	Aug. 7, 1759	Aug. 7, 1759
THOMAS GLEN	July 31, 1726 July 27, 1730	Rheims St. Andrews	Nov. 6, 1759	May 6, 1760
ROBERT RAMSAY	Dec. 10, 1757	Edinburgh	Dec. 11, 1759	May 5, 1761
EDWARD WRIGHT	June 15, 1753	Edinburgh	Feb. 5, 1760	May 5, 1761
JOHN GARDINER	Dec. 29, 1759	Edinburgh	Aug. 5, 1760	Aug. 4, 1761
JOHN HOPE	Jan. 29, 1750	Glasgow	Nov. 6, 1759	Feb. 2, 1762
ADAM AUSTIN	May 15, 1749	Glasgow	Aug. 7, 1753	Aug. 3, 1762
THOMAS YOUNG	Nov. 30, 1761	Edinburgh	Dec. 8, 1761	Nov. 2, 1762
WILLIAM BUTTER	Sept. 16, 1761	Edinburgh	Aug. 7, 1763	Nov. 1, 1763
JAMES WALKER	May 28, 1757	St. Andrews	Nov. 1, 1763	Feb. 7, 1764
JAMES GRAINGER	March 14, 1753	Edinburgh	Nov. 1, 1763	Feb. 7, 1764
THOMAS LIVINGSTONE	Dec. 1752	Aberdeen	Feb. 7, 1764	May 1, 1764
ROBERT PETRIE	May 30, 1750	Edinburgh	Feb. 7, 1764	May 1, 1764
ANDREW WILSON	June 22, 1749	Edinburgh	Aug. 7, 1764	Nov. 6, 1764
MAXWELL GARTSHORE	May 8, 1764	Edinburgh	June 12, 1764	Nov. 6, 1764
JOHN GREGORY	March 13, 1746	Aberdeen	March 5, 1765	Aug. 6, 1765
JOHN MORGAN	July 18, 1763	Edinburgh	March 5, 1765	Aug. 6, 1765
JOHN STEEDMAN	Nov. 15, 1740	Rheims	Aug. 7, 1764	Nov. 5, 1765
JAMES HAY	Nov. 8, 1758	St. Andrews	Feb. 5, 1765	Aug. 5, 1766
JOSEPH BLACK	June 11, 1754	Edinburgh	Feb. 3, 1767	May 5, 1767
ARTHUR NICOLSON	March 10, 1765	Aberdeen	May 5, 1767	Aug. 4, 1767
JAMES McKITTRICK	Sept. 12, 1766	Edinburgh	Aug. 4, 1767	Nov. 3, 1767
WILLIAM SHIPPEN, Jun.	Sept. 16, 1761	Edinburgh	Nov. 3, 1767	Feb. 2, 1768
WILL. MACFARLANE	Aug. 8, 1725 March 15, 1727	Rheims St. Andrews	Nov. 7, 1727	Dec. 12, 1768
JAMES SPENCE	Sept. 4, 1764	St. Andrews	March 30, 1769	Aug. 1, 1769
JAMES AIKMAN	July 6, 1768	Aberdeen	Feb. 7, 1769	May 1, 1770
JAMES LIND	Sept. 12, 1768	Edinburgh	Nov. 7, 1769	Nov. 6, 1770
ANDREW DUNCAN	Oct. 25, 1769	St. Andrews	May 1, 1770	May 7, 1771
GEORGE TAILOUR	Jan. 27, 1768	Glasgow	Feb. 5, 1771	May 7, 1771
MARTIN ECCLES	Aug. 21, 1753	St. Andrews	June 20, 1771	Nov. 5, 1771
WILLIAM BUCHAN	June 2, 1761	Edinburgh	Aug. 6, 1771	Nov. 3, 1772
JAMES HAMILTON	June 12, 1771	Edinburgh	Nov. 5, 1771	Nov. 3, 1772
NATHANIEL SPENS	June 4, 1773	St. Andrews	Aug. 3, 1773	July 7, 1774
ROBERT HAMILTON	May 12, 1766	St. Andrews	Nov. 3, 1773	Feb. 1, 1774
EDWARD SPRY	Jan. 4, 1759	Aberdeen	Feb. 1, 1774	May 3, 1774
JAMES HUNTER	June 2, 1747	St. Andrews	Feb. 24, 1774	July 14, 1774
ROBERT LANGLANDS	July 4, 1750	Edinburgh	May 2, 1775	May 7, 1776
DANIEL RUTHERFORD	Sept. 12, 1772	Edinburgh	Feb. 6, 1776	May 6, 1777
JAMES GREGORY	June 18, 1774	Edinburgh	Feb. 6, 1776	May 6, 1777
ARNOLD H. BEEREN-BROK	June 24, 1774	Leyden	Aug. 11, 1777	Feb. 3, 1778
MATTHEW POWELL	Aug. 27, 1773	St. Andrews	Nov. 4, 1777	Aug. 1, 1778
JAMES HAMILTON	Aug. 13, 1771	Aberdeen	Nov. 2, 1779	Feb. 1, 1780
WILLIAM WRIGHT	Oct. 25, 1761	St. Andrews	Feb. 1, 1780	May 2, 1780
THOMAS GILLESPIE	Dec. 1, 1766	Aberdeen	Nov. 2, 1779	Nov. 7, 1780

Names of Fellows.	Dates of their Diplomas.	Places where they received their Degrees.	Dates of their Licences to Practise.	Dates of their admission as Fellows.
THOMAS MEIK .	May 11, 1772	St. Andrews	Feb. 6, 1781	May 1, 1781
JOHN LIND .	Jan. 4, 1777	St. Andrews	Feb. 6, 1781	May 1, 1781
WILLIAM GRIEVE .	Sept. 10, 1770	Edinburgh	May 1, 1781	May 7, 1782
HENRY CULLEN	June 24, 1780	Edinburgh	Aug. 6, 1782	Nov. 5, 1782
JOHN ELLISON .	Nov. 30, 1782	St. Andrews	May 6, 1783	Aug. 5, 1783
ROBERT STEVENSON	June 24, 1778	Edinburgh	Aug. 5, 1783	Nov. 4, 1783
JOHN JOSEPH SUE .	Aug. 26, 1783	St. Andrews	Sept. 1, 1783	Nov. 4, 1783
JOHN MARSHALL	Aug. 26, 1783	St. Andrews	Nov. 4, 1783	Dec. 4, 1783
JAMES WOOD .	Sept. 10, 1776	Edinburgh	Feb. 3, 1784	May 4, 1784
ROBERT GRANT	Aug. 24, 1780	Aberdeen	May 4, 1784	Aug. 3, 1784
ANDW. FARQUHARSON	Oct. 27, 1784	St. Andrews	Nov. 2, 1784	Feb. 1, 1785
THOMAS KERR . .	Nov. 25, 1784	Aberdeen	Dec. 2, 1784	Feb. 1, 1785
JOHN CLARK	June 7, 1773	St. Andrews	March 23, 1785	May 3, 1785
WILL. FARQUHARSON	Sept. 28, 1778	Aberdeen	March 23, 1785	May 3, 1785
JAMES CAMPBELL .	Oct. 17, 1781	St. Andrews	Nov. 1, 1785	Feb. 7, 1786
HENRY M'LAGGAN .	Sept. 20, 1784	Glasgow	Nov. 1, 1785	Feb. 7, 1786
ROBERT FREER .	Feb. 23, 1779	Aberdeen	Feb. 7, 1786	May 2, 1786
DAVID MORTON .	Sept. 1, 1768	Aberdeen	May 2, 1786	Aug. 1, 1786
THOMAS STEVENSON	July 24, 1786	St. Andrews	Aug. 1, 1786	Nov. 7, 1786
THOMAS COCHRANE	Nov. 27, 1784	Glasgow	Nov. 7, 1786	Nov. 6, 1787
SAMUEL SPALDING .	Sept. 26, 1785	St. Andrews	May 1, 1787	Aug. 7, 1787
GEO. BACHMATIEV .	Sept. 10, 1786	Edinburgh	Aug. 7, 1787	Aug. 21, 1787
THOMAS SPENS .	Sept. 13, 1784	Edinburgh	Nov. 6, 1787	Feb. 5, 1788
JOHN DRUMMOND .	June 8, 1786	St. Andrews	Nov. 6, 1787	Feb. 5, 1788
PAT. BARON SETON	Sept. 10, 1787	Edinburgh	Nov. 6, 1787	Feb. 5, 1788
WILLIAM SPINK .	Aug. 1, 1788	St. Andrews	Aug. 5, 1788	Aug. 19, 1788
CHARLES STUART .	Sept. 10, 1781	Edinburgh	March 4, 1783	Feb. 3, 1789
ALEX. HAMILTON .	Mar. 19, 1783	St. Andrews	Feb. 5, 1788	Feb. 3, 1789
ALEX. GRANT CLUGSTON	Sept. 6, 1788	St. Andrews	Jan. 13, 1789	Feb. 3, 1789
JOHN CRAIGIE . .	Dec. 27, 1788	Aberdeen	Jan. 13, 1789	Feb. 3, 1789
CHARLES WEBSTER .	Sept. 12, 1777	Edinburgh	Feb. 1, 1780	May 5, 1783
CHARLES CONGALTON	April 4, 1771	St. Andrews	Feb. 5, 1788	May 5, 1789
THOMAS GILLIES .	July 28, 1788	Aberdeen	May 5, 1789	Aug. 3, 1789
JAMES CLARK .	Sept. 17, 1773	Aberdeen	May 5, 1789	Aug. 3, 1789
WILLIAM ROXBURGH	Jan. 12, 1790	Aberdeen	Feb. 7, 1790	Feb. 13, 1790
GEORGE WILSON .	Jan. 7, 1790	Aberdeen	Aug. 3, 1790	Nov. 3, 1790
JOHN LORIMER .	April 29, 1764	St. Andrews	May 3, 1791	Aug. 2, 1791
WIL. MONCRIEFF .	Sept. 12, 1768	Edinburgh	June 1, 1791	....
ANDREW FILLAN .	May 4, 1791	Aberdeen	June 1, 1791	Aug. 2, 1791
JAMES HOME .	Sept. 18, 1751	Edinburgh	Feb. 1, 1791	Nov. 1, 1791
JAMES CURRIE .	March 30, 1780	Glasgow	Aug. 2, 1791	....
JO. COAKLEY LETSOM	June 20, 1769	Leyden	Oct. 25, 1791	Dec. 1, 1791
NICOLAS BINDON .	Sept. 12, 1788	Edinburgh	Nov. 1, 1791	....
THOMAS ARNOLD .	Nov. 29, 1766	Edinburgh	Nov. 24, 1791	..
JOHN YULE . .	Sept. 12, 1785	Edinburgh	....	.. .
JOSEPH FOX .	Feb. 1, 1783	St. Andrews	Feb. 7, 1792	March 6, 1792
JAMES M'DONNELY .	Sept. 13, 1784	Edinburgh	....	....
JAMES HAMILTON, Jun.	Feb. 8, 1792	St. Andrews	Feb. 17, 1792	March 6, 1792

Names of Fellows.	Dates of their Diplomas.	Places where they received their Degrees.	Dates of their Licences to Practise.	Dates of their admission as Fellows.
ANDREW YOUNG . .	June 22, 1793	Aberdeen	Aug. 22, 1793	Nov. 5, 1793
JAMES M'KITTRICK ADAIR . . . }	Sept. 12, 1783	Edinburgh	Nov. 15, 1792	Dec. 5, 1793
ANGUS M'DONALD . .	Jan. 10, 1789	St. Andrews	Dec. 5, 1793	Feb. 3, 1794
ALEX. PHILIP WILSON .	June 25, 1790	Edinburgh	Feb. 3, 1794	Feb. 3, 1795
JAMES BUCHAN . . .	Sept. 12, 1792	Edinburgh	Aug. 5, 1794	Aug. 4, 1795
JAMES GASKING . .	June 10, 1789	Leyden	Oct. 27, 1795	Feb. 2, 1796
ALEX. STEWART . .	Nov. 2, 1795	St. Andrews	Dec. 2, 1795	Feb. 2, 1796
SIR WALTER FARQUHAR, BART. . . . . }	Jan. 19, 1796	Aberdeen	March 1, 1796	May 3, 1796
JO. HUTTON COOPER .	March 12, 1796	St. Andrews	March 15, 1796	. . . .
SIR ALEX. DOUGLAS, BART. . . . }	July 11, 1760	St. Andrews	May 10, 1796	May 18, 1796
THO. CHA. HOPE . .	Sept. 12, 1787	Edinburgh	Nov. 5, 1795	Nov. 1, 1796
GEORGE DICKSON . .	Aug. 8, 1796	St. Andrews	Sept. 6, 1796	Dec. 1, 1796
ANDREW DUNCAN . .	Sept. 12, 1794	Edinburgh	Nov. 1, 1796	. . . .
ANDREW KELTIE . .	. . . .	Aberdeen	. . . .	. . . .
ALEX. MONRO . . .	Sept. 12, 1797	Edinburgh	Nov. 5, 1797	Nov. 30, 1797
COLIN LAUDER . . .	July 24, 1786	St. Andrews	Nov. 30, 1797	May 1, 1798
GEO. GAVIN BROWN .	Aug. 22, 1797	St. Andrews	Dec. 6, 1798	May 7, 1799
ALEXANDER WILSON .	Dec. 17, 1796	St. Andrews	Feb. 5, 1799	. . . .
MATTHEW POOLE . .	Aug. 18, 1798	St. Andrews	Aug. 6, 1799	Nov. 5, 1799
ROBERT KENNEDY . .	Sept. 12, 1794	Edinburgh	May 7, 1799	Aug. 5, 1800
WILLIAM KENNEDY .	April 12, 1800	Aberdeen	Aug. 5, 1800	Nov. 4, 1800
THOMAS JAMIESON .	Jan. 15, 1791	Aberdeen	Dec. 5, 1799	Nov. 4, 1800
NICOLAS ROMAYNE . .	June 24, 1780	Edinburgh	Aug. 28, 1800	Nov. 4, 1800
SIR ALEX. MORISON .	Sept. 12, 1799	Edinburgh	May 6, 1800	May 11, 1801
WILLIAM WARD . . .	Sept. 12, 1800	Edinburgh	Feb. 3, 1801	May 5, 1801
JAMES ROBERTSON . .	Oct. 14, 1794	Aberdeen	March 30, 1800	May 4, 1802
DONALD SMITH . . .	May 6, 1783	St. Andrews	May 3, 1803	Aug. 2, 1803
OSWALD HUNTER . .	June 24, 1803	Edinburgh	Aug. 2, 1803	Nov. 1, 1803
WILLIAM DICK . . .	Feb. 24, 1803	Aberdeen	June 1, 1804	Nov. 6, 1804
WILLIAM FRANKLIN .	July 7, 1795	Aberdeen	Aug. 7, 1804	Nov. 6, 1804
ROBINSON FOXLEY . .	Oct. 8, 1804	St. Andrews	Feb. 5, 1805	May 7, 1805
JOHN GRAY	May 11, 1805	Aberdeen	Aug. 6, 1805	Nov. 5, 1805
SAMUEL M'DOWELL .	June 14, 1805	St. Andrews	Aug. 6, 1805	Nov. 5, 1805
THOMAS BROWN . .	Sept. 12, 1803	Edinburgh	Feb. 5, 1805	Feb. 4, 1806
ALEX. MACKENZIE . .	March 13, 1803	St. Andrews	May 6, 1806	Aug. 5, 1806
JOHN BARCLAY . . .	June 24, 1796	Edinburgh	Nov. 5, 1805	Nov. 4, 1806
WILLIAM WIGHTMAN .	June 3, 1799	St. Andrews	Aug. 5, 1806	Nov. 4, 1806
JAMES MACGREGOR .	Feb. 17, 1804	Aberdeen	Nov. 26, 1806	May 5, 1807
GEORGE ALLEY . . .	April 11, 1807	St. Andrews	Nov. 3, 1807	Feb. 2, 1808
WILLIAM GOURLAY . .	June 24, 1782	Edinburgh	Feb. 2, 1808	May 3, 1808
THOMAS GRAY . . .	April 7, 1800	Aberdeen	Aug. 2, 1808	Nov. 1, 1808
JOSHUA H. DAVIDSON .	June 24, 1807	Edinburgh	Aug. 2, 1808	Aug. 1, 1809
ALEXANDER WYLIE .	July 2, 1808	St. Andrews	Nov. 1, 1808	Nov. 7, 1809
ADAM BURT . . .	March 26, 1808	St. Andrews	Aug. 1, 1809	Nov. 7, 1809
JOHN CHEYNE . . .	June 24, 1795	Edinburgh	Feb. 22, 1810	May 1, 1810

Names of Fellows.	Dates of their Diplomas.	Places where they received their Degrees.	Dates of their Licences to Practise.	Dates of their admission as Fellows.
JAMES MUTTLEBURY .	April 21, 1810	St. Andrews	May 1, 1810	Aug. 7, 1810
JAMES PROUD JOHNSON	Sept. 23, 1805	St. Andrews	Aug. 7, 1810	Nov. 6, 1810
HENRY HARDIE .	Sept. 12, 1809	Edinburgh	Feb. 5, 1811	May 7, 1811
JAMES ANDERSON . .	Sept. 21, 1810	Aberdeen	Nov. 6, 1810	Nov. 5, 1811
DAVID DANIEL DAVIS .	May 4, 1801	Glasgow	Feb. 4, 1812	May 5, 1812
JOHN BIGSBY . .	June 2, 1810	St. Andrews	Feb. 4, 1812	May 5, 1812
WIL. ELFORD LEACH .	Jan. 18, 1812	St. Andrews	Feb. 4, 1812	May 5, 1812
WILLIAM FERGUSON .	March 21, 1812	St. Andrews	May 5, 1812	Aug. 4, 1812
WIL. PULTENEY ALISON	Sept. 12, 1811	Edinburgh	Nov. 5, 1811	Nov. 3, 1812
ALEX. MACLARTY .	Sept. 12, 1795	Edinburgh	Feb. 1, 1813	May 4, 1813
BENJAMIN BARTLET } BUCHANAN . .	Sept. 12, 1808	Edinburgh	Aug. 4, 1812	Aug. 3, 1813
JOHN WARROCH PUR- } SELL	Sept. 12, 1798	Edinburgh	March 2, 1810	Aug. 3, 1813
JOHN CLARK . . {	Aug. 5, 1806 / Aug. 1, 1821	St. Andrews } Edinburgh }	March 2, 1813	Aug. 3, 1813
WILLIAM MAXTON . .	Sept. 22, 1804	St. Andrews	Nov. 2, 1813	Feb. 1, 1814
JOHN WILLIAMSON .	Oct. 20, 1813	St. Andrews	Nov. 2, 1813	Feb. 1, 1814
SAMUEL FERGUSSON .	Nov. 6, 1813	St. Andrews	Dec. 2, 1813	May 3, 1814
ROBERT BRIGGS . .	Sept. 12, 1806	St. Andrews	Dec. 18, 1813	May 3, 1814
JOHN BOWEN . .	Oct. 9, 1809	St. Andrews	Feb. 1, 1814	May 3, 1814
BENJAMIN LARA . .	May 17, 1802	Aberdeen	Feb. 12, 1814	Aug. 2, 1814
GEORGE MAGRATH .	Aug. 3, 1805	St. Andrews	Aug. 2, 1814	Nov. 1, 1814
WILLIAM BEATTY .	Feb. 28, 1806	Aberdeen	Aug. 2, 1814	Nov. 1, 1814
HENRY DEWAR . .	June 25, 1804	Edinburgh	Feb. 1, 1814	Feb. 7, 1815
ANTHONY LINDSAY .	Dec. 16, 1814	Aberdeen	Feb. 7, 1815	May 2, 1815
JAMES MURDOCH . .	July 9, 1814	St. Andrews	Aug. 2, 1814	Aug. 1, 1815
ANDREW NICOLL .	Sept. 12, 1810	Edinburgh	May 2, 1815	Aug. 1, 1815
JOHN MURRAY . .	Oct. 17, 1814	St. Andrews	Nov. 1, 1814	Nov. 7, 1815
GEORGE DRYSDALE .	June 1, 1815	St. Andrews	July 15, 1815	Nov. 7, 1815
HEN. EVANS HOLDER .	Aug. 24, 1801	St. Andrews	Nov. 7, 1815	Feb. 6, 1810
WILLIAM PYM . . .	April 2, 1799	St. Andrews	Feb. 6, 1816	May 7, 1816
DAVID AIRD . .	Sept. 12, 1805	Edinburgh	Feb. 6, 1816	May 7, 1816
ISAAC WILSON . .	Dec. 23, 1796	St. Andrews	May 7, 1816	Aug. 6, 1816
DAVID JAMES HAMIL- } TON DICKSON . .	Aug. 18, 1806	Aberdeen	May 7, 1816	Aug. 6, 1816
ROBERT JOHN HUME .	Jan. 12, 1816	St. Andrews	Aug. 6, 1816	Nov. 5, 1816
JAMES CLARK . . .	Feb. 7, 1817	Aberdeen	Feb. 25, 1817	Aug. 5, 1817
WALTER OGILVIE . .	April 14, 1817	St. Andrews	May 6, 1817	Aug. 5, 1817
WILLIAM WYNNE .	Dec. 7, 1816	St. Andrews	May 6, 1817	Aug. 5, 1817
JOHN RAMSAY . .	Sept. 12, 1810	Edinburgh	May 16, 1817	Nov. 4, 1817
PAT. CAMPBELL BAIRD .	March 7, 1818	St. Andrews	May 5, 1818	Aug. 4, 1818
WILL. MONCRIEFF .	June 24, 1814	Edinburgh	Nov. 4, 1817	Nov. 3, 1818
SAMUEL SPROULE . .	July 4, 1818	St. Andrews	Aug. 4, 1818	Nov. 3, 1818
WM. PRESTON LAUDER	March 4, 1809	St. Andrews	May 5, 1818	May 4, 1819
ANDREW KENNEY . .	June 24, 1812	Edinburgh	May 5, 1818	May 4, 1819
JAMES THOS. BROWN } WATT	June 24, 1809	Edinburgh	Dec. 19, 1818	May 4, 1819

Names of Fellows.	Dates of their Diplomas.	Places where they received their Degrees.	Dates of their Licenses to Practice.	Dates of their admission as Fellows.
WALTER ADAM . . .	Aug. 1, 1816	Edinburgh	Nov. 3, 1818	Nov. 2, 1819
AUGUSTUS WEST . .	Dec. 5, 1818	St. Andrews	Aug. 5, 1819	Nov. 2, 1819
EDWARD TURNER . .	Aug. 2, 1819	Edinburgh	Aug. 3, 1819	Nov. 2, 1819
ALEX KENNEDY . .	Jan. 30, 1819	Aberdeen	March 3, 1819	May 2, 1820
JAMES MILLAR . .	June 24, 1795	Edinburgh	May 4, 1819	May 2, 1820
STEPH. MACMULLEN .	Jan. 7, 1815	St. Andrews	Feb. 1, 1820	May 2, 1820
JAMES GILLIES . .	May 13, 1816	Aberdeen	Feb. 1, 1820	May 2, 1820
Sir JAS. RO. GRANT .	June 20, 1814	Aberdeen	May 2, 1820	Aug. 1, 1820
EBENEZER GAIRDNER .	Aug. 2, 1819	Edinburgh	Aug. 1, 1820	Nov. 7, 1820
ROBERT GRAHAM . .	Sept. 12, 1808	Edinburgh	Feb. 1, 1820	Feb. 6, 1821
JAMES GEORGE PLAY-FAIR . . . }	Aug. 2, 1819	Edinburgh	Feb. 1, 1820	May 1, 1821
JOHN BUTTER . .	Aug. 1, 1820	Edinburgh	Aug. 7, 1821	Nov. 6, 1821
WILLIAM ARNOLD . .	Oct. 4, 1821	Aberdeen	Nov. 6, 1821	Feb. 5, 1822
DAVID CAMPBELL . .	Jan. 18, 1771	Leyden	Aug. 6, 1822	Nov. 5, 1822
ROBERT RENTON . .	June 24, 1814	Edinburgh	Feb. 5, 1822	Feb. 4, 1823
Sir R. CHRISTISON, Bart.	Aug. 2, 1819	Edinburgh	Feb. 5, 1822	Feb. 4, 1823
THOMAS KIDD . .	May 10, 1819	Aberdeen	Aug. 6, 1822	Feb. 4, 1823
JOHN ABERCROMBIE .	June 4, 1803	Edinburgh	Aug. 6, 1822	Aug. 4, 1823
ROBERT GROAT. . .	Sept. 12, 1783	Edinburgh	Nov. 5, 1822	Nov. 4, 1823
G. AUGUSTUS BORTH-WICK . . . }	June 24, 1808	Edinburgh	Feb. 4, 1823	Feb. 3, 1824
ROBERT CARNEGY . .	Aug. 1, 1817	Edinburgh	Feb. 4, 1823	Feb. 3, 1824
JOHN YOUNG . .	April 10, 1803	Glasgow	May 6, 1823	May 4, 1824
THOMAS MAGRATH .	June 3, 1809	St. Andrews	May 4, 1824	Aug. 3, 1824
WILLIAM BEILBY .	Aug. 1, 1816	Edinburgh	Aug. 4, 1823	Nov. 2, 1824
EDWARD MILLIGAN .	Aug. 1, 1815	Edinburgh	Nov. 4, 1823	Nov. 2, 1824
JOHN MACWHIRTER .	Jan. 6, 1816	St. Andrews	Nov. 4, 1823	Nov. 2, 1824
THOMAS SHORTT .	Aug. 1, 1815	Edinburgh	Feb. 3, 1824	Feb. 1, 1825
JAMES WOOD .	Sept. 12, 1809	Edinburgh	May 4, 1824	May 3, 1825
ALEXANDER BOYLE .	Aug. 28, 1812	Aberdeen	Feb. 1, 1825	May 3, 1825
JOHN MURRAY . .	Feb. 5, 1825	Aberdeen	May 3, 1825	Aug. 2, 1825
RICHARD POOLE .	Feb. 16, 1805	St. Andrews	Nov. 2, 1824	Nov. 1, 1825
ROBERT GRANT .	June 24, 1814	Edinburgh	Dec. 28, 1825	Feb. 6, 1827
RICHARD HAWLEY .	June 24, 1807	Edinburgh	Feb. 7, 1826	Feb. 6, 1827
JAMES MELLIS . .	Jan. 4, 1806	Aberdeen	Nov. 7, 1826	Feb. 6, 1827
Sir ANDW. HALLIDAY .	June 24, 1806	Edinburgh	Nov. 4, 1817	Aug. 7, 1827
JAMES MACDONALD .	May 21, 1806	St. Andrews	Feb. 5, 1828	May 6, 1828
JOHN THATCHER .	June 24, 1806	Edinburgh	May 7, 1815	May 6, 1828
JAMES CRAWFURD GREGORY . . }	Aug. 2, 1824	Edinburgh	Nov. 6, 1827	June 24, 1828
PETER RAMSAY .	March 3, 1817	St. Andrews	June 24, 1828	Nov. 4, 1828
WILLIAM GREGORY .	July 10, 1828	Edinburgh	Aug. 5, 1828	Aug. 4, 1829
EDWARD DUFFIN ALLI-SON . . . }	Aug. 20, 1827	Aberdeen	Jan. 13, 1829	Feb. 2, 1830
JOHN THOMSON .	Jan. 11, 1808	Aberdeen	Feb. 7, 1815	Aug. 3, 1830
JOHN PRICE .	July 3, 1821	Aberdeen	. . . .	Aug. 3, 1830
ROBERT LEWINS .	June 24, 1823	Edinburgh	Nov. 3, 1829	Nov. 2, 1830

Names of Fellows.	Dates of their Diplomas.	Places where they received their Degrees.	Dates of their admission as Fellows.
DAVID BOSWELL REID	July 12, 1830	Edinburgh	Aug. 2, 1831
JOHN MACKENZIE	Aug. 2, 1824	Edinburgh	Nov. 1, 1831
MONTGOMERY ROBERTSON	Oct. 16, 1829	Aberdeen	Feb. 7, 1832
ANDREW COMBE	Aug. 1, 1825	Edinburgh	May 1, 1832
JOHN HUME PEEBLES	Sept. 30, 1828	Pisa	Aug. 7, 1832
DAVID CRAIGIE	Aug. 1, 1816	Edinburgh	Aug. 7, 1832
PETER FAIRBAIRN	Aug. 2, 1819	Edinburgh	Feb. 5, 1833
THOS. STEWART TRAILL	Sept. 13, 1802	Edinburgh	May 7, 1833
ALEX. GEORGE HOME	Aug. 1, 1823	Edinburgh	May 7, 1833
JACOB D. HUNTER	July 12, 1831	Edinburgh	May 7, 1833
PATRICK CHARLES	July 12, 1828	Edinburgh	Aug. 6, 1833
WILLIAM GLOVER	Aug. 17, 1818	St. Andrews	Aug. 6, 1833
WILLIAM THOMSON	April 1, 1831	Aberdeen	Oct. 12, 1833
JOHN WILSON ANDERSON	Aug. 1, 1820	Edinburgh	Oct. 12, 1833
JOHN SMITH	Aug. 1, 1823	Edinburgh	Oct. 12, 1833
JAMES PATTERSON	July 12, 1832	Edinburgh	Feb. 4, 1834
J. D. MORRIES STIRLING	July 12, 1831	Edinburgh	Feb. 4, 1834
ROBERT SPITTAL	March 11, 1832	Giessen	May 6, 1834
JAMES BURNES	Aug. 7, 1824	St. Andrews	Sept. 23, 1834
CHARLES RANSFORD	July 12, 1833	Edinburgh	Feb. 3, 1835
RALPH RICHARDSON	Aug. 1, 1834	Edinburgh	Feb. 3, 1835
ARCHIBALD ROBERTSON	Aug. 1, 1817	Edinburgh	Aug. 4, 1835
THOS. B. HARNESS	April 28, 1835	St. Andrews	Nov. 3, 1835
WILLIAM MACDONALD	Aug. 1, 1818	Edinburgh	Feb. 2, 1836
SAMUEL HOBART	Aug. 30, 1835	Erlangen	Feb. 2, 1836
JOHN TILSTONE	Aug. 24, 1835	Heidelberg	Aug. 2, 1836
WILLIAM SELLER	Aug. 1, 1821	Edinburgh	Oct. 4, 1836
JOHN REID	July 12, 1830	Edinburgh	Oct. 4, 1836
Sir JAMES Y. SIMPSON, Bart.	July 12, 1832	Edinburgh	Oct. 4, 1836
HENRY ATKINSON	Aug. 1, 1835	Erlangen	Oct. 4, 1836
WILLIAM REID	Aug. 2, 1824	Edinburgh	Feb. 7, 1837
JOHN SPENS	Aug. 1, 1835	Edinburgh	Feb. 7, 1837
Sir JAMES COX	Aug. 1, 1835	Edinburgh	Feb. 7, 1837
CHARLES BELL	April 27, 1836	Glasgow	Feb. 7, 1837
EDMUND B. LOCKYER	July 8, 1836	Jena	Feb. 7, 1837
MARTIN BARRY	July 12, 1833	Edinburgh	July 15, 1837
JOHN MOIR	July 12, 1828	Edinburgh	July 15, 1837
GEORGE PATERSON	July 12, 1833	Edinburgh	July 15, 1837
PATRICK ROLLAND	May 28, 1837	Keil	July 15, 1837
JOHN HOME	July 13, 1829	Edinburgh	Feb. 6, 1838
WILLIAM HENDERSON	July 12, 1831	Edinburgh	Feb. 6, 1838
JAMES MARR	Dec. 6, 1837	St. Andrews	Feb. 6, 1838
JOHN MACNAUGHT	April 7, 1815	Aberdeen	Feb. 6, 1838
JAS. LYNCH O'CONNER	Nov. 24, 1820	Aberdeen	May 1, 1838
JNO. T. INGLEBY	May 28, 1838	Heidelberg	Nov. 6, 1838
ROB. GEO. HOLLAND	June 12, 1838	Erlangen	Nov. 6, 1838
JNO. WARD DOWSLEY	Feb. 11, 1826	St. Andrews	Nov. 6, 1838
JOHN MILLER	June 24, 1805	Edinburgh	Feb. 5, 1839

Names of Fellows.		Dates of their Diplomas.	Places where they received their Degrees.	Dates of their admission as Fellows.
ANDREW HENDERSON	. . .	Aug. 1, 1823	Edinburgh	Feb. 5, 1839
J. STEVENSON BUSHNAN	. . .	May 14, 1836	Heidelberg	Feb. 5, 1839
RALPH F. AINSWORTH	. . .	March 13, 1836	Berlin	Feb. 5, 1839
JAMES STARK	. . .	July 12, 1833	Edinburgh	May 7, 1839
THOMAS RADFORD	. . .	April 4, 1839	Heidelberg	Aug. 6, 1839
KEITH IMRAY	. . .	June 28, 1836	Pisa	Feb. 4, 1840
JAMES ANDREW	. . .	July 2, 1839	Cambridge	May 5, 1840
ROB. BOWES MALCOLM	. . .	July 12, 1831	Edinburgh	Aug. 4, 1840
GEORGE LUND	. . .	Aug. 1, 1837	Edinburgh	Aug. 4, 1840
EVAN P. CAMERON	. . .	....	....	Aug. 4, 1840
THOMAS R. COLLEDGE	. . .	Dec. 16, 1839	Aberdeen	Aug. 4, 1840
ALEXANDER WOOD	. . .	Aug. 1, 1839	Edinburgh	Nov. 3, 1840
JOHN WILLET	. . .	May 5, 1840	St. Andrews	Nov. 3, 1840
Sir JNO. ROSE CORMACK	. . .	Aug. 1, 1837	Edinburgh	Feb. 2, 1841
GEORGE HULL	. . .	June 6, 1825	St. Andrews	Feb. 2, 1841
HENRY HAWKINS	. . .	March 16, 1838	Erlangen	Aug. 3, 1841
HENRY LONSDALE	. . .	Aug. 1, 1838	Edinburgh	Aug. 3, 1841
JNO. HUGHES BENNETT	. . .	Aug. 1, 1837	Edinburgh	Sept. 30, 1842
DONALD MACFARLANE	. . .	Aug. 1, 1836	Edinburgh	Nov. 1, 1842
WILLIAM ROBERTSON	. . .	Aug. 1, 1839	Edinburgh	Feb. 7, 1843
AN. HALLIDAY DOUGLAS	. . .	Aug. 1, 1840	Edinburgh	Feb. 7, 1843
JOHN G. MACDONALD BURT	. . .	Nov. 9, 1836	Giessen	May 2, 1843
WILLIAM HALL RYOTT	. . .	Jan. 10, 1842	Erlangen	May 2, 1843
WILLIAM MACLEOD	. . .	May 2, 1843	St. Andrews	Aug. 1, 1843
ALEXANDER JACKSON	. . .	Aug. 1, 1838	Edinburgh	Nov. 7, 1843
THEODORE F. WOOD	. . .	Aug. 1, 1843	Edinburgh	Nov. 7, 1843
JOHN BEEVOR	. . .	Aug. 3, 1841	St. Andrews	Feb. 6, 1844
WILLIAM HUTCHESON	. . .	Aug. 1, 1839	Edinburgh	Feb. 6, 1844
W. M. ADAMS	. . .	Aug. 9, 1843	Giessen	Nov. 5, 1844
JOHN SCOTT	. . .	Aug. 1, 1820	Edinburgh	Feb. 4, 1845
EDWARD GREENHOW	. . .	Sept. 24, 1835	Erlangen	Feb. 4, 1845
JOHN COLDSTREAM	. . .	Aug. 1, 1827	Edinburgh	Feb. 4, 1845
ARCHIBALD MAKELLAR	. . .	April 25, 1832	Glasgow	Feb. 4, 1845
ROBERT PATERSON	. . .	Aug. 1, 1836	Edinburgh	Feb. 4, 1845
GEORGE S. KEITH	. . .	Aug. 1, 1841	Edinburgh	Feb. 4, 1845
WILLIAM BOWIE	. . .	Sept. 12, 1812	Edinburgh	May 6, 1845
NEVILLE WOOD	. . .	Aug. 1, 1844	Edinburgh	May 6, 1845
ALEXANDER PEDDIE	. . .	Aug. 1, 1835	Edinburgh	May 27, 1845
BEN. NORTH ARNOLD	. . .	April 6, 1840	Giessen	May 27, 1845
THOMAS SMITH MACCALL	. . .	April 24, 1838	St. Andrews	May 27, 1845
THOMAS HUGHES	. . .	Aug. 1, 1825	Edinburgh	Aug. 5, 1845
WILLIAM MACKINNON	. . .	Aug. 1, 1836	Edinburgh	Aug. 5, 1845
THOMAS HEAD	. . .	May 6, 1845	St. Andrews	Aug. 5, 1845
WILLIAM SCOTT	. . .	May 6, 1845	St. Andrews	Aug. 5, 1845
SAMUEL D. LEES	. . .	Aug. 1, 1837	Edinburgh	Nov. 4, 1845
ALEXANDER SMITH	. . .	Jan. 28, 1826	Aberdeen	Nov. 4, 1845
JOHN G. HARRISON	. . .	June 6, 1842	Giessen	Nov. 4, 1845
BENJAMIN ROBINSON	. . .	May 7, 1839	St. Andrews	Nov. 4, 1845

Names of Fellows.	Dates of their Diplomas.	Places where they received their Degrees.	Dates of their admission as Fellows.
CHARLES CHADWICK . . .	Aug. 1, 1837	Edinburgh	Nov. 20, 1845
J. CALTHROP WILLIAMS . .	Aug. 2, 1824	Edinburgh	Nov. 20, 1845
ROBERT BRENT	July 1, 1845	St. Andrews	Aug. 4, 1846
WILLIAM HENRY LOWE . .	Aug. 1, 1840	Edinburgh	Nov. 4, 1846
ALFRED CRABB	May 5, 1846	St. Andrews	Nov. 7, 1846
JOHN FERGUSON	June 1, 1815	Edinburgh	Feb. 2, 1847
JOHN SCOTT	Aug. 1, 1819	Edinburgh	Feb. 2, 1847
JAMES BEGBIE	Aug. 2, 1821	Edinburgh	Feb. 2, 1847
JOHN TAYLOR	July 12, 1830	Edinburgh	Feb. 2, 1847
THOMAS GRAHAM WEIR . .	Aug. 2, 1835	Edinburgh	Feb. 2, 1847
THOMAS STRETHILL WRIGHT	Aug. 1, 1845	Edinburgh	May 4, 1847
JOHN BROWN	July 12, 1833	Edinburgh	Aug. 3, 1847
EDWARD MACKAY . . .	Sept. 25, 1844	Giessen	Nov. 2, 1847
NATH. AYLAN TRAVIS . .	Aug. 1, 1825	Edinburgh	Dec. 2, 1847
DAVID MACLAGAN . . .	Sept. 12, 1805	Edinburgh	Feb. 1, 1848
FRED. BELL HUNT . . .	May 6, 1845	St. Andrews	Feb. 1, 1848
JAMES YORK	Dec. 15, 1832	Erlangen	May 1, 1848
JOHN CHARLES HALL . .	June 27, 1840	Erlangen	May 1, 1848
CHAS. RADCLYFFE HALL . .	Feb. 16, 1848	Erlangen	Aug. 1, 1848
EDWARD WATERS . . .	Aug. 2, 1847	Edinburgh	Aug. 1, 1848
ALEXANDER KEILLER . .	Aug. 4, 1835	St. Andrews	April 5, 1849
C. LOCKT. ROBERTSON . .	May 5, 1845	St. Andrews	May 1, 1849
THOS. HILL PATTISON . .	July 12, 1831	Edinburgh	Nov. 6, 1849
JNO. YOUNG MYRTLE . .	July 12, 1833	Edinburgh	Nov. 6, 1849
SAMUEL SOMERVILLE . .	Aug. 1, 1836	Edinburgh	Nov. 6, 1849
WILLIAM CUMMING . .	Aug. 6, 1839	St. Andrews	Nov. 6, 1849
FORBES BENJ. WINSLOW . .	April 13, 1849	Aberdeen	Feb. 5, 1850
WM. TENNANT GAIRDNER .	Aug. 1, 1845	Edinburgh	May 7, 1850
WM. CHARLES WOOD . .	May 5, 1846	St. Andrews	May 7, 1850
ALEX. A. RENTON . . .	Aug. 1, 1849	Edinburgh	Feb. 4, 1851
JAMES MATT. DUNCAN . . .	Oct. 16, 1846	Aberdeen	May 6, 1851
PETER NIDDRIE	April 29, 1835	Glasgow	Dec. 4, 1851
J. WARBURTON BEGBIE . .	Aug. 2, 1847	Edinburgh	Feb. 3, 1852
AWLY P. BARRON . . .	Dec. 31, 1851	St. Andrews	May 4, 1852
THOS. ALEX. WISE . . .	Aug. 2, 1824	Edinburgh	Aug. 3, 1852
DANIEL RUTHERFORD HALDANE	Aug. 1, 1848	Edinburgh	Aug. 3, 1852
THOMAS T. WINGETT . .	Aug. 4, 1846	St. Andrews	May 3, 1853
W. R. SANDERS	Aug. 1, 1849	Edinburgh	May 3, 1853
HENRY C. GURNEY . . .	July 2, 1845	Pisa	Nov. 1, 1853
ALEXR. ZIEGLER . . .	May 6, 1845	St. Andrews	Nov. 1, 1853
JOHN SCOTT	Aug. 1, 1836	Edinburgh	Feb. 7, 1854
JOHN H. WALKER . . .	Oct. 1853	Aberdeen	March 2, 1854
COURTLAND S. SHAW . .	Oct. 1853	Aberdeen	May 2, 1854
CHARLES WILSON . . .	Aug. 1, 1827	Edinburgh	Feb. 6, 1855
JAMES ALLAN	Aug. 1, 1838	Edinburgh	Feb. 6, 1855
THOMAS GIBSON . . .	April 25, 1827	Glasgow	May 1, 1855
WILLIAM J. MARTIN . . .	April 24, 1855	St. Andrews	May 15, 1855
THOMAS PRITCHARD . . .	April 24, 1844	Glasgow	July 10, 1855

Names of Fellows.	Dates of their Diplomas.	Places where they received their Degrees.	Dates of their admission as Fellows.
JOHN S. STEEL	April 7, 1854	Aberdeen	Dec. 5, 1855
THOMAS LAYCOCK	July 19, 1839	Göttingen	Feb. 5, 1856
GEORGE SAMPSON	Aug. 3, 1855	Aberdeen	Aug. 5, 1856
FREDERICK COLLINS	Aug. 6, 1851	Aberdeen	Aug. 5, 1856
WILLIAM E. TAYLOR	May 6, 1845	St. Andrews	Nov. 4, 1856
WILLIAM KINGSLEY	July 1, 1845	St. Andrews	Feb. 3, 1857
ARCHD. W. P. PINKERTON	Aug. 1, 1350	Edinburgh	Aug. 4, 1857
JOSEPH MARCUS JOSEPH	April 28, 1852	Glasgow	Aug. 4, 1857
CHARLES COATES	Oct. 1856	Aberdeen	Aug. 4, 1857
FREDERICK JOHN BIRD	May 4, 1841	St. Andrews	Feb. 2, 1858
JAMES GEO. ATKINSON	Aug. 2, 1841	Edinburgh	Feb. 9, 1858
JAMES GAMMELL STEWART	Aug. 1, 1846	Edinburgh	Feb. 9, 1858
DONALD C. CAMPBELL	April 24, 1844	Glasgow	May 4, 1858
WILLIAM FINLAY	May 6, 1845	St. Andrews	May 18, 1858
JOSEPH SEATON	May 6, 1845	St. Andrews	May 13, 1858
T. HARRINGTON TUKE	Aug. 2, 1849	St. Andrews	Aug. 26, 1858
GEORGE ALTHAM	Sept. 27, 1842	Paris	Aug. 26, 1858
GEORGE HARLEY	July 30, 1850	Edinburgh	Aug. 26, 1858
W. OVEREND PRIESTLEY	Aug. 1, 1853	Edinburgh	Aug. 26, 1858
JOHN MAULE SUTTON	Nov. 1, 1853	St. Andrews	Aug. 26, 1852
JOHN SHAND	Aug. 1, 1844	Edinburgh	Nov. 23, 1858
KEATS ROBINSON RISK	Oct. 24, 1851	Aberdeen	Nov. 23, 1858
JAMES JOSEPH CREGEEN	Oct. 21, 1853	St. Andrews	Nov. 23, 1855
JOHN HAYBALL PAUL	May 6, 1854	St. Andrews	Nov. 23, 1858
THOS. BEATH CHRISTIE	May 6, 1854	St. Andrews	Nov. 23, 1858
ROBERT CROSS	Aug. 1, 1854	Edinburgh	Nov. 23, 1858
HENRY KINGSLEY	Oct. 18, 1854	Aberdeen	Nov. 23, 1858
JOHN COCKER	Jan. 2, 1845	Erlangen	Dec. 7, 1858
THOS. HAYES JACKSON	Sept. 30, 1854	Erlangen	Dec. 9, 1858
A. M'NAMEE WALKER	Nov. 7, 1856	Giessen	Dec. 2, 1858
WILLIAM HELPS	May 6, 1854	St. Andrews	Dec. 28, 1858
JOHN GODFREY	May 6, 1854	St. Andrews	Dec. 29, 1858
W. FRED. HUTCHIESON RAMSAY	Aug. 2, 1843	Glasgow	May 3, 1859
J. DRUMMOND M'GAVIN	April 24, 1844	Glasgow	May 3, 1859
JAMES HOPE WATSON	Jan. 8, 1840	Jena	Aug. 2, 1859
G. MATHIESON OGILVIE	May 5, 1840	St. Andrews	Oct. 18, 1859
JOHN CHALLICE	April 12, 1850	Aberdeen	Feb. 28, 1860
ROBERT BOWMAN	Aug. 1, 1852	Edinburgh	Dec. 21, 1860
GEORGE WILLIAM BALFOUR	May 6, 1845	St. Andrews	Aug. 6, 1861
JAMES STRUTHERS	Aug. 1, 1848	Edinburgh	Aug. 6, 1861
ROBERT PEEL RITCHIE	Aug. 1, 1856	Edinburgh	Aug. 6, 1861
THOMAS GRAINGER STEWART	Aug. 1, 1858	Edinburgh	Aug. 6, 1861
WILLIAM ZIEGLER	Aug. 1, 1849	Edinburgh	Nov. 5, 1861
THOMAS JOHN GRAHAM	April 24, 1828	Glasgow	Nov. 19, 1861
DAVID CHRISTISON	Aug. 1, 1851	Edinburgh	May 6, 1862
LEWIS QUIER BOWERBANK	Aug. 1, 1836	Edinburgh	Aug. 5, 1862
R. EDMUND SCORESBY-JACKSON	Aug. 1, 1857	Edinburgh	Aug. 5, 1862
Sir DOUGLAS MACLAGAN	Aug. 1, 1833	Edinburgh	May 3, 1864

Admitted under Charter, dated 31st October 1861.

Names of Fellows.	Qualifications.	Dates of admission as Members.	Dates of admission as Fellows.
REGINALD READ	L.R.C.P.Ed., 1859	Feb. 3, 1863	Feb. 7, 1865
JOHN LINTON	M.D. Edin., 1861	Feb. 2, 1864	May 2, 1865
RICHARD FERNANDEZ FREEBORN	L.R.C.P.Ed., 1859	Feb. 3, 1863	Aug. 1, 1865
CHARLES ROBINSON	L.R.C.P.Ed., 1860	Nov. 3, 1863	Aug. 1, 1865
JOHN ALEXANDER SMITH	M.D. Edin., 1840	Aug. 2, 1864	Nov. 7, 1865
ALEXANDER RUSSELL SIMPSON	M.D. Edin., 1856	Aug. 2, 1864	Nov. 7, 1865
ALEXANDER CRUM BROWN	M.D. Edin., 1861	Aug. 2, 1864	Nov. 7, 1865
ANDREW SMART	M.D. Edin., 1862	Aug. 2, 1864	Nov. 7, 1865
CLAUD MUIRHEAD	M.D. Edin., 1862	Aug. 2, 1864	Nov. 7, 1865
JAMES RUTHERFORD	M.D. Edin., 1863	Aug. 1, 1865	Aug. 7, 1866
ROBERT CRAIG MACLAGAN	M.D. Edin., 1860	May 2, 1865	Nov. 6, 1866
ANDREW DAVIDSON	L.R.C.P.Ed., 1862	Feb. 7, 1865	Nov. 6, 1866
WILLIAM ROSS	M.D. Glas., 1830	Aug. 2, 1864	Feb. 5, 1867
JOHN GEORGE SINCLAIR COGHILL	M.D. Edin., 1857	Feb. 7, 1865	May 7, 1867
WILLIAM HENRY BRACE	L.R.C.P.Ed., 1860	May 1, 1865	Aug. 6, 1867
DAVID JAMES BRAKENRIDGE	M.D. Edin., 1863	May 1, 1866	Aug. 6, 1867
ALLEN DALZELL	M.D. Edin., 1853	Nov. 6, 1866	Nov. 5, 1867
THOMAS HARDIE	M.D. Edin., 1858	Aug. 1, 1865	Feb. 4, 1868
JOHN STEWARD	L.R.C.P.Ed., 1859	Feb. 7, 1865	Nov. 3, 1868
THOMAS ALEX. GOLDIE BALFOUR	M.D. Edin., 1851	Aug. 6, 1867	Feb. 2, 1869
GRIFFITH RICHARD JENKINS	L.R.C.P.Ed., 1867	Feb. 4, 1868	May 4, 1869
ANGUS MACDONALD	M.D. Edin., 1864	May 5, 1868	May 4, 1869
THOMAS RICHARD FRASER	M.D. Edin., 1862	May 5, 1868	Aug. 3, 1869
JOHN MILLAR	M.D. Edin., 1863	May 7, 1867	Aug. 3, 1869
WILLIAM JAMES HUNT	L.R.C.P.Ed., 1859	Nov. 3, 1868	Nov. 2, 1869
JOHN WYLLIE	M.D. Edin., 1865	May 4, 1869	May 3, 1870
JAMES ANDREW	M.D. Edin., 1866	May 4, 1869	May 3, 1870
CHARLES GAGE BROWN	M.D.St.And., 1851	Nov. 5, 1867	Aug. 2, 1870
THOMAS COSSAR	M.D. Edin., 1841	Aug. 3, 1869	Nov. 1, 1870
WILLIAM GORDON	M.D. Edin., 1862	Nov. 2, 1869	Nov. 1, 1870
ROBERT JAMES WILSON	L.R.C.P.Ed., 1859	Nov. 3, 1863	Feb. 7, 1871
WILLIAM WATSON CAMPBELL	M.D. Edin., 1862	May 1, 1866	Feb. 7, 1871
JOHN BATTY TUKE	M.D. Edin., 1856	Aug. 2, 1870	Nov. 7, 1871
FRANCIS WALTER MOINET	M.D. Edin., 1867	Feb. 7, 1871	May 7, 1872
JAMES MURRAY FOSTER	L.R.C.P.Ed., 1865	May 2, 1871	Aug. 6, 1872
HENRY WILLIAM HAIGH	L.R.C.P.Ed., 1869	Aug. 1, 1871	Aug. 6, 1872
JOHN GRAY M'KENDRICK	M.D. Aberd., 1864	May 2, 1871	Aug. 6, 1872
MORRISON WATSON	M.D. Edin., 1867	May 2, 1871	Aug. 6, 1872
ARTHUR GAMGEE	M.D. Edin., 1862	Feb. 7, 1871	Nov. 5, 1872
FRANCIS KENNEDY DICKSON	L.R.C.P.Ed., 1864	May 7, 1873	May 6, 1873
THOMAS STRETCH DOWSE	M.D. Aberd., 1868	May 7, 1872	May 6, 1873
JAMES CUMMING	M.D. Edin., 1871	Feb. 6, 1872	Aug. 5, 1873
JAMES BELL PETTIGREW	M.D. Edin., 1861	Aug. 6, 1872	Aug. 13, 1873
THOMAS SMITH CLOUSTON	M.D. Edin., 1861	Nov. 5, 1872	Nov. 4, 1873

Names of Fellows.	Qualifications.	Dates of admission as Members.	Dates of admission as Fellows.
SAMUEL CARTRIGHT REED	M.D. St. And., 1862	Feb. 4, 1873	May 5, 1874
ALEXANDER JAMES SINCLAIR	M.D. Edin., 1872	Feb. 4, 1873	May 5, 1874
PETER ALEXANDER YOUNG	M.D. Edin., 1870	May 6, 1873	May 5, 1874
JOHN JANET KIRK DUNCANSON	M.D. Edin., 1871	May 6, 1873	May 5, 1874
JOSEPH DOUGALL	M.D. Edin., 1872	Nov. 4, 1873	Nov. 3, 1874
JAMES CARMICHAEL	M.D. Edin., 1864	Feb. 3, 1874	Feb. 2, 1875
JOHN RICHARD CARMICHAEL	L.R.C.P.Ed.,	May 7, 1872	May 4, 1875
FRANCIS BOYNTON LEE	L.R.C.P.Ed., 1869	Feb. 3, 1874	May 4, 1875
JAMES ORMISTON AFFLECK	M.D. Edin., 1869	May 5, 1874	May 4, 1875
THOMAS CHAMBERS	L.R.C.P.Ed., 1860	Nov. 7, 1871	Aug. 3, 1875
WALTER ALFRED SATCHELL	L.R.C.P.Ed., 1873	Nov. 3, 1874	May 2, 1876
JOSEPH JOHN BROWN	M.B. Edin., 1871	Feb. 7, 1875	May 2, 1876
JOHN PLAYFAIR	M.B. Edin., 1872	Feb. 2, 1875	May 2, 1876
JOHN SIBBALD	M.D. Edin., 1854	Feb. 6, 1872	Aug. 1, 1876
HERBERT TIBBETS	L.R.C.P.Ld., 1865	May 5, 1874	Aug. 1, 1876
CHARLES EDWARD UNDERHILL	M.B. Camb., 1870	Aug. 3, 1875	Aug. 1, 1876
JOHN PARKIN	L.R.C.P.Ed., 1859	Nov. 2, 1875	Nov. 7, 1876
KEITH NORMAN MACDONALD	L.R.C.P.Ld., 1863	Aug. 3, 1875	Nov. 7, 1876
THOMAS ANDERSON	M.B. Edin., 1871	Aug. 4, 1874	Nov. 7, 1876
ALEXANDER BALLANTYNE	M.D. Edin., 1860	Feb. 1, 1876	Feb. 6, 1877
ALEXANDER MONTGOMERIE BELL	M.D. Edin., 1863	Aug. 7, 1866	May 1, 1877
JOHN CONNEL	M.D. Edin., 1873	Feb. 1, 1876	May 1, 1877
DAVID HOPE WATSON	L.R.C.P.Ed., 1859	May 2, 1876	May 1, 1877
WILLIAM RUTHERFORD	M.D. Edin., 1863	May 2, 1876	May 1, 1877
WILLIAM ALLAN JAMIESON	M.B. Edin., 1865	May 2, 1876	May 1, 1877
CHARLES FRERE WEBB	L.R.C.P.Ed., 1871	May 5, 1874	Aug. 7, 1877
HENRY MORRIS	L.R.C.P.Ld., 1875	Aug. 1, 1876	Nov. 6, 1877
EDWARD CHARLES ROBSON ROOSE	L.R.C.P.Ed., 1871	May 4, 1875	Dec. 14, 1877
WILLIAM JOHN HENRY LUSH	L.R.C.P.Ed., 1873	Feb. 1, 1876	Dec. 14, 1877
ALEXANDER JAMES	M.D. Edin., 1877	Aug. 7, 1877	Dec. 14, 1877
CHARLES FIELD GOLDSBRO'	L.R.C.P.Ed., 1860	Feb. 1, 1876	Feb. 5, 1878
JAMES FOULIS	M.B. Edin., 1872	Feb. 6, 1877	May 7, 1878
THOMAS NGLIS	L.R.C.P.Ed., 1874	Feb. 6, 1877	May 7, 1878
HENRY JECKELL KENDRICK VINES	L.R.C.P.Ed., 1869	May 1, 1877	May 7, 1878
GEORGE HERON AITCHISON	M.B. Edin., 1872	May 1, 1877	May 7, 1878
FREDERICK EMMET BECK	L.R.C.P.Ed., 1867	Feb. 6, 1877	Aug. 6, 1878
WILLIAM MILSTED HARMER	L.R.C.P.Ed., 1864	Feb. 7, 1865	Nov. 5, 1878
WILLIAM STEWART	L.R.C.P.Ed., 1864	May 1, 1877	Nov. 5, 1878
REGINALD LOUIS VERLEY	L.R.C.P.Ed., 1872	Aug. 4, 1874	Feb. 4, 1879
THOMAS RUTHERFORD RONALDSON	M.B. Edin., 1874	Aug. 7, 1877	Feb. 4, 1879
HERVEY EUSTACE ASTLES	L.R.C.P.Ed., 1867	Nov. 6, 1877	May 6, 1879
HENRY MACDONALD CHURCH	M.D. Edin., 1874	Feb. 5, 1878	May 6, 1879
JOHN BROWN BUIST	M.D. Edin., 1871	May 7, 1878	May 6, 1879
THOMAS OUTTERSON WOOD	L.R.C.P.Ed., 1868	Nov. 3, 1874	Aug. 5, 1879
PETER M'BRIDE	M.B. Edin., 1876	May 6, 1879	May 4, 1880
RICHARD JAMES MAITLAND COFFIN	L.R.C.P.Ed., 1871	Aug. 4, 1874	Aug. 3, 1880
BYROM BRAMWELL	M.D. Edin., 1877	Aug. 5, 1879	Aug. 3, 1880
GEORGE ALEXANDER GIBSON	M.B. Edin., 1876	Aug. 5, 1879	Aug. 3, 1880

Names of Fellows.	Qualifications.	Dates of admission as Members.	Dates of admission as Fellows.
JAMES MURDOCH BROWN	M.B. Edin., 1874	May 1, 1877	Nov. 2, 1880
JOHN HALLIDAY CROOM	M.B. Edin., 1868	Feb. 5, 1878	Nov. 2, 1880
DAVID BERRY HART	M.B. Edin., 1877	May 6, 1879	Nov. 2, 1880
WALTER WEIR	M.B. Edin., 1878	Aug. 5, 1879	Nov. 2, 1880
JAMES ALEXANDER RUSSELL	M.B. Edin., 1868	Nov. 4, 1879	Nov. 2, 1880
THOMAS WHITEHEAD REID	L.R.C.P.Ld., 1875	Feb. 3, 1880	May 3, 1881
STEPHEN COULL MACKENZIE	M.D. Edin., 1864	Aug. 2, 1870	Aug. 2, 1881
CHARLES ORTON	L.R.C.P.Ed., 1865	May 6, 1879	Aug. 2, 1881
ALFRED BOYLE THOMPSON	L.R.C.P.Ed., 1860	Feb. 3, 1880	Aug. 2, 1881
ALFRED JAMES AITKINSON	L.R.C.P.Ed., 1871	May 4, 1875	Nov. 1, 1881
CHARLES BROWNE	L.R.C.P.Ed., 1874	May 4, 1880	Nov. 1, 1881
JAMES ALLAN GRAY	M.B. Edin., 1876	Aug. 3, 1880	Nov. 1, 1881
WILLIAM SMITH GREENFIELD	M.D. Lond., 1874	Aug. 2, 1881	Nov. 1, 1881
PETER YOUNG	M.D. Edin., 1857	Feb. 1, 1881	Feb. 7, 1882
JOHN JAMES GRAHAM BROWN	M.D. Edin., 1878	May 3, 1881	May 2, 1882
MARCUS HENRY ALLEN	L.R.C.P.Ed., 1871	May 6, 1873	Aug. 1, 1882
GEORGE FOWLER	L.R.C.P.Ed., 1864	Aug. 5, 1873	Aug. 1, 1882
GERMAN SIMS WOODHEAD	M.B. Edin., 1878	May 4, 1880	Nov. 7, 1882
JOSEPH CARNE ROSS	M.B. Edin., 1880	May 3, 1881	Nov. 7, 1882
THOMAS SMITH	L.R.C.P.Ld., 1861	Aug. 2, 1881	Feb. 6, 1883
ALFRED ELLIOTT BENTHALL	L.R.C.P.Ed., 1880	Aug. 2, 1881	Feb. 6, 1883
ALEXANDER HUGH FREELAND BARBOUR	M.B. Edin., 1879	Feb. 1, 1881	May 1, 1883
WILLIAM TAYLOR	M.D. Edin., 1867	Feb. 7, 1882	May 1, 1883
ALEXANDER BLACK	M.B. Edin., 1877	Feb. 7, 1882	May 1, 1883
THOMAS FRANCIS SPITTAL CAVERHILL	M.B. Edin., 1878	Feb. 7, 1882	May 1, 1883
ALEXANDER BRUCE	M.B. Edin., 1879	Feb. 7, 1882	May 1, 1883
FREDERICK WILLIAM DYCE FRASER	M.B. Edin., 1878	May 2, 1882	May 1, 1883
ROBERT COOPER PARKE	L.R.C.P.Ed., 1868	Feb. 1, 1876	Nov. 7, 1883
JAMES RITCHIE	M.B. Edin., 1872	May 2, 1882	Nov. 7, 1883
HIBBERT SULLIVAN PARKER	L.R.C.P.Ed., 1880	May 2, 1882	Nov. 7, 1883
ALEXANDER WILLIAM MACFARLANE	M.D. Glas., 1872	Feb. 7, 1882	Feb. 5, 1884
WILLIAM CAMPBELL	M.B. Edin., 1872	Aug. 1, 1882	Feb. 5, 1884
WILLIAM JAMES TIVY	L.R.C.P.Ed., 1873	Aug. 1, 1882	May 6, 1884
ARTHUR DOUGLAS WEBSTER	L.R.C.P.Ed., 1878	Feb. 6, 1883	Aug. 5, 1884
ARTHUR EDWARD WELLINGTON FOX	M.B. Edin., 1870	Feb. 5, 1884	May 5, 1885
CHARLES SPENCER WALLER COBBOLD	L.R.C.P.Ed., 1874	May 4, 1880	Aug. 4, 1885
JOHN MEIKLE	L.R.C.P.Ed., 1867	Aug. 1, 1876	Nov. 3, 1885
JAMES WILLIAM HOPE	L.R.C.P.Ed., 1874	Aug. 6, 1878	Nov. 3, 1885
WILLIAM WILBERFORCE DUNKLEY	L.R.C.P.Ed., 1872	May 2, 1882	May 4, 1886
ALEXANDER SOMERVILLE CUMMING	M.B. Edin., 1884	Feb. 4, 1885	May 4, 1886
ROBERT MILNE MURRAY	M.B. Edin., 1879	Feb. 1, 1881	Aug. 3, 1886
JOHN THORNTON DUNCAN	L.R.C.P.Ed., 1880	May 2, 1882	Aug. 3, 1886
ORMOND HALDANE GARLAND	M.B. Edin., 1868	May 2, 1876	Nov. 2, 1886
ADOLPHUS EDWARD BRIDGER	M.D. Edin., 1880	May 3, 1881	Feb. 1, 1887
WILLIAM JOHN HARNETT	L.R.C.P.Ed., 1865	Aug. 1, 1862	Feb. 1, 1887
ALEXANDER BRUCE LOW	M.D. Edin., 1881	Nov. 4, 1884	Feb. 1, 1887
WILLIAM RUSSELL	M.D. Edin., 1884	May 5, 1885	Feb. 1, 1887

Names of Fellows.	Qualifications.	Dates of admission as Members.	Dates of admission as Fellows.
ALBERT HIRST	L.R.C.P.Ed., 1871	Aug. 3, 1875	May 3, 1887
JAMES MURRAY LINDSAY	M.D.St.And., 1859	Feb. 3, 1885	May 3, 1887
GEORGE HARRY MELVILLE DUNLOP	M.D. Edin., 1884	Nov. 3, 1885	May 3, 1887
DIARMID NOËL PATON	M.D. Edin., 1885	May 4, 1886	May 3, 1887
NATHANIEL THOMAS BREWIS	M.B. Edin., 1882	Aug. 3, 1886	Aug. 2, 1887
ROBERT WILLIAM PHILIP	M.B. Edin., 1882	Aug. 3, 1886	Aug. 2, 1887
JOHN THOMSON	M.B. Edin., 1884	May 3, 1887	May 1, 1888
FRANCIS WILLIAM NICOL HAULTAIN	M.B. Edin., 1882	May 3, 1887	May 1, 1888
WILLIAM HENRY MILLER	M.B. Edin., 1883	May 3, 1887	Aug. 7, 1888
THOMAS WILLIAM DEWAR	M.B. Edin., 1884	Nov. 1, 1887	Aug. 7, 1888
RICHARD GREENE	L.R.C.P.Ed., 1868	May 3, 1885	Nov. 6, 1888
JOHN WILLIAM BALLANTYNE	M.B. Edin., 1883	Aug. 2, 1887	Nov. 6, 1888
ROBERT SWAN AITCHISON	M.B. Edin., 1882	Nov. 1, 1887	Nov. 6, 1888
JOHN BATTY TUKE, Jun.	M.B. Edin., 1884	May 3, 1887	Feb. 5, 1889
AUGUSTUS ALEXANDER MATHESON	M.D. Edin., 1876	Feb. 7, 1882	Feb. 5, 1889
GEORGE HENRY DARWIN	L.R.C.P.Ed., 1880	Aug. 2, 1881	Aug. 6, 1889
ALEXANDER MORISON	M.D. Edin., 1878	Feb. 1, 1887	Aug. 6, 1889
JAMES HAIG FERGUSON	M.B. Edin., 1884	May 3, 1887	Aug. 6, 1889
RALPH STOCKMAN	M.D. Edin., 1886	May 7, 1889	Aug. 6, 1889
CHARLES PITT WETHERILL NEATE	L.R.C.P.Ed., 1879	Feb. 3, 1880	Nov. 5, 1889
JAMES STEWART	L.R.C.P.Ed., 1872	Aug. 3, 1880	Nov. 5, 1889
THOMAS ERNEST GEE	L.R.C.P.Ed., 1882	Aug. 7, 1888	Feb. 4, 1890
JAMES STITT THOMSON	L.R.C.P.Ed., 1875	Aug. 1, 1882	May 6, 1890
JOHN ROSS HOME ROSS	M.B. Edin., 1886	Feb. 5, 1889	May 6, 1890
GEORGE LOVELL GULLAND	M.B. Edin., 1886	May 1, 1888	July 29, 1890
THOMAS JACKSON THYNE	M.B. Edin., 1883	Nov. 6, 1888	July 29, 1890
GUTHRIE RANKIN	M.B. Glas., 1880	Feb. 7, 1882	Nov. 4, 1890
JAMES WILLIAMSON MARTIN	M.D. Edin., 1887	Feb. 7, 1888	Feb. 3, 1891
GEORGE HUNTER	M.D. Edin., 1869	May 6, 1890	May 5, 1891
DAWSON FYERS DUCKWORTH TURNER	M.B. Edin., 1888	May 6, 1890	May 5, 1891
JAMES CRAUFURD DUNLOP	M.B. Edin., 1887	July 29, 1890	Aug. 4, 1891
WILLIAM GEORGE AITCHISON ROBERTSON	M.B. Edin., 1887	July 29, 1890	Aug. 4, 1891

LIST

OF

Honorary Members of the College

FROM ITS ERECTION, WITH THE DATES OF THEIR ADMISSION.

— ◆◆◆ — —

The Record is wanting from December 1682 to the year 1691.

Names of Honorary Members.	Dates of their admission.	Names of Honorary Members.	Dates of their admission.
EARL OF MARCHMONT .	May 15, 1696	M. DE SENAC . . .	Nov. 4, 1760
LORD WHITEHILL . .	....	JOHN EARL OF BUTE .	Nov. 3, 1761
LORD ANSTRUTHER .	Nov. 6, 1699	DR. JAMES MOUNSEY .	Nov. 2, 1762
DR. DAVID GREGORY .	Aug. 22, 1705	COUNT CARBURY . .	Nov. 5, 1765
DR. ROBERT GRAY . .	Oct. 4, 1705	SIR CHARLES LINNEUS .	Nov. 3, 1772
SIR HANS SLOAN . .	Oct. 4, 1705	BARON ALBERT VON ⎱ HALLER . . . ⎰	Nov. 3, 1772
EARL OF WEMYSS . .	Dec. 13, 1705		
LAIRD OF POSSO . . .	Nov. 14, 1706	HENRY DUKE OF BUC- ⎱ CLEUCH . . . ⎰	Dec. 2, 1773
EARL OF LEVEN . . .	April 22, 1707		
EARL OF ERROLL . .	June 3, 1707	DR. H. GAUBIUS . .	Dec. 2, 1773
EARL OF GLASGOW . .	....	DR. JAS. FLINT, ex officio .	May 3, 1774
LORD PRESTONHALL .	June 18, 1707	DR. ANT. STÖRCK . .	Nov. 5, 1776
LORD MINTO . . .	....	DR. J. G. ZIMMERMAN .	Dec. 5, 1782
DR. JOHN ARBUTHNOT .	Dec. 12, 1707	DR. J. M. DE LASSONE .	Dec. 5, 1782
DR. ALEX. RUSSELL .	Feb. 12, 1712	SIR JOS. BANKS, BART. .	....
DR. WILL. COCKBURN .	May 5, 1724	DR. JOHN ROGERSON .	....
DR. GEORGE CHEYNE .	....	GEORGE DUKE OF MON- ⎱ TAGUE . . . ⎰	Dec. 17, 1782
DR. JAMES CAMBELL .	May 2, 1727		
DR. WILL. FULLERTON .	Nov. 5, 1728	DR. P. CAMPER . . .	....
DR. GEORGE MARTIN .	Aug. 5, 1740	DR. FEL. VICQ. D'AZYR .	Feb. 2, 1790
DR. DAVID BALFOUR .	Feb. 7, 1744	DR. JO. AND. MURRAY .	....
DR. JOHN JOHNSTON .	....	DR. AUG. GOT. RICH-⎱ TER . . . ⎰	Dec. 1, 1791
DR. THOMAS SIMPSON .	Feb. 7, 1744		
DR. RICHARD MEAD .	May 7, 1745	DR. JO. GOT. WALTER .	....
DR. JAS. M'KENZIE . .	Oct. 2, 1755	SIR GEO. BAKER, BART. .	Mar. 27, 1792
DR. JOHN HUXHAM . .	Oct. 2, 1755	COUNT RUMFORD . .	Nov. 4, 1800
DR. G. VAN SWIETEN .	Nov. 4, 1755	DR. EDWARD JENNER .	May 20, 1806
ARCH. DUKE OF ARGYLE .	Nov. 30, 1758	DR. MATTHEW BAILLIE .	Nov. 13, 1809

LIST

OF

Presidents of the College

FROM ITS ERECTION.

✦✦✦

SIR ARCHIBALD STEVENSONE, elected President 8th December 1681, and continued till 1684.

SIR ROBERT SIBBALD elected 4th December 1684.

From 1684 to 1693 the Record is wanting.

Names of Presidents.	Dates of their Election.	Names of Presidents.	Dates of their Election.
SIR ARCH. STEVENSONE	Nov. 30, 1693	DR. JOHN GARDINER .	Dec. 5, 1782
DR. ROBERT TROTTER .	Dec. 6, 1694	DR. JOHN HOPE. . .	Dec. 2, 1784
SIR THOMAS BURNET .	Dec. 3, 1696	DR. JAMES HAY . .	Nov. 30, 1786
DR. MAT. SINCLARE. .	Dec. 1, 1698	DR. JOSEPH BLACK .	Dec. 4, 1788
DR. ROBERT TROTTER .	Dec. 5, 1700	DR. AND. DUNCAN . .	Dec. 2, 1790
DR. ALEX. DUNDAS .	Dec. 3, 1702	DR. JAMES HAMILTON .	Dec. 6, 1792
DR. JAMES HALKET .	Nov. 30, 1704	DR. NATHANIEL SPENS .	Dec. 4, 1794
DR. WILLIAM ECCLES	Dec. 5, 1706	DR. D. RUTHERFORD .	Dec. 1, 1796
DR. MAT. SINCLARE. .	Dec. 2, 1708	DR. JAMES GREGORY .	Dec. 6, 1798
DR. WILL. STEWART .	Dec. 4, 1716	DR. WILL. WRIGHT . .	Dec. 3, 1801
DR. JAMES FORREST .	Dec. 5, 1719	DR. THOMAS SPENS . .	Dec. 1, 1803
DR. JOHN DRUMMOND .	Dec. 6, 1722	DR. CHARLES STUART .	Dec. 4, 1806
DR. FRANCIS PRINGLE .	Nov. 30, 1727	DR. JAMES HOME . .	Nov. 30, 1809
DR. JOHN RIDDELL . .	Dec. 2, 1731	DR. J. HAMILTON, Jun. .	Dec. 3, 1812
DR. ROBERT LOWIS . .	Dec. 4, 1735	DR. THOS. CHAS. HOPE .	Nov. 30, 1815
DR. JOHN CLERK . .	Dec. 4, 1740	DR. JAMES BUCHAN . .	Dec. 2, 1819
DR. WILL. COCHRAN .	Dec. 6, 1744	DR. AND. DUNCAN, Jun. .	Dec. 5, 1822
DR. W. PORTERFIELD .	Dec. 1, 1748	DR. AND. DUNCAN, Sen. .	Dec. 4, 1824
DR. JO. RUTHERFORD .	Nov. 30, 1752	DR. ALEX. MONRO . .	Dec. 1, 1825
SIR ALEX. DICK . . .	Dec. 2, 1756	SIR ALEX. MORISON. .	Dec. 6, 1827
DR. ROBERT WHYTT .	Dec. 1, 1763	DR. J. H. DAVIDSON . .	Dec. 3, 1829
SIR S. THRIEPLAND .	Dec. 4, 1766	DR. J. MACWHIRTER .	Dec. 1, 1831
DR. JOHN BOSWELL .	Dec. 6, 1770	DR. J. H. DAVIDSON . .	Dec. 5, 1833
DR. COLIN DRUMMOND.	Dec. 3, 1772	DR. JOHN THOMSON .	Dec. 4, 1834
DR. WILLIAM CULLEN .	Aug. 3, 1773	DR. W. P. ALISON . .	Dec. 1, 1836
DR. FRANCIS HOME .	Nov. 30, 1775	SIR R. CHRISTISON . .	Dec. 6, 1838
DR. GREGORY GRANT	Dec. 4, 1777	DR. R. GRAHAM . . .	Dec. 3, 1840
DR. ALEX. MONRO .	Dec. 3, 1779	DR. R. RENTON . . .	Dec. 1, 1842

Names of Presidents.	Dates of their Election.	Names of Presidents.	Dates of their Election.
Dr. W. BEILBY	Dec. 5, 1844	Dr. A. H. DOUGLAS	Dec. 2, 1869
Sir R. CHRISTISON	Dec. 3, 1846	Dr. R. PATERSON	Nov. 30, 1871
Dr. W. SELLER	Nov. 30, 1848	Dr. W. H. LOWE	Dec. 4, 1873
Sir J. Y. SIMPSON	Dec. 5, 1850	Dr. ALEX. KEILLER	Dec. 2, 1875
Dr. THOS. S. TRAILL	Dec. 2, 1852	Dr. ALEX. PEDDIE	Dec. 6, 1877
Dr. JAMES BEGBIE	Nov. 30, 1854	Dr. D. R. HALDANE	Dec. 4, 1879
Dr. DAVID MACLAGAN	Dec. 4, 1856	Dr. GEORGE WILLIAM BALFOUR	Nov. 30, 1882
Dr. ALEXANDER WOOD	Dec. 2, 1858		
Dr. DAVID CRAIGIE	Dec. 5, 1861	Sir DOUGLAS MACLAGAN	Dec. 4, 1884
Dr. JOHN G. M. BURT	Dec. 3, 1863	Dr. ROBT. PEEL RITCHIE	Dec. 1, 1887
Dr. JOHN SMITH	Nov. 30, 1865	Dr. THOMAS GRAINGER STEWART	Dec. 5, 1889
Dr. JOHN MOIR	Dec. 5, 1867		

HISTORICAL SKETCH

ROYAL COLLEGE OF PHYSICIANS.

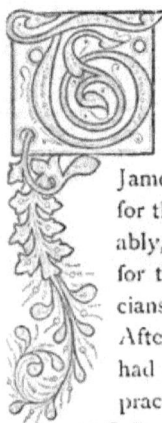

THE attempt to incorporate the Practitioners of Medicine in Scotland, for the purpose of raising the standard both of the character and acquirements of Physicians, originated in 1617. King James I. of England, to whom an application for that purpose was made, received it favourably, and issued an Order to the Parliament for the establishment of a College of Physicians in Edinburgh. This Order is still extant. After reciting the evils which the community had suffered from the intrusion of irregular practitioners, it directs the Parliament to form a College of Physicians, appoints seven persons to examine those who proposed to practice Medicine, and makes it illegal for any person to exercise the art and science of Physic within Edinburgh and the neighbourhood without the Diploma of the College.

Early attempts at formation of a College.

Order of James I.

His Majesty also further suggests that warrant should be given to the College to appoint yearly three of its number to visit the Apothecaries' shops in the burgh, to examine the state of the drugs exposed for sale, and to destroy such as might be found corrupt or insufficient.

How frustrated.

Dissensions, chiefly of a religious kind, had the effect of preventing the wishes of the King from being carried out.

Renewal of attempt, 1630.

In 1630 the attempt was renewed, and King Charles I. referred the matter to his Privy Council ; but, owing chiefly to the unsettled state of public affairs, nothing more was done in his reign.

Patent by Cromwell, 1656.

The matter was warmly taken up by Cromwell during his Protectorate ; and a Patent, still extant, was made out in 1656, instituting a College of Physicians of Scotland, "who shall have power and authority to oversie, rule, and order, what may concerne the right administratioune of Physike to the people of Scotland in all pairts and places of the said nation, with power to them to censure and punish all persons who shall presume to practise, exercise, or profess Physike, or give medicines, or ordaine Physicall Praescriptiones in any pairt or place in Scotland, being not members of the said Colledge, or not being approved and licensed by the said Praesident and Colledge under their Common Seal." Further, in this Patent of Incorporation, it was proposed to give to the said President and College the power to practise the Art of Surgery : "forasmuch as the Science of Physick doth comprehend, include, and containe in it the knowledge of Chirurgery, being a special part of the same and member thereof." By it, also, the power of examining and licensing Apothecaries, and of visiting their shops, was to be conferred on the proposed College ; and, lastly, the College was to be entitled to receive from the magistrates of the several

cities and burghs, and the sheriffs of the respective
counties, "such dead bodies of malefactors executed as
they shall desyre, for making of dissection and anatomic
for the use of the Colledge."

The extensive powers thus proposed to be conferred
naturally created jealousies among the other public
Medical bodies, and before the various conferences for the
adjustment of these differences were ended, the death of
the Protector put a stop for a time to the whole scheme.

Eventually, though not without great opposition on
the part of the Surgeons, the Universities, the Municipal
Corporation, and even the Bishops and Archbishops, a
Charter of Incorporation was, chiefly by the exertions
of Sir Robert Sibbald, and the assistance of the Earl of
Perth, obtained from Charles II., and the Great Seal was
appended to this Charter on St. Andrew's Day, 1681.

This Charter commenced by laying down the necessity which existed for ascertaining that those who design
to practise any profession should be examined as to their
capacity for doing so, and stated that from the absence
of any regulation of this kind regarding Medicine, great
confusion had arisen, and many very ill qualified persons
exercised the healing art. It then proceeded to institute
the College of Physicians as a great and powerful means
of correcting this abuse. It ordained that the College
should consist of certain individuals who were named,
and of all others who might be chosen by them as Colleagues and Fellows of their Society, within the city of
Edinburgh, its Suburbs and Liberties : so that they and
their successors should be united and conjoined into one
Body, Community, and College, in all time coming. The
Charter further provided for the election of a Council
President, and other Office-Bearers, and conferred on
the College the power to enact Laws for its due govern-

Frustrated by
other Medical
Bodies and death
of Cromwell.

Charter of 1681.

Summary of
contents of
Charter of 1681.

c

ment and welfare, and for promoting the Science and regulating the practice of Medicine within the city of Edinburgh and Leith, their Suburbs and Liberties.

It prevented, under certain penalties, any one from practising Medicine within the jurisdiction of the College who had not obtained its Licence or Diploma.

It conferred on the College the power, under certain regulations, of calling before it and fining unlicensed practitioners, and also of punishing all Physicians, Doctors of Medicine, Licentiates, and Fellows practising within their jurisdiction, who might violate any of the Laws of the College.

The College was further invested by the Charter with power to examine, along with a magistrate and chemist, the Medicines kept in the Apothecaries' shops, and to destroy such as were not found to be of good quality.

The Charter also prevented the Magistrates from allowing any one to open an Apothecary's shop until he had, by an examination, satisfied the President and Censors of the College that he had a competent knowledge of drugs.

The Charter further provided, that no Fellow of the College should be cited as a juror on any assize in town or country, or be called out to watch or ward, or on any pretext whatever be withdrawn from his patients.

The College continued to discharge its functions under this Charter for many years, although it eventually abandoned in practice the exclusive rights conferred on it, and ceased to exercise any inspection over the shops of the Apothecaries. In fact, the changes of social position necessarily caused many of the provisions to fall into abeyance.

The College had not been insensible to the advantages that would accrue to it from obtaining a new

Charter, more especially that it might thereby free itself from the obligation laid on it of admitting to its licence all Scottish University Graduates, without examination and without a ballot, and also that it might get rid of the clause prohibiting it from being connected with a Medical School, and further, that it might obtain the power of expelling unworthy Members.

The subject of a new Charter had repeatedly been considered by the College, but was always delayed, in the hope of the settlement of the long-vexed question of Medical Reform.

In 1843, when the late Sir James Graham, then Home Secretary, had all but succeeded in carrying a Bill for Medical Reform, the College instructed the late Mr. Richard Mackenzie, W.S., to prepare the draft of a new Charter, which, after revision by the College, was finally adjusted in 1845 by Mr. Drinkwater Bethune, the Government official, but the abandonment by Sir James Graham of his Bill caused it to be laid aside.

Draft of a new Charter prepared in 1843.

Adjusted in 1845. Subsequently postponed.

On the 9th of May 1854 the long-forgotten draft was referred to the Medical Reform Committee for its consideration and amendment, and the Committee reported on the 1st May following. Fresh discussions on Medical Reform again interrupted procedure regarding it, and it was not until the Medical Act had received the Royal Assent in July 1858 that the subject was again resumed. On the 21st of September of that year the Committee of the College on Medical Reform presented to the College a very full and exhaustive Report on the manner in which the College would probably be affected by the Medical Act (21 and 22 Victoriæ, 1858).

Consideration of new Charter resumed in 1854.

Report to College on the effect on its interests of the Medical Act.

This Report fairly brought before the College the propriety of obtaining a new Charter, as it was

Reasons why a new Charter was considered to be desirable.

authorized to do by clause 49 of the Act. The objects
to be kept in view were stated in this Report to be,
First, To give the College a wider designation, The
Royal College of Physicians of Scotland; *Second*, To
get rid, if possible, of the restrictive clauses in the
existing Charter; *Third*, To introduce an order of
Members; *Fourth*, To obtain power to examine, should
the College choose it, all applicants for the Licence,
whether University Graduates or not; *Fifth*, Should
the power of examination not be given or exercised,
to have power to apply the ballot; *Sixth*, To have the
undoubted power of the suspension and expulsion of
unworthy Members vested in the College.

A new Charter
resolved on.

On the 21st of December the College took this part
of the Report into consideration, and resolved to apply
for a new Charter. At several meetings thereafter
(28th and 29th December 1858, and 18th February and
1st March 1859) the College discussed the draft of the

Difference of
opinion as to its
provisions.

proposed Charter. Considerable difference of opinion
was manifested, chiefly in regard to whether the College
should admit to its Fellowship other than University
Graduates, and whether the College should get rid of
the restriction which prevented it from erecting a
Medical School. Both these questions were at length
decided in the affirmative. The College also introduced
a clause to enable it to hold property in its corporate
name. Between the period when the new Charter
was agreed to by the College and the date of its being
granted, the College, on a Report by the Council, agreed

The College
resolves to retain
the name of
" Edinburgh "
in preference to
" Scotland."

to retain the name of Royal College of Physicians
of Edinburgh, in preference to that of Royal College
of Physicians of Scotland, which the Medical Act
authorized Her Majesty to bestow. This resolution
was come to on the 5th February 1861, and the new

Charter was obtained, dated the 16th August, and sealed and registered on the 31st October 1861.

This Charter sets out by reciting the petition of the College for the grant of a new Charter. Clause first constitutes the President, the Vice-President, the Members of Council of the College and their successors, and the other existing Fellows and all who shall hereafter be admitted Fellows or Members, a body corporate, with all the rights and privileges usually appertaining to corporate bodies.

Clause 2 gives to the College, as constituted by the new Charter, the right to all property, of whatever description, which belonged to it under the former Charter.

Clause 3 constitutes the existing Fellows the first Fellows of the College as newly incorporated.

Clause 4 gives power to admit new Fellows and Members under such regulations, and on payment of such fees, as the College may from time to time ordain.

Clause 5 gives power to grant Licences.

Clause 6 gives power to the College, with consent of three-fourths of the Members present, to censure, suspend, or depose any Fellow, Member, or Licentiate of the College who has obtained admission by false pretences, or violated any of the Bye-Laws.

Clauses 7 to 10 regulate the Ordinary and Extraordinary Meetings of the College.

Clauses 11 to 17 regulate the appointment of the Office-Bearers.

Clause 18 arranges for the management of the property and affairs of the College.

Clause 19 secures the validity of the acts of the College, notwithstanding any informality in the election of the President or of any Councillor.

Clause 20 gives to the College power to make

bye-laws for promoting the Science of Medicine, for duly ordering the practice of the same, and for the good government, order, and direction of the College.

Clause 21 continues the existing Bye-Laws in force until new ones are passed.

Clause 22 gives to the new College, its Fellows, Members, and Licentiates, all the powers enjoyed by the existing College, and those connected with it.

Among the other changes effected by this Charter was the power given to the College to elect its President directly, and not through the intervention of the Council; and the abolition of the offices of Censors and Fiscal, the duties of which having long been in abeyance, the names were now finally relinquished.

Returning to the history of the College after the first Charter (1681) had been obtained, we find it enter with great zeal on the discharge of the duties committed to it.

The publication of a Pharmacopœia was undertaken, and arrangements were made for regular attendance on the sick poor.

The loss of the earlier Minutes renders it very difficult to ascertain where the meetings of the College were at first held. Dr. Beilby, in his Address at the opening of the present Hall, stated that the first and several subsequent meetings were held in the house of Sir Robert Sibbald, but there seems no sufficient authority for this; and it is evident that what follows in Dr. Beilby's narrative is founded on his having misread the name of Dr. (afterwards Sir Archibald) Stevenson for that of Johnstone.

The cause of the door being locked in the faces of the President and Fellows by Dr. Stevenson, which Dr. Beilby was unable to explain, is rendered sufficiently clear by a reference to the disputes in which Dr. Pitcairn and Sir Archibald Stevenson were so conspicuous, all mention of which were, however, erased from the Minutes by authority of the College.[*]

Mr. Livingstone's House.

On the 24th May 1697, the Treasurer was authorized to pay £3, 10s. to Mr. William Livingstone for a year's rent of the room in which the College met, and half a dollar to the maid.

On 17th April 1698, the College resolved unanimously to buy a house of its own, and two days afterwards a Committee was authorized to offer £75 for the house of Mr. Livingstone, where the College then met. This offer probably proved insufficient, as the College continued to meet in apartments rented for the purpose, until, in 1704, it acquired the house and grounds of Sir James Mackenzie, in Fountain Close in the High Street.

First Hall in Fountain Close, 1704.

Situation of first Hall.

This property, purchased for £194, 8s. 10d., immediately adjoined that of the Marquis of Tweeddale; and when, seven years subsequently, the College acquired the land belonging to Bailie Jeffrey (price £127, 14s. 11d.), which lay between their first purchase and the then fashionable Cowgate, the extent of the gardens and shrubbery were the envy of the neighbouring Peers, to several of whom the privilege of walking in them was, at their request, permitted as a favour.

Its extensive Gardens.

It throws a curious light on the manners and customs of our ancestors, and on the absence of what are now considered indispensable arrangements for personal comfort in every private dwelling, to find that the College converted certain ruinous buildings which bordered on the Cowgate, into a pavilion-shaped cold bath, which was open to the inhabitants generally, at a charge for each ablution of 12 shillings Scots and

Its Public Bath.

[*] Paterson's Abstract of the Minutes.

one penny to the servant. But those who subscribed
one guinea annually might resort to it as often as they
pleased.

At first a Committee of the Physicians appears to
have attended to receive the fees and superintend the
ablutions ; but this having been found inconvenient, the
President was allowed to let the bath on lease.

In 1714 the bath was let to Alexander Murray and
John Russell of Bradshaw, W.S. The speculation does
not seem to have been a successful one, as they and
several successive tenants were continually craving for
an abatement of the rent, while the bath was as continually requiring repair.

In 1722 a new Hall was erected in the garden, the
necessary funds having been borrowed from Robert
Marshall, merchant in Edinburgh.

" Notwithstanding," says Dr. Beilby, " all the sums
that had been expended in the erection of a *new* building, and in the repair of the *old*, the former seems to
have been slight and insufficient, and the latter was in
so dilapidated a condition, that in 1760 it was resolved
to build a new Hall upon the premises then held by the

College, and a plan was obtained and approved, the
execution of which was to cost £800, a sum that was
declared to be within the means of the College ; but
before commencing the work, it was determined to
submit the design to the judgment of Mr. Robert Adam,
the King's Architect, who, after inspecting it, gave it as
his opinion that it was unsuitable, and quite unworthy
of the Body for which it was intended ;—and, with great

liberality, Mr. Adam gave, spontaneously and gratuitously, a plan of his own, the execution of which was
estimated to cost between £5000 and £6000, exclusive
of the statues, busts, and bas-reliefs, which he recom-

mended as appropriate and almost necessary. This plan, after being handed about and admired, was laid aside as unsuitable to the finances of the College.

"At length, however, such was the state of the College buildings, that the books were suffering great injury, and it became absolutely necessary to remove them without further delay. Application was made to the Managers of the Royal Infirmary for permission to deposit the Library in a spare apartment of that building, and also for liberty to hold the meetings of the College in the Manager's Board-room. These requests were readily granted, and the privilege was continued to the College for fifteen years. The Library had now become so extensive, that it was insured for £600. *Royal Infirmary affords a Temporary Asylum.*

"By this time a design had been formed, and some progress had already been made, towards laying out a New Town in the northern vicinity of the city. To this situation the eyes of the College were turned, as being greatly preferable to that which it had hitherto occupied. A petition was presented to the Town Council for a site, and the negotiation was nearly concluded for the lot of ground on which the Register Office now stands, for which the College was to have paid a feu-duty of £8 sterling per annum; but Mr. Adam, the architect who was employed by Government to give a design for the Register Office, perceiving how peculiarly desirable that situation was for the noble building he intended to erect, had influence enough to prevent the consummation of the transaction, and to secure that site for himself. *New Town. Site sought there.* *Site of present Register Office all but obtained.*

"The Town Council then agreed to give a site just where the Scott Monument has been erected; but this was deemed by the College ineligible. A choice of two sites was next offered,—the one in George Square and the other in George Street, the latter of *Site of present Scott Monument offered and rejected.*

the objecting Fellows, to endeavour to get the transaction rescinded by an appeal to the Courts of Law. In
the end the College relinquished all intention of selling
the building, and all trace of the proceedings relative to
it was removed from the Minutes. It was now resolved
to take possession of the New Hall without further
delay, submitting to whatever inconvenience might be
sustained from the yet unfinished state of the interior.
The College assembled in it for the first time on the
7th of August 1781, just one hundred years after being
first incorporated."

During the subsequent removal of that building,
after being disposed of by the College under circumstances to be immediately narrated, the foundation-
stone was discovered in May 1845. A well-cut inscription on this interesting relic sets forth that it was
laid on the 27th November 1775 by the President,
Dr. Cullen. Enclosed in the stone, a bottle was
found, containing, 1st, A Parchment Roll, on which
are beautifully inscribed the names of the Fellows of
the College at the time ; 2nd, Several British Coins of
date 1771 ; 3rd, A Silver Medal, representing on the
one side the future College, surmounted by the words,
"ARTI SALUTIFERAE SACRUM," at its base a
serpent entwined round a club ; on the other side—

AEDES

COLL. REG. MED.

EDINE.

HIC POSITAE

XXVII NOV. A.D. MDCCLXXV

CURANTE PRAESIDE

GULIELMO CULLEN

ARCHITECTO

JAC. CRAIG.

Hall in George
Street.

Foundation
Stone.

Laid by Pro-
fessor Cullen.

Inscription on
Medal.

4th, Another Silver Medal, having the Arms of the City of Edinburgh on the one side, and on the other an inscription, bearing that this memorial had been presented to Mr. Craig, Architect, by the Council of the City of Edinburgh, in compliment to his professional talents, in the year 1767. It is as follows :—

Memorial to Architect.

JACOBO CRAIG

ARCHITECTO

PROPTER OPTIMAM

EDINBURGI NOVI

ICHONOGRAPHIAM

D . D

SENATUS

EDINBURGENUS

M·DCCLXVII.

These interesting relics of an age gone by are now in the possession of the College.

Hall in George Street sold.

The same poverty which had prevented the College from availing itself of the plans of Adam, and which had caused it to desire to part with its New Hall in George Street, even before it had entered on its occupation, still pressed heavily on it. Having at that time no funded capital, it was entirely dependent on the entrance fees paid by Fellows, a fluctuating and inadequate source of income. Besides, beautiful as the George Street Hall was in its outward proportions, its internal arrangements were not so convenient as might have been desired, and it is therefore not to be wondered at that when the College found that its site was coveted by a wealthy banking corporation, its poverty and not its will consented; and in 1843 the George Street Hall was sold to the Commercial Bank for £20,000,—a sum which it was hoped would suffice to

Purchased by Commercial Bank.

build a more commodious, if less imposing, Hall, and leave a surplus to secure a certain annual income.

Although the transaction was obviously an advantageous one for the College, it was not without some difficulty that many of the Fellows made up their minds to part with a building of which they were justly proud.

On the 8th of August 1844, the foundation-stone of the present Hall, designed by Mr. Thomas Hamilton, was laid by the President, Dr. Renton, in presence of the Fellows of the College, and various representative persons. As is customary on such occasions, a bottle containing various memorials was deposited in the stone. In this instance these were—1st, A copy of the last edition of the Edinburgh Pharmacopœia, containing a list of the Fellows of the College; 2nd, A work regarding the private affairs of the College, printed several years previously; 3rd, An Edinburgh Almanac for the current year; 4th, Several British Coins of the day; and lastly, A silver plate with an inscription in Latin suitable to the occasion.

During the erection of the Hall the College rented for its use a private house, No. 121 George Street, from which, in 1846, it removed to its present building.

Ample as the accommodation of the Hall appeared to be at the date of its erection, the rapid additions to the Library, and the great increase in the number of Fellows, consequent on a reduction of the entry money, and other changes, soon rendered some extension necessary.

After long and anxious deliberation, and much delicate negotiation, the Trustees, on the recommendation of the Council, agreed to purchase from the Trustees of the late Dr. Reid, formerly Principal of the

Edinburgh Institution for Languages and Mathematics, the building in which the business of that Seminary was conducted.

The purchase was made in 1865 for £6000, but the house was then under a lease to the successors of the late Dr. Reid, which did not expire until May 1867. This house, No. 8 Queen Street, which immediately adjoins the Hall on the east, had been built and occupied as his residence by Baron Orde, and considerably exceeds in size the other houses in the street.

Plans of Library Extension.

Considerable difference of opinion existed as to how the new purchase could be made most available for the extension of the present Hall. Mr. Bryce, as instructed by the Council, prepared a plan for a new Library, to extend along the back of the existing Hall and of the new purchase, and this plan was laid before the College It was ultimately, however, agreed to carry out so far the design of Mr. Hamilton, the architect who planned

Alteration of Hall.

the original building, and double the size of the existing Hall, by extending it backwards, at the same time completely altering the character of the roof according to suggestions made by Mr. Bryce, with the view of increasing the light and improving the acoustic properties of the Hall. Additional accommodation for books was provided by arranging round the new Hall dwarf bookcases, which would, it was supposed, contain all the additions which the Library was likely to

New Building.

acquire for some years to come. At the same time a spacious building was erected at the back of the adjoining house, which was leased for a term of years to the proprietors of the Institution, with a view to its ultimately affording additional accommodation for the Library. But so rapidly has the accumulation of books gone on, that it was soon found necessary to connect this building with the Hall, and convert it into a Library capable of containing about twenty-five thousand volumes.

It will be apparent to every one who has perused the preceding pages, that the College of Physicians was not, until very recently, a wealthy body; and yet, as has been observed by Dr. Poole (Appendix to Report on Licensing), " it has throughout its career manifested a conduct that would do honour to a rich community." . . . " It appears to have existed purely for the welfare of society."

On the 7th February 1738, the Members were recommended to encourage the design of founding an Orphan Hospital. In return for the assistance afforded, the President of the College is still *ex officio* a Governor of that Institution.

On the 3rd of May 1744, £50 was unanimously voted by the College to aid in the erection of an Episcopal Chapel on the site formerly possessed by the College in Fountain Close. This building is now in possession of, and used by, the Roman Catholics.

On the 20th March 1775, fifty guineas was subscribed towards the erection of the High School, which was afterwards converted into part of the Surgical Hospital; and this at a time when extraordinary efforts were being made to raise the necessary funds to erect the Hall in George Street.

On the 13th November 1789, the sum of £150 was subscribed to assist in the erection of the University of Edinburgh; and when, rather more than eighty years later, a scheme was set on foot for extending the scientific and educational buildings of the University, the College, on the 6th May 1873, subscribed a sum of one thousand guineas in aid of it. The College subsequently, on the 4th February 1885, subscribed a further sum of five hundred guineas towards the completion of the new University Buildings.

On examining the Minutes it will be found that many of our oldest Charitable Institutions were indebted to the College for pecuniary aid—as the Blind Asylum, the Lunatic Asylum (more than once), and the Charity Workhouse.

Blind Asylum, Lunatic Asylum, Charity Workhouse.

To other Charitable Institutions.

In 1874, one hundred guineas was voted in aid of the Building Fund of the Royal Maternity Hospital, and in 1875, fifty guineas in aid of the Livingstone Medical Missionary Memorial Dispensary. In 1889 the College voted the sum of two hundred and fifty guineas to Queen Victoria's Jubilee Institute for Nurses.

Contributions to various Objects.

In 1871, fifty guineas was subscribed to the local fund for defraying the expenses of the reception of the British Association in Edinburgh; in 1881, fifty pounds was voted towards defraying the expenses of the International Medical Congress which met in London; and in 1891 a sum of twenty-five guineas was voted in aid of the International Congress of Hygiene and Demography held in London.

Among other liberal donations may also be chronicled one to the National Monument in 1822, of fifty guineas; and the same day (30th August) one of a like amount for a statue to commemorate the visit of George IV. to his Scottish metropolis; one of fifty pounds for a statue of Dr. Jenner at Gloucester, 4th November 1823; one to the Scottish National Memorial of the late Prince Consort of twenty-five guineas, on the 20th June 1862; and one of twenty-five guineas to the fund for erecting a statue to Dr. David Livingstone, African explorer. On 5th May 1863, one hundred pounds was voted by the College to assist in repairing the tomb of the late Dr. Cullen, in Kirknewton burial ground. On the 24th February 1880, the sum of one hundred guineas was voted in aid of the fund for the Restoration of the Cathedral Church of St. Giles.

Two hundred pounds was voted for the relief of the poor in the famine of 1796. On the 24th December 1878, a sum of two hundred and fifty guineas was voted in aid of the fund for the relief of the sufferers by the failure of the City of Glasgow Bank.

On the 15th February 1796, £200 was voted towards the defence of the country "in the present exigency of public affairs." In return for this liberality, the Government, judging of the capabilities of the College more by its generosity than by its actual income, imposed a Stamp Duty upon the Diplomas of its Licentiates and Fellows—the former of which was only, after repeated application, removed in 1859; while the latter still exists.

Besides these donations to public objects, the College seem to have been not unmindful of the claims of their own Fellows, and occasional contributions to the widows of deceased Fellows are recorded in the Minutes. Sundry donations to the College also seem to have called forth a pecuniary return, as when, on two occasions (August 4, 1713; January 11, 1715) the College voted a guinea to Mr. Alexander Bruce for a book he had presented to the Library; and, in 1717, two guineas to Mr. Gordon, surgeon, Aberdeen, "for a great excresence he had removed from a person's cheek, and complimented the College therewith." In 1696 the College presented to the University a Boat, honestly avowing that it was because there was no place in the College to keep it, to which is appended the additional reason, that the University had already the oars and the skirt of the barbarous man that was in it. This

Marginal notes:
National Defence Fund.

Tax imposed upon Fellows and Licentiates.

Donations to Widows of Fellows.

Curious presents, and their acknowledgment.

boat seems to have come into possession of the College as one of Sir A. Balfour's curiosities.

Care for the
Sick Poor.

To the College of Physicians also the public are indebted for the origin of some of our best Medical Charities. A care for the sick poor manifested itself at a very early period of its history; for we find that, at the third meeting of the College (10th February 1682), two Physicians were appointed to serve the poor of the City and Suburbs.

Erection of
Infirmary first
suggested by
College.

These appointments continued to be regularly made; but the Physicians, "in serving the poor," found all their efforts often unavailing, from the want of suitable accommodation, diet, and nursing, and accordingly about 1725 the plan of an Infirmary was suggested by the College to several well-disposed persons; and the scheme having been favourably received by them, a public meeting was called to make the proposal known. Thereafter, on the 1st February 1726, we find the following Minute:—

Minute regard-
ing commence-
ment of Infir-
mary, February
1726.

"The President represented to the College that according to their desire, he and several of the members had set on foot a subscription for erecting and maintaining an Infirmary or Hospital for the sick poor, and had pretty good success; and recommended to all the Members of the College to use their best endeavours to procure more subscriptions for accomplishing so good and charitable a work."

Undertake the
Medical charge
of the Infirmary
gratuitously.

On 1st August 1727, the College bound itself by a Minute, "that one or more of their number shall attend the said Hospital faithfully and freely, without any prospect of reward or salary, until the Stock of the said Hospital shall be so increased that it can afford a reasonable allowance for one or two physicians."

On 7th November 1727, appears a Minute, "That the Members of the College had sett this charitable work on foot;" and on the 7th May 1728, the College memorialized, and sent a deputation to the General Assembly of the Church of Scotland, calling the attention of that Reverend Body to the value of the proposed charity.

On the 5th August 1729, the Minutes of the College show that a temporary Hospital was established by it, in which the sick poor were attended by its Fellows.

It will be seen from the History of the Royal Infirmary, published by authority (1778), that as soon as £2000 had been subscribed, "The College of Physicians called the Contributors together; at this meeting a Committee was appointed, who prepared a report regarding the management, which was submitted to a second meeting, when twenty Managers were elected." The Infirmary was incorporated by Royal Charter, 25th August 1736. By this Charter it was provided that five of the Managers *at least*, must be Fellows of the College. By the new Charter, granted to the Royal Infirmary 20th June 1870, the number of the Representatives of the College on the Board of Management was reduced to two.

At a meeting of the College, 7th February 1738, a letter was read from the Managers of the Royal Infirmary, stating that it had been resolved for the future that none but Fellows of the College were to act as Physicians to that charity.

1st August 1738.—The College attended as a body at the laying of the foundation-stone of the Royal Infirmary; and the next day voted thirty guineas to the funds, to be raised by voluntary contribution.

On the 2nd November 1742, the College ordained

that each Fellow should, on admission to the College,
pay twenty shillings to the Infirmary.

2nd February 1785.—The College voted fifty guineas
to the funds of the Royal Infirmary.

On the 2nd February 1819, the College, on account
of the expense incident to the prevalence of fever, voted
fifty guineas to the Infirmary, and ten guineas to the
Society for preventing Contagious Fever.

It having been decided to remove the Royal
Infirmary to a new site, and a public subscription
having been instituted to provide the necessary funds,
the College, on the 18th February 1868, voted the sum
of £1000 in aid of this object.

On the 3rd May 1879, the College agreed to contribute a sufficient sum (£630) to furnish two Medical
Wards in the New Royal Infirmary.

On the 29th October 1879, the College attended as a
Body at the inauguration of the New Royal Infirmary.

There are many other Minutes showing the close
and intimate relationship subsisting between the College
and the Infirmary ; and it should be known to all the
Fellows that the College can insist that none but its
Fellows shall act as Physicians to the noble institution
which it was mainly instrumental in founding.

The Royal Edinburgh Asylum for the Insane at
Morningside also owes its origin to the enlightened
liberality of the College of Physicians. On the 2nd of
August 1791, a Committee reported to a Quarterly
Meeting of the College on the propriety of placing the
Private Asylums under regulation, and also of erecting
a Public Asylum near Edinburgh, similar to one at
York. This Report pointed out that if Trustees in
whom the public had confidence were appointed to
manage the proposed Asylum, donations and bequests

might be expected to come in. It further suggested that the Trustees, to whom a sum of money had been left by the late Mr. Watson to establish a Foundling Hospital, should be applied to, to give it to the proposed Lunatic Asylum, as being a charity of a less doubtful character. It also proposed the names of those who should be Trustees. This Report was unanimously adopted by the College, and was the first movement which led to the formation of the present magnificent establishment at Morningside.

The publication of a Pharmacopœia engaged much of the attention of the College, and it was issued in 1799; from that time the publication of successive editions enabled the College to keep pace with the progress of scientific discovery.

Pharmacopœia, first edition, 1699.

When, however, the Medical Act of 1858 conferred on the General Council of Medical Education and Registration the power of issuing a Pharmacopœia, which should be obligatory in all three divisions of the kingdom, the College, on the 1st of July 1862, gave its formal assent to the introduction into Parliament of a Bill, the effect of which was that the British Pharmacopœia, published by the General Medical Council, superseded in Scotland the Pharmacopœia published by the College of Physicians.

Power of issuing Pharmacopœia relinquished in 1862.

The College, restricted by its original Charter in many ways—prevented from connecting itself with any Medical School—compelled to receive, without examination and without ballot, the Graduates of all Scottish Universities, and having allowed any power of licensing which it had possessed to pass from it by desuetude, occupied a position of a very peculiar character among the Medical Bodies. Highly respectable and respected, containing among its Fellows the most

Position of the College among Medical Bodies.

eminent Physicians in Edinburgh, and the Medical Professors of the University, full of good works and charity, it never comprised any large proportion of those practising medicine in Edinburgh, or in Scotland, who usually joined the College of Surgeons.

Privileges of its Fellows.

This state of matters existed, notwithstanding the exclusive privileges which the Fellows of the College possessed, of being the only Physicians of the Infirmary, and of certain of the Dispensaries in the city. The unsatisfactory condition of such a state of matters, as bearing upon the real interest and due importance of the College, pressed itself at various times on the attention of the Fellows.

Licence of College.

Up to 1829 the College had issued a Licence to practise ; but this was given, as the Charter required, to all University Graduates, without examination. It was conferred on no others ; and on 1st November 1763, the Licentiateship was made a necessary stepping-stone to the Fellowship of the College. Finding, however, that by making each fellow pass through the grade of Licentiate the College compelled him to pay a double tax to Government, this regulation was abolished in 1829, and, the Fellows being elected without passing through the inferior grade, the old order of Licentiates ceased to exist.

Discontinuance of Licentiates.

Committees twice report in favour of Licensing other than University Graduates.

On two several occasions an elaborate Report was drawn up and printed, strongly recommending the College to admit another class of Licentiates, who should derive their Qualification to practise directly from the College ; but, besides that such a measure was of doubtful legality, influences were at work within the College which were sufficient to frustrate all efforts in that direction.

Changes in composition of College.

In the meantime, however, certain changes in the Extra-Academical School, particularly the working of a regulation which required every Teacher of Medicine or Surgery to belong to, and subsequently to be examined as to his capabilities for teaching by, a College of Physicians or Surgeons, were gradually introducing a new element into the College, and associating it with interests very different from those with which, in its earliest years, it had been inseparably connected.

It would be a tedious task to enumerate all the keen discussions to which the struggle between the party which had long been dominant in the Councils of the College, and that which was gradually springing up, gave rise; even the copious Minutes of the Meetings held during the protracted contendings scarcely serve to record their extent; suffice it to say, that the passing of the Medical Act of 1858 inaugurated a new era in the history of the College. An elaborate Report on the manner in which the Act would affect the College was presented by the Council to the College on the 21st September 1859, in which it was argued that the admission of Licentiates other than University Graduates was, in the altered state of the whole medical profession, absolutely essential for the credit of the profession, as well as for the very existence of the College. It will probably appear strange to those Fellows who have joined the College since 1860, and who hear read at each Quarterly Meeting the long list of Licentiates admitted by examination, that the proposal to examine and confer a Licence on gentlemen who had not previously obtained a University degree was strenuously resisted, not only by Professors of the University, but by a large number of Fellows who had no direct connection with that Body, and that it was ultimately carried on the 5th of April 1859 only by the vote of one Fellow; and that there actually appears in

[marginal notes:]
Struggles in College.

Report on Medical Act.

Recommends a new order of Licentiates.

Proposal to License other than University Graduates.

Strenuously resisted.

Carried by one vote.

Protested against.

the Minutes of the College (26th April 1859) a protest, signed by ten Fellows, against the Licence being conferred on any but University Graduates.

Regulations for Licence.

The College having, however, resolved to examine and admit to the profession, as Licentiates of their Body, gentlemen who had no other qualifications to practise, or who might wish to possess the Licence of the College in addition to qualifications already obtained, proceeded to consider a report of the Council, suggesting the regulations under which the Licence should be conferred. As one of these regulations was unfortunate enough to provoke keen discussions in the College, as

Alleged sale of Licences.

well as hostile criticisms on its policy from without; and as the proceedings of the College in this respect have been, and still are, the subject of misrepresentation, it appears essential, even in this slight sketch of its history, to enter somewhat fully into an explanation of the motives which actuated the College in a matter which has been the subject of so much controversy.

Sufficiency of Study and Examination.

With regard to the permanent regulations, the amount of study and of examination required of Candidates for the Licence has never been considered otherwise than sufficient, it was the exceptional admissions, during what was termed the Year of Grace, which excited all the clamour with which the College was assailed.

Exceptional admissions in "Year of Grace."

The College had been compelled, by its Charter of 1681, drawn up under the influence of the Scottish Universities, to admit all Graduates of these Bodies within its ranks without examination. There existed various Licensing Bodies, which required of their Licentiates an education and examination equal to that of any, and superior to that of some, of these Universities. The London College of Physicians had passed regulations extending for one year the privilege of becoming Licentiates of their Body to all Graduates or Licentiates of Universities in Great Britain, simply requiring of them the recommendation of three Fellows, and the test of the ballot. The Commissioners for the Improvement of the Scottish Universities had intimated that the Degrees of these Bodies were henceforth to be considered as Licences for general practice. Under these circumstances, it was strongly urged upon the Council of the College that it would be a right and fitting thing to inaugurate the new era in Medical practice, by extending for a limited period, to men equally well educated and equally qualified to practise, the privilege long enjoyed by University Licentiates, of entering the Body without examination. This Act of Grace was intended for a large body of men of mature age, who, having begun life as Surgeons or Apothecaries, had established their position as good Practitioners, and were naturally anxious to be connected with a Body of higher position than a Trading Company.

Many young men did, undoubtedly, apply for admission, but, with few exceptions, they were told that they must undergo an examination, as the Regulations of the "Year of Grace" were only intended for Practitioners of mature age. The securities instituted by the College to prevent the conferring of the Licence on unsuitable persons were the following:—

1. That the Candidate had passed the examination of one or more of the Licensing Boards.
2. That he must give up the sale of drugs, if he had previously dealt in them.
3. That he must produce certificates of his fitness to be a Licentiate of a College of Physicians from Hospital Physicians, or men of eminence in the profession.

Regulations of London College.

Reasons for the relaxation.

Intended for men of mature age.

Young men refused.

Securities taken in regard to admission.

4. That his claims for admission must be carefully
   scrutinized by the Council of the College.

5. That these claims must be subjected to a ballot in the
   College, a majority of two-thirds of those who voted
   being essential to his admission.

Supposed to be
better tests in
the circum-
stances than a
mere examina-
tion.

These appeared to the College to be better tests of
the fitness of men to be Licentiates of the College,
than the subjecting them to an examination framed
for Students fresh from their studies. They were in
strict accordance with the principles of an *ad eundem*
admission which almost every Licensing Body at that
time permitted.

Large number
of Applicants.

The boon thus offered was sought for with an eager-
ness which startled even those who had been most forward in urging it. In fact, it was its very success which
provoked the attacks made upon it. Another circum-
stance, naturally calculated to excite jealousy, was, that
many of the Licentiates of the College, possessing no
University Degree, at once proceeded to call themselves

Assumption by
Licentiates of
title of Doctor.

"Doctors of Medicine." Unjustifiable as this was, the
Edinburgh College of Physicians was not chargeable
with any blame in the matter; it had encouraged no such
assumption of titles. The mistake, as far as it could be
traced, seemed to have arisen from the old practice of the
London College of Physicians to style all its Licentiates

Practice of the
London College
of Physicians.

Doctors. That this is no mere surmise appears from
the fact, that the then newly appointed Registrar under
the Medical Act, who had long been Registrar to the
London College of Physicians, at first gave the title of
Doctor to the Licentiates of the Edinburgh College in
the receipt granted to them for their Registration-fee;
and from the other fact, that as the agitation proceeded,

Practice of
Registrar and
Medical Council.

the title of M.D., which had long stood after the names
of many gentlemen in the Army and Navy Lists, who

had no other claim to that title than that these gentlemen were Licentiates of the London College of Physicians, began rapidly to disappear from these Lists.

It may be, as indeed was afterwards admitted, that a privilege which, in the opinion of the College, might safely have been extended to gentlemen who had previously been examined and licensed in Medicine, ought not to have been offered to those who only held a Surgical Qualification, and who had undergone no examination in Medicine.

Probably those who proposed the scheme, at a time when the requirements of the various Licensing Bodies were not so well known as they now are, overlooked the fact that there were Bodies licensing for practice which did not examine in Medicine; certain it is that the mistake was no sooner pointed out than it was rectified, by the institution of an examination in Medicine alone, to be passed by those Candidates who had not already been subjected to that ordeal.

The jealousy and rancour which had been excited were not, however, to be easily appeased. The Medical Press still reiterated their charge against the College, of "selling Licences" to practise. The London College of Physicians was induced to remonstrate with the Edinburgh College, which it did in the most courteous terms. A reply, equally courteous, was forwarded to it, pointing out the reasons which had induced the Edinburgh College to modify its terms of admission; and regulations subsequently passed by the London College would appear to show that in some important respects it had become converted to the views of the Edinburgh College. It indeed was the inventor of what was called a Year of Grace, during which it agreed to admit certain men to its Licence without

further examination. The Edinburgh College imitated
its example; but, in consequence of the different state
of Medical practice in Scotland, and its consequently
different position, its admissions were on a wider scale.
If the giving of Licences without examination be a
crime, and if it is to be stigmatised as a Sale of Licences,
both Colleges are reprehensible, as well as every other
Examining Board which admitted *ad eundem* Licentiates,
as most of them did at that period.

Non-graduated
Licentiates not
inferior to
University
Graduates.

It would be difficult to prove that the Licentiates of
the various Bodies who were admitted without examination to the Edinburgh College, were inferior in medical
knowledge and ability to practise their profession, to
many Licentiates of Universities who were eligible for
admission to the Licence, without examination.

Extraordinary
proceeding of
British Medical
Association.

The British Medical Association, a Body which contained in its ranks a large number of Fellows of the
Royal College of Physicians of Edinburgh, and which,
during its recent meeting in Edinburgh, had received
the utmost hospitality and encouragement from the
Edinburgh College, acting on the unwarrantable publication of a private letter, addressed by a Fellow of the
Edinburgh College to one of its Members, without requesting or even giving any opportunity for explanation
from the College or any of its Fellows, passed a
resolution condemnatory of its Regulations,—a piece of
interference, on the part of a self-constituted body, of a
most reprehensible kind, and which had the effect of
causing a number of its most distinguished Edinburgh
Members to withdraw from its ranks. Ultimately, at a
meeting of the Medical Council, Sir D. J. Corrigan,
on the 8th of August 1859, moved, "That the General
Medical Council is of opinion that any Degree or
Licence obtained since the passing of the Medical

Act, without regular examination by the University or College granting such Degree or Licence, ought not to be placed on the *Register*, excepting *ad eundem* Degrees, or Degrees and Licences in Medicine or Surgery of any University in the United Kingdom, admitted to the Fellowships or Licentiateships of the several Colleges of Physicians and Surgeons." This motion was strenuously resisted. Dr. Alexander Wood, the President of the Edinburgh College, and its Representative in the Medical Council, showed the real position of the question, and the unfair advantage which such a resolution would give to the Graduates and Licentiates of Universities; after which the Medical Council adopted an amendment to Sir D. Corrigan's motion, proposed by Dr. Wood, namely, "That the General Medical Council are of opinion that for the future no Licence or Degree should be given by any of the Bodies in Schedule (A) to the Medical Act, without examination."

Since the publication of this opinion no one has received a Licence without examination; but the examination is modified and restricted in the case of gentlemen already holding a Licence to practise. It may not be out of place to state here, that, long before the passing of the Medical Act, it had become the conviction of the leading Fellows of the College that it had been a highly impolitic proceeding on the part of the London College of Physicians to refuse the offer made to it by the Government, in the year 1815, to undertake the licensing of General Practitioners in England, as by so doing that important office was thrown into the hands of a trading Company of Apothecaries, and thereby the name of Apothecary, as that of a Medical Practitioner, was legalised, instead of one of

Proceedings of General Medical Council.

Resolution of the General Council of Medical Education and Registration.

No Licence now given without examination.

Modified Examination.

the time-honoured names—Physician or Surgeon ; that
they were desirous of having the name Apothecary,
as applied to a Medical Practitioner, wiped out without
delay ; that, at the same time, they recognised the
excellence of the Regulations acted on for a number of
years by the Apothecaries' Company with regard to
their curriculum and examinations, and therefore they
felt themselves called on, as soon as it was in the power
of the College, to offer to those gentlemen who had
been compelled, for many years, to put up with the title
of Apothecary, the opportunity of exchanging it for that
of a Licentiate of a College of Physicians, provided they
could produce testimonials of respectability and ability
in the past conduct of their practice.

Such is a brief outline of this most critical part of
the history of the College, with which it is incumbent
on every Fellow to be acquainted, and regarding which
explanations are often asked even at the present day.

But the College had still a serious difficulty to
contend against in the shape of a tax of Fifteen Pounds
imposed on every Licence which was issued. By the
Medical Act all exclusive privileges enjoyed by certain
Bodies had been swept away, and the Licentiates of any
of the Bodies in Schedule (A) to the Medical Act had
an equal right to practise Medicine and Surgery, or
Medicine or Surgery, in any part of Her Majesty's
dominions. The Licentiates of Colleges of Physicians,
and the Graduates of Universities, were alone subjected
to a Stamp Duty, and this proved an important obstacle
to any increase in their number. Various attempts had
been made at various periods to obtain a remission of
these duties, but without success.

On the 27th November 1858, Dr. Alexander Wood,
then President of the College, and its representative in

Government
Tax on
Licentiates.

Failure of re-
peated attempts
to obtain its
removal.

Renewed efforts
in 1858.

the Medical Council, moved that Body to memorialize the Lords of Her Majesty's Treasury on the subject. This memorial was not prepared or transmitted till the 5th February 1859. No effect having been produced by it, Dr. Wood endeavoured to organize a joint deputation from the three Royal Colleges of Physicians, to the Treasury, but without success. Ultimately, at the request of the Council, he proceeded to London, and on the 20th May 1859 he received the announcement that the Stamp Duty of Fifteen Pounds on the Diploma of Licentiates would be remitted. For his services on this occasion the President received a special vote of thanks from the College at its meeting on the 14th June 1859; and for his other invaluable services in placing the College on the advantageous footing which it had lately attained, it was unanimously resolved, in the following year, to present him with his portrait, painted by Sir John Watson Gordon.

Stamp Duty on Diploma of Licentiates removed.

Acknowledgment of services of Dr. Wood.

Other difficulties still beset the College in regard to its new Licence. The English Poor Law Board, and the Army Medical Board, not being previously aware of its existence, refused to recognise it as a sufficient Medical Qualification. This led to a correspondence between the heads of these Bodies and the President of the College, and eventually Dr. Wood, proceeding to London, succeeded in obtaining the recognition of the Licence of the College, which was thereafter regarded as a sufficient Medical Qualification.

Recognition by Poor Law Board and Army Medical Board.

In 1859 important arrangements were made with the Royal College of Surgeons of Edinburgh and the Faculty of Physicians and Surgeons of Glasgow, both of which have the right to license in Surgery. In combination with each of these Bodies the College granted a "Double Qualification," conferring upon

Arrangement with College of Surgeons of Edinburgh and Glasgow Faculty for " Double Qualification."

the holder the right to practise all branches of the profession in every part of Her Majesty's dominions.

The terms on which these alliances were formed will be best understood from the following proposals submitted, by the two Edinburgh Colleges, to the General Council of Medical Education and Registration, on the 6th of August 1859, and approved of by that Body on the 8th of the same month :—

"1. By Clause 19 of the Medical Act, 'any two or more of the Colleges and Bodies mentioned in Schedule (A) may, with the sanction and under the directions of the General Medical Council, unite or co-operate in conducting the Examinations for Qualifications to be registered under this Act.' Hence it is quite competent for a College of

Physicians and a College of Surgeons to combine, in order, by a Joint Examination, to give a Double Qualification, embracing Medicine and Surgery.

"2. Co-operation between a College of Physicians and a College of Surgeons being legal, as stated above, the Colleges of Physicians and Surgeons of Edinburgh propose, with the sanction of the General Medical Council, to make an arrangement for the purpose of granting, by a series of Examinations, Preliminary and Professional, their respective Licences in Medicine and Surgery, so as to constitute a Double Qualification.

"3. It is proposed that the Preliminary Examination in Literature and Science, and also the Examinations on those professional subjects which are common to Medicine and Surgery, shall be conducted conjointly by a Board formed of Examiners in equal proportions from the two Colleges.

"4. It is proposed that the Examinations in *Medicine* shall be conducted exclusively by Examiners from the College of Physicians, and the Examinations in *Surgery* exclusively by Examiners from the College of Surgeons.

"5. It is proposed that the decision as to the competency of the Candidate, in all the branches except Medicine and

Surgery, shall rest with the conjoined Board of Examiners from the two Colleges; but that the decision as to his competency in Medicine and in Surgery shall rest entirely, in the one case with the Examiners from the College of Physicians, in the other case with the Examiners from the College of Surgeons.

"6. It is proposed that, having passed through the final Examinations, the Candidate shall receive two separate Diplomas —one from each College—signed by the Office-Bearers of each respectively, so that he may be enabled to produce them to the Registrar under the Medical Act, and to register two separate Qualifications—viz., L.R.C.P. Ed., and L.R.C.S. Ed.

"7. The Colleges wish it to be clearly understood, that such co-operation is not to interfere in any degree with the right of each College to grant its Diploma separately, as heretofore, to those who may wish a Single Qualification, or with the right of each College to make similar arrangements with other Licensing Bodies, if deemed expedient, and if sanctioned by the Medical Council.

"8. For the purpose of carrying out the objects stated above, the Colleges have prepared a Series of Regulations, which they beg now to submit to the Medical Council for their consideration."

These "Double Qualifications" were eagerly sought after; and the College was thus enabled, after long and arduous struggles, to exercise the licensing functions legitimately appertaining to such a Body, and, while containing on its Roll of Fellows the names of the most distinguished Physicians in Scotland, to confer the right to practise Medicine on a numerous and increasing body of general Practitioners. *Success of the Scheme.*

Several changes have in recent years been effected in regard to the admission of Licentiates. *Later Changes.*

On the 5th February 1884 the College resolved not to grant the Licence as a Single Qualification, excep-

Arrangement
with other
Scottish
Corporations

to those who have already obtained a registrable Diploma in Surgery.

During the same year, 18th March 1884, the College approved of and adopted a scheme for conferring the Licence in association with the other two Scottish Corporations as a Triple Qualification, and the two Double Qualifications were superseded. The scheme then adopted, which was approved of by the General Council of Medical Education and Registration, 31st March 1884, and which has worked most successfully, may be quoted in its entirety:—

Conditions of
Triple
Qualification.

" I. That each of the three Medical Corporations of Scotland—namely, the Royal College of Physicians of Edinburgh, the Royal College of Surgeons of Edinburgh, and the Faculty of Physicians and Surgeons of Glasgow—while reserving to itself liberty to confer its Higher Qualification or Qualifications as it may deem proper, resolves, That on and after the 1st day of October 1884, it shall abstain from the exercise of its power of granting its Licence separately and independently, except only in the cases herein provided for :—That is to say, the Royal College of Physicians of Edinburgh may, notwithstanding this Agreement, grant its Licence to Candidates already possessed of one or other of the Surgical Qualifications mentioned in Schedule (*A*) of the Medical Act, 1858 ; and the Royal College of Surgeons of Edinburgh, and the Faculty of Physicians and Surgeons of Glasgow, may each grant its Licence to Candidates already registered Licentiates of one of the Colleges of Physicians of the United Kingdom, or Graduates in Medicine of a British or Irish University mentioned in Schedule (*A*) of the Medical Act.

"II. That the three Medical Authorities above mentioned shall co-operate to form an Examining Board to conduct their Examinations in combination ; and that from the date to be fixed for the commencement of this Scheme, the Agreement or Convention at present subsisting between the Royal College of Physicians of Edinburgh, and the Royal College of Surgeons of Edinburgh, by which, under Section XIX. of the Medical Act, 1858, these two Colleges conduct Examinations in combination, and the similar Agreement or Convention at present subsisting between the Royal College of Physicians of Edinburgh, and the Faculty of Physicians and Surgeons of Glasgow, by which these two Bodies conduct Examinations in combination, shall cease and terminate; and the provisions of this present Agreement, in respect to Combined Examinations, shall alone be valid.

"III. That each of the co-operating Medical Authorities shall elect two Members of a Committee, herein called the Committee of Management. Of this Committee of six Members three Members shall retire annually, that is to say, one elected by each of the Authorities; but they shall be eligible for re-election, but shall not at same time hold office as Examiners. To the Members of this Committee reasonable remuneration shall be paid for attendance at the Meetings.

"IV. That the duties of the Committee of Management shall be—

(*a*) To elect annually a Chairman, who shall also be Convener, and have both a deliberative and casting vote.

(*b*) To fix the periods and places of Examination under the provisions of this Scheme.

(*c*) To convene the Examiners, and to apportion their work at the different periods and places of Examination, in accordance with the provisions of this Scheme.

(*d*) To appoint a General Treasurer and any other Executive Officers they may consider necessary.

(*e*) To determine the Fees to be paid to the Examiners and other Officers.

(*f*) To arrange for the visitation of Examinations.

Conditions of Triple Qualification.

(*g*) To act generally as a Committee of Superintendence and Reference under the provisions of this
Scheme, and also in all matters concerning the
Examinations which are not specially provided
for in this Scheme.

"V. That each of the co-operating Medical Authorities
shall elect its own Examiners to examine on special or allied
subjects, each of these Authorities determining the number
to be elected on each subject, and the period for which they
shall hold office; and notification of the names of the
Examiners, with the subjects for which they are appointed,
shall be duly made to the Committee of Management.

"VI. That the Examination on the Principles and Practice
of Medicine (including Clinical Medicine) and in Therapeutics, and except only so far as is provided otherwise in
the note appended to this Article, shall be conducted wholly
by the Examiners on these subjects appointed by the Royal
College of Physicians of Edinburgh; that the Examination on
the Principles and Practice of Surgery (including Clinical
Surgery) and on Surgical Anatomy shall be conducted wholly
by the Examiners on these subjects appointed by the Royal
College of Surgeons of Edinburgh, and by the Faculty of
Physicians and Surgeons of Glasgow; and that in all the
other subjects the Examinations shall, subject to the provisions of Article VII., be conducted by the Examiners of the
three co-operating Authorities.

> Note.—At the Examinations to be held in Glasgow, the Examina-
> tion in Clinical Medicine shall be conducted by Examiners
> of the Faculty of Physicians and Surgeons of Glasgow, being
> Hospital Physicians, and by the Examiners of the Royal
> College of Physicians of Edinburgh.

"VII. In arranging for the Examinations at the different
periods and places, the Committee of Management shall
apportion the Examiners in the different subjects of the three
co-operating Authorities, on the plan provided for in the
Schedule appended to this Agreement, which plan may from

time to time be modified, with the consent of the three co-operating Authorities.

"VIII. The Examinations shall be held in Edinburgh and in Glasgow, it being arranged that at every third period they shall be held in Glasgow, and at the other periods in Edinburgh.

"IX. That there shall be three Professional Examinations, named herein the First, the Second, and the Third Examinations.

> To the First Examination, Candidates shall be admissible at the end of the first year (embracing a Summer and Winter Session) of study, on producing Certificates of Attendance on the prescribed Courses of subjects embraced in the Examination.

> To the Second Examination, Candidates shall be admissible at the end of the second year of study, on producing Certificates of attendance on the prescribed Courses of subjects embraced in the Examination.

> To the Third Examination, Candidates shall be admissible at the end of the full period of study, on producing Certificates of having completed the entire Curriculum.

"X. That the Subjects of the First Examination shall be—
> Chemistry.
> Practical Chemistry.
> Elementary Anatomy and Histology.

That the Subjects of the Second Examination shall be—
> Anatomy.
> Physiology.
> Materia Medica and Pharmacy.

That the Subjects of the Third Examination shall be—
> Principles and Practice of Medicine, including Therapeutics, Medical Anatomy, and Pathology.

Clinical Medicine.

Principles and Practice of Surgery, including
Surgical Anatomy, Operative Surgery, and
Pathology.

Clinical Surgery.

Midwifery and Diseases of Women.

Medical Jurisprudence and Hygiene.

" XI. That a Candidate on passing the Third Examination
shall be admitted and receive the Diplomas; as

Licentiate of the Royal College of Physicians
of Edinburgh.

Licentiate of the Royal College of Surgeons of
Edinburgh.

Licentiate of the Faculty of Physicians and
Surgeons of Glasgow.

" XII. That the total fees payable by Candidates in respect
of the Examinations and Qualifications shall be Twenty-five
guineas. Of this there shall be paid—

At the First Examination—Five guineas.

At the Second Examination—Five guineas.

At the Third Examination—Fifteen guineas.

For each Examination after rejection—

At the First Examination—Three guineas.

At the Second Examination—Three guineas.

At the Third Examination—Five guineas.

" XIII. That all moneys received in respect of the Examinations shall be paid into a common fund under the control of
the Committee of Management, which fund, prior to apportion-
ment annually, shall be liable to the following charges :—

(*a*) Remuneration to Members of Committee
of Management.

(*b*) Fees of Examiners and Officers.

(*c*) Expenses of Printing and of Material for
Examining purposes.

(*d*) Such other expenses as the Committee of
Management may deem necessary for the
proper carrying out of this Scheme.

"XIV. That after deduction of the aforesaid charges, the
Surplus Funds shall be apportioned to the co-operating
Authorities in the manner as follows:—

> To the Royal College of Physicians of Edin-
> burgh—Five-tenths.
> To the Royal College of Surgeons of Edinburgh
> —Three-tenths.
> To the Faculty of Physicians and Surgeons of
> Glasgow—Two-tenths.

"XV. That this Agreement shall come into operation on
the said 1st day of October 1884, and remain in full force
and effect for the period of five years from and after that
date; but declaring that the same shall come to an end and
shall cease and determine on the said 1st day of October 1889,
provided one or other of the said parties shall have given
to the said first, second, or third parties one year's previous
notice in writing of their intention that the said Agreement
shall be so terminated; and, failing such notice, the same shall
continue in full force and effect from and after the said 1st
day of October 1889, until the expiration of one year after
such notice shall have been given as aforesaid."

On 5th May 1885 the College, with the approval
of the General Council of Medical Education and
Registration, determined to hand over the Preliminary
Examination to the Educational Institute of Scotland,
and on 2nd February 1886, it was resolved to admit
Women to the Examinations for the Conjoint Qualification.

As already stated, the College obtained power by its
Charter of 1861 to institute an order of Members who
should be intermediate in rank between the Licentiates

Order of
Members.

and the Fellows. No special privileges were conferred upon the Members ; but a Law was passed to the effect that no one should be eligible for the Fellowship until he had been at least one year a Member of the College.

Conditions of
admission.

At first the only qualifications for the Membership were, that the Candidate should be a Licentiate of a College of Physicians, or a Graduate of a British or Irish University ; that he should have attained the age of twenty-four years ; that he should produce satisfactory testimonials as to his social and professional status ; and that a motion for his election should be carried by a majority of not less than three-fourths of the Fellows voting. Under these conditions a large and constantly increasing number of Members was admitted. In course of time, however, the opinion began to gain ground among the Fellows, that these conditions of admission

Proposal to
establish an
Examination.

were unsatisfactory, and that it was desirable that an examination should be instituted, which all candidates for the Membership should be required to pass. The subject was brought before the College from time to time, but was delayed in the hope that some comprehensive measure of Medical Reform would be introduced by the Government. As years, however, passed, and no such measure was proposed, the subject was taken up seriously, and on the 24th February 1880 a Committee was appointed to consider the Laws relative to admission to the Membership and Fellowship of the College. After a good deal of discussion at several meetings of the College, the Report of the Committee was, on the 1st February 1881, approved of, and the new Laws relative to admission were agreed to. A few minor alterations

Laws as to
admission to
Membership.

were adopted on 30th October 1890, when the Laws of the College were revised. In conformity with these Laws, Candidates for the Membership are required,

before they are balloted for, to pass an examination
on Medicine and Therapeutics, as well as on one of
the following subjects, to be selected by themselves :—
(*a*) One or more departments of Medicine specially
professed; (*b*) Psychological Medicine; (*c*) General Pathology and Morbid Anatomy; (*d*) Medical Jurisprudence;
(*e*) Public Health; (*f*) Midwifery; (*g*) Diseases of
Women. Power is, however, given to the Council to
exempt from examination Candidates over forty years
of age who have been Registered Practitioners for not
less than ten years, and who have been highly distinguished for their scientific or practical attainments.

In certain cases
examination
may be dis-
pensed with.

The College, looking to the increasingly important
position occupied by the subject of Public Health,
resolved, on the 29th December 1874, to establish a
certificate of Qualification in that subject; and on the
4th May 1875, agreed to the Regulations under which
it is now granted. The Regulations for the Diploma
in Public Health were revised and altered on 21st
November 1889.

Qualification in
State Medicine.

The Regulations regarding the Diploma in Public
Health are as follows :—

Regulations for
Diploma in
Public Health.

I.—GENERAL REGULATIONS.

1. Candidates shall not appear for the final Examination
for the Diploma in Public Health till twelve months after
receiving a registrable qualification.

2. Candidates shall be required to produce evidence that
they have worked in a Public Health Laboratory, specially
recognised by the College, for a period of not less than six
months, and for not less than fifteen hours a week ; and that
they have for six months practically studied the duties of Out-
door Sanitary Work under the Medical Officer of Health of a
County or Large Urban District.

3. Candidates shall be subjected to two Examinations, and there shall be an interval of not less than six months between them.

4. The Examination shall be written, oral, and practical.

5. The Examination shall be held in the Physicians' Hall, or elsewhere if found more convenient.

6. Rejected Candidates shall not be admitted for re-examination till after the expiry of six months.

7. Holders of the Diploma are designated as "Diplomates in Public Health, R.C.P.E."

*** The *Rules* as to study shall not apply to—

    (*a.*) Medical Practitioners registered on or before January 1, 1890.

    (*b.*) Registered Medical Practitioners who have for a period of three years held the position of Medical Officer of Health to any County, or to any Urban District of more than 20,000 inhabitants, or to any entire Rural Sanitary District.

II.—EXAMINATIONS.

1. The First Examination shall embrace—

    (1.) *Physics.* — Especially Pneumatics, Hydrostatics, Hydraulics, and Engineering in relation to Sanitary Operations, including a knowledge of Architectural and other Plans.

    (2.) *Meteorology.*—Including Climate, Topographical and Seasonal Influences in relation to Health and Disease.

    (3.) *Laboratory Work*, including—

        (*a.*) Chemical and Bacteriological Examination of Air, Water, and Sewage.

        (*b.*) Chemical Examination of Foods:—Milk, Butter, Bread, Animal Food, Tea, Coffee, Cocoa, Alcoholic and other beverages.

(*c.*) Bacteriological methods as applied to Public Health, including preparation of Nutrient Media, cultivation and identification of Micro-organisms.

Two days will be allowed for Laboratory work, which will embrace both qualitative and quantitative Analysis.

2. THE SECOND EXAMINATION SHALL EMBRACE—

(1.) *Epidemiology and Endemiology.*—Including the corresponding departments in the Diseases of Animals and Plants,—Contagious Diseases,—Diseases of Periods of Life, Professions, Trades, Seasons, and Climates.

(2.) *Practical Hygiene.*—Duties of a Health Officer; Food; Water Supply, Sewerage, and Drainage; Nuisances; Construction of Hospitals, Public Buildings; Dwellings; Manufactories; Slaughter-Houses; Cemeteries, including the explanation and drawing of Plans.

(3.) *Sanitary Law and Vital Statistics.*

3. Meetings for both Examinations shall be held annually in April and October. The First Examination shall begin on the second Tuesday of the month, with the Examination in Physics and Meteorology, and be followed on the two next days by Practical Laboratory work. The Second Examination shall begin on the third Tuesday of April and October, and shall occupy two days.

4. The Examinations must be passed in their order, First and Second, and at least six months shall elapse between each.

5. A Candidate remitted at either Examination will be allowed to come up again after a further period of six months.

III.—FEES.

1. The fees for Examinations must be paid at least a week before the day of Examination.

2. The whole charges by the College for the Diploma amount to Ten guineas.

3. The fee for the First Examination is Five guineas; and the fee for the Second Examination is Five guineas.

4. Candidates forfeit the fee for the Examination which they have been unsuccessful in passing.

From the date of its Incorporation in 1681, the attention of the College appears to have been steadily directed to the formation of a Library. Sir Robert Sibbald, to whose exertions the College is mainly indebted for its Charter, was a large contributor to the Library. Two years after the Incorporation of the College a Librarian was appointed. The Library was, during the earlier years of its existence, enriched by donations from Fellows of the College, eminent Physicians, and individuals of distinction not even connected with the Medical Profession.

The following Chronological Notes as to the progress of the Library may be interesting, from the references made in them to many of the former Fellows to whom the College is indebted for valuable services in connection with it, which have helped to bring the Library to its present satisfactory condition.

In 1683 Dr. Archibald Stevenson was elected Librarian, and Dr. Pitcairne, Deputy-Librarian.

In 1696 a law was enacted, that every Intrant should contribute a book or books to the Library; and numerous donations of single books are noticed from time to time in the Minutes of several following years— one consequence of which was, that duplicates, and works unsuited to a Medical Library, began to accumulate, which were every now and then ordered to be sold, and new medical books to be purchased in their stead.

In 1713 it was resolved that the Fellows should have the option of buying such Duplicates before they were put up to auction.

In 1705 a considerable addition was made to the Library by the purchase of the books of the late Patrick Murray, Laird of Livingstone, for 300 merks Scots (about £16, 13s.). The first Library Committee seems to have been appointed at the end of that year; for the Minutes bear, that on December 13, Sir R. Sibbald, Drs. Smelholm, Riddell, and Luitfoot, with the President, Censors, and Library-keeper, were appointed Curators and Overseers of the Library.

Purchase of the Laird of Livingstone's Books.

In 1741 the College came into possession of the library of a former President, Dr. John Drummond, after his decease, by the Bequest of David Drummond, Advocate, his brother and heir. Two conditions were attached to the Bequest, namely, that these books should be kept in presses by themselves, and that none of them should be lent out unless the full value was deposited with the Keeper of the Library. The College formally accepted the conditions, and took measures to comply with them; but by the lapse of time, and by the repeated transferences of the Library, these conditions were unfortunately lost sight of, and can now no longer be fulfilled. It seems probable that this neglect is to be accounted for, in a great measure, by the sudden removal of the books in 1766 from the Old Hall in the Cowgate (where they were suffering from the insufficiency of the roof) to the Royal Infirmary, in which they were accommodated for fifteen years, until the Hall in George Street was built, and ready for their reception. A printed Catalogue of the Drummond books was presented along with them, and a copy of this Catalogue, still extant, has appended to it the legal

Bequest of Books of Dr. John Drummond.

Printed Catalogue of Drummond Books.

documents of conveyance and acceptance, signed in due
form. This Catalogue contains a list of 1250 works in
all, many of which are no longer in the Library, having
in all probability been exchanged, together with other
duplicates and non-medical books, in order to enable

the College to enlarge its medical collection. Like so
many of the books themselves, this copy of the Catalogue had at one period gone astray, and was not re-
covered till 1820, as appears from an inscription on the
title-page, in the handwriting of the late Dr. Duncan,
Senior, containing an anathema upon any one who
should thereafter take it away. On further inquiry, it
was found that the College was indebted for its restoration to Mr. David Laing, Librarian to the Society of
Writers to the Signet, who, on returning it to the
Library, stated that he purchased it at a sale of books
in Edinburgh ; and seeing, from the official documents
appended to it in writing, that it had belonged to the
Royal College of Physicians, he presented it through
the late Dr. Alexander Wylie, at that time Librarian.
Dr. Poole has since written on the blank leaves some
interesting entries, chiefly taken from the Minutes, calculated to throw light on the fate of this Drummond

Collection. It cannot but be deemed a cause of regret
that the conditions of the Bequest have been so completely lost sight of, and the Library Committee would
gladly have done what was possible towards complying
with their spirit, on the occasion of the removal to the
Hall in Queen Street in 1846; but, from the great dis-
persion of the Collection, and the difficulty in replacing
the books long since disposed of, which appear from
the printed Catalogue to have been partly theological,
it was found impossible.

In 1756 a considerable addition to the Library was

obtained from Messrs. Hamilton and Balfour, booksellers, in return for the copyright of the Pharmacopœia published in that year, and for duplicates and other books considered to be unfit for a Medical Library.

In 1761 the College was presented with the library of a former Fellow, Dr. Edward Wright of Kersie, by Sir Alexander Gibson of Clifton Hall, to whom it had fallen by inheritance. About the same time Dr. James Mackenzie, another Fellow, bequeathed to the College seventy-nine quarto volumes, being the Transactions of the Academy of Sciences of Paris from 1666 to 1755.

In 1763 a proposal from the Principal of the University for the union of the Library with the Library of the University, on conditions represented as favourable to the Fellows, came before the College ; but after some deliberation, a Report against the proposal was finally adopted. Another proposal to the same effect was made soon after by Dr. Robert Whytt, then Professor of the Institutes of Medicine, and a Fellow of the College ; but neither was this entertained. In the same year the insurance of the Library is mentioned for the first time, to the amount of £600.

In 1766, owing to the defective condition of the roof of the Old Hall, accommodation, as already noticed, was obtained for the books in the Royal Infirmary. Among the donors to the Library at this period is found John, Earl of Bute, who presented the twenty-six magnificent folios of Sir John Hill's Vegetable System.

In 1767 the first Catalogue of the Library was printed. This Catalogue, which shows that the Library must have been a large and valuable collection for the period, contains a list of 2346 works. It was printed in 12mo ; but there is no notice in the Minutes of the College as to the person by whom it was compiled.

Singularly enough, no copy of this interesting little volume had been preserved in the Library, and it was entirely unknown to the Library Committee of 1849, when engaged in preparing the Preface to the Catalogue issued in that year. The College is indebted for the copy now in the Library, probably the only one in existence, to William Brown, Esq., F.R.C.S.E., who, finding it bound up in a volume of pamphlets in his library, lately presented it to the College.

Removal to George Street

In 1781 the Library was removed from the Infirmary to the New Hall in George Street. In the same year Sir John Pringle presented to the College ten volumes of MS. Annotations, on condition that they were never to be lent out, and never to be published; conditions which have been faithfully adhered to.

Purchases at sale of Dr. Cullen's Books.

In 1791 the Library Committee were empowered to expend £100 in the purchase of books at the sale of Dr. Cullen's library. The new shelving of the Library being by this time completed, a Press Catalogue was prepared, and from it a printed Alphabetical Catalogue was formed, and brought out in 1793. This Catalogue was completed under the care of Dr. Thomas Spens, at that time Librarian. In the same year, on the proposal of Dr. Duncan, then Professor of the Institutes of Medicine, it was resolved to allow the Professors of the University the privilege of borrowing books from the Library, on condition that the Fellows of the College should enjoy a similar privilege in regard to that of the University. The Senatus Academicus agreed to a trial of this arrangement for one year, but it does not appear to have remained in operation longer.

Library to be annually inspected.

In 1800 a law was made that all books borrowed should be called in once a year.

In 1801, on the occasion of the retirement of Dr.

James Home from the office of Librarian, the first notice appears of the useful practice of appointing a Special Committee to take the Library off the hands of the retiring Librarian, and hand it over to his successor.

In 1821 an Appendix to the Catalogue was printed, containing the additions made to the Library from 1793 to that time.

In 1823 the appointment of an Assistant Librarian, with a salary, was first resolved on, and Mr. John Small, senior, was appointed to the office. Up to this time, and indeed throughout the whole history of the Library, much difficulty seems to have been experienced in preventing the books from being taken away in an irregular manner, and in getting the whole of the borrowed books returned.

In 1826 the subject of access for the Fellows to the University Library was again agitated, and a Committee was appointed for the furtherance of this object. This Committee continued in existence for nearly four years, and successively memorialized the Patrons of the University, and the Royal Commission on the Scottish Universities, but finally met with a refusal from both.

In 1826 Dr. William Moncrieff was requested to undertake a Catalogue raisonnée of the Library, and in the following year thanks were voted to him for the progress he had made in it. Several years later, after Dr. Moncrieff's death, a Committee was formed to prosecute the same object, while Dr. William Thomson was Librarian; but after some progress had been made it was relinquished, chiefly because the state of the College funds would not permit of its being printed.

In 1828, by the Bequest of Dr. Andrew Duncan, Senior, the College came into possession of a large collection of manuscript Notes and Lectures, being the

F

Lectures of the Founders of the Edinburgh School of
Medicine, and his own Practical Observations used as
notes for his Clinical Lectures. The whole collection
includes about 180 volumes. A portion of the Practical
Observations, however, seems to have been presented by
Dr. Duncan during his lifetime.

In 1830, on a Report of the Council as to the low
state of the funds applicable to the purchase of books,
it was resolved that each Fellow should contribute two
guineas annually for this purpose. This resolution,
however, was suspended almost as soon as passed, and
appears in no instance to have been enforced.

In 1831 Dr. Walter Adam presented to the Library
the twelve folio volumes of Montfauçon's Antiquité
Expliquée.

In 1833 Dr. Thomas Spens presented four Engraved
Prints of Medical Practitioners, with a view to make
a commencement of a collection of such Prints. The
collection rapidly increased, and a list of these Engravings
is appended to the Library Catalogue.

In 1835 the Librarian was authorized to have an
Appendix to the Library Catalogue printed, but the
resolution was not at that time carried into effect.

In 1836 the College, by the Bequest of Dr. William
Moncrieff, acquired his medical books, consisting of two
hundred and twenty-five volumes, of which twenty-one
were notes of lectures, etc., in manuscript.

In 1844 the Library Committee was empowered,
under certain conditions, to make temporary regulations
in regard to the Library, owing to the inconvenience
arising from the necessity of making a formal application
to the College on every new emergency, however trivial.

In 1845 the Library was increased by two considerable
donations of books; one by Dr. James Home, just

before his death, the other by the family of Dr. John Abercrombie, after his death. The former consisted of two hundred and forty volumes, including manuscript lectures by St. Clair, Alston, Cullen, Rutherford, Black, Francis Home, and Gregory. The latter donation comprised about eighty volumes.

In 1846 the Library, which during the previous three years had been placed in the temporary apartments of the College at 119 George Street, was removed to the New Hall in Queen Street. In the same year, on the occasion of the opening of the New Hall, an important donation to the Library falls to be noticed, consisting of a number of scarce and curious old Medical Books presented by Dr. Beilby, who was at that time President.

Immediately upon being settled in the New Hall, the Library Committee took measures for preparing for the press a new Alphabetical Catalogue, and the work was entered upon by the late Mr. Small, senior. From the progress made, it was hoped that the printing might have been commenced in the summer of 1847. But unforeseen obstacles were interposed in consequence of the illness and death of Mr. Small, and the subsequent illness of the Librarian, who was for a considerable time rendered incapable of superintending the work. In these circumstances the task was taken up by certain members of the Library Committee, who in the end of the year went through the labour of comparing the MS. Catalogue left by Mr. Small, with the books themselves, and by great exertions brought the work to a successful termination in 1849.

Since 1849 the Library has increased very rapidly. By the additional funds placed at its disposal, the Committee have made many valuable additions, particularly in 1852, when they purchased a large portion of the

Donations by Dr. James Home and the Family of Dr. John Abercrombie.

Removal to Queen Street.

Donation by Dr. Beilby.

New Catalogue commenced.

New Catalogue published in 1849.

Rapid increase of Library.

Library of the late Dr. John Thomson, Professor of General Pathology in the University of Edinburgh.

Among the benefactors to the Library, between the years 1849 and 1854, were Drs. Begbie, Bennett, Brown, Jackson, Seller, Robertson, and Simpson.

In 1854 an Appendix to the Catalogue of 1849 was printed, incorporating these additions to the Library.

Dr. Cullen's MSS. presented.
In 1860, agreeably to an arrangement contemplated by the late Dr. John Thomson, there were presented to the College, by Dr. Allen Thomson and Dr. Craigie, twenty-two volumes of manuscript writings by Dr. Cullen; one complete manuscript copy of his Lectures; several editions of his First Lines, especially that by Dr. Peter Reid; a German translation of the First Lines, and some smaller articles by the same physician.

All the donations now mentioned, with many others, as well as numerous purchases, have added greatly to the extent of the Library. In the year 1849, when the third edition of the Catalogue was printed, the number of volumes contained in the Library was estimated at about 9000. At present it is calculated that there are in the Library between thirty and forty thousand volumes.

Progress of Library.
In order to indicate the progress of the Library, the following statement of the annual additions made to it during the last twenty years is presented :—

Vols. added.	Vols. added.	Vols. added.
1870 422	1877 389	1884 540
1871 301	1878 432	1885 488
1872 314	1879 440	1886 471
1873 350	1880 539	1887 412
1874 377	1881 612	1888 632
1875 397	1882 505	1889 770
1876 450	1883 590	1890 820

Total number of volumes added, 10,251.

In 1861 the previous edition of the Catalogue having been all but exhausted, the preparation of a new one was undertaken by Mr. John Small, junior, who had succeeded his father as Assistant Librarian, and by his able management, under the supervision of Dr. David Craigie, the President, was completed in about two years. The complete Catalogue was published in a handsome volume in January 1863, and on the 5th May 1863 the sum of £105 was voted to Mr. Small for his labours. Since that time two Supplements have been published, and the preparation of a Catalogue raisonnée is being proceeded with by the Librarian, Dr. G. W. Balfour, with the aid of the Sub-Librarian, Mr. J. Matheson Shaw.

New Edition of Catalogue printed.

The formation of the Museum of Materia Medica may be dated from the 4th August 1835, when a Committee appointed to consider the sale or improvement of the College Hall in George Street reported—" That it had occurred to the Committee that it might be desirable to commence a Museum of Materia Medica, for the reception of which the Hall, or other part of the building, might gradually, as required, be fitted up." A Committee was appointed to take all measures which should appear to them to be proper for commencing such a Museum.

Museum of Materia Medica.

The Committee accordingly invited the Fellows and others to contribute Donations to the Museum, and entered into a correspondence with Lord Glenelg the Colonial Secretary, and with the Heads of the Army and Navy Medical Boards, for the purpose of procuring, through their influence, objects of interest for the Museum.

In the meantime Donations began to be received, and Dr. Jonathan Davidson had the honour of being the first Contributor, presenting the first three specimens on the 3rd November 1835. Dr. Christison's Donations

Progress of Museum.

were the most numerous and valuable, numbering twenty-nine by April 1837.

The first Honorary Curator, Dr. James Stark, appointed in 1839, entered vigorously on the discharge of his duties; and it was chiefly through his exertions that many Donations were obtained.

In 1839 Dr. Christison put the duplicates he might receive for his own collection at the disposal of the College, and became a contributor to the Museum of valuable specimens not otherwise attainable. Mr. Duncan (of Duncan & Flockhart), Mr. J. F. Macfarlan, and others, also made numerous donations. The Messrs.

Lawson & Son, on a list being furnished to them of such articles as they could easily procure, kindly presented the collection of cereals now in the Museum; and the Botanical Society of Edinburgh, on being furnished with a list of the medicinal plants of Great Britain, generously presented select specimens of the whole, amounting to 338 species, to the Museum of the College. Through the kindness of Professor Graham, and Mr. Macnab, the College also obtained from the

Royal Botanical Gardens specimens of such medicinal plants as flowered or bore fruit there, and from this source several interesting specimens were procured, which have been preserved both in the green and in the dried states.

To forward the formation of the Museum, Dr. James Wood gave a donation of £10, 10s., and the College, from its entertainment fund, gave £25, to be expended in purchase of articles of the Materia Medica. These sums were spent in adding to the Museum 301 specimens, which were placed there on or before the 9th November 1841.

Very few additions were made to the Museum from the above date till 1847, when the College, having heard that Dr. Theodore Martius of Erlangen, the brother of the celebrated Brazilian traveller, wished to dispose of his splendid and very complete collection of Materia Medica, resolved to purchase it. After considerable correspondence, it was announced to the College at its meeting on the 3rd August 1847, that Dr. Martius' collection had been secured for the College for the sum of £250. Through the influence of Sir William Gibson-Craig, then M.P. for Edinburgh and one of the Lords of the Treasury, the whole collection was not only passed free of duty, but was allowed to be forwarded to the College Hall before being opened.

No time was lost in getting suitable cases and show-tables fitted up for the exhibition of this collection, and on the 1st of May 1848 the Martius Collection was arranged and ready for inspection.

The Animal Preparations in the Martius Collection		
amount to	. . .	164
Vegetable do.		1401
Mineral do.		309
	TOTAL,	1874

During the years 1848, 1849, and 1850, the Museum received a valuable addition in the form of a complete series of Cinchona and allied Barks, presented by John Elliot Howard, Esq. of Tottenham. This series embraced specimens of all Barks met with in British commerce, and also a series of the Lichens growing on the Barks.

On a rough calculation, the preparations in the Museum may be arranged as follows :—

Present state of Museum.

Animal Preparations,		169
Vegetable do.		2396
Mineral do.		561
	TOTAL,	3126

When the Museum of Science and Art was established by Government, some idea existed of presenting
the College Museum to it. This, however, was set aside
by a Report from a Committee on increased Library
Accommodation, which was drawn up by a Committee,
of which Dr. Christison was chairman, and unanimously
adopted by the College on 18th November 1862. The
following Excerpt relates to the Museum :—

"It was next suggested, that time might be given for beginning the extension of the Hall, by converting the present
Museum room into a Library room, which would provide for
the increase of books for a period of ten years at least. For
this purpose it would be necessary to part with the Museum
of Materia Medica; and it was further suggested that the
Museum might be presented to the Museum of Science and
Art, or the University, where it would be more accessible,
and more widely visited than in Physicians' Hall. The Committee resolved, however, almost unanimously, to recommend
the College, if possible, not to part with the Museum. The
Museum and Cases, together with the special embellishment
of the apartment, cost the College about £750. The Collection is a unique one in this country, being an almost complete
Collection of the "Medicamina Simplicia" of the Materia
Medica, as it stood at the time of its purchase from
Dr. Martius of Erlangen; and as the specimens are choice
and in excellent order, the Collection will always be an object
of interest on this historical ground, even although the College
should never add to it. The Committee, indeed, are assured
that it is a subject of interest to strangers, and that its existence in the College is well known to the cultivators of Materia
Medica. They do not think that the College would willingly
part with a Collection which cost them so much, and which
brings the College some credit. The Committee have come
to the resolution to recommend the retention of the Museum,
all the more willingly, because they see a plan for leaving

it untouched, for obtaining increased Library Accommodation, and for extending the Hall without delay, by a single scheme which will not unduly encroach on the College Funds."

For some years there had been a growing feeling on the part of many Fellows of the College that its opportunities might be turned to good account in furthering those scientific researches to which modern medicine owes so much ; and this feeling led to the institution of a Laboratory devoted to physiological and pathological research.

On the motion of Dr. John Batty Tuke, a Committee was appointed on 4th February 1885, to consider and report on means for furthering the prosecution of original research in connection with the College. The Committee, on 7th July 1885, reported in favour of founding and maintaining a Laboratory in connection with the College, and submitted a scheme for carrying out this design. A majority of the College voted in favour of a formal motion for the adoption of the Report ; but as no motion tending to alienate the property of the College, or to apply it to other than the ordinary purposes of the College, can be adopted unless approved of at three meetings by three-fourths of the Fellows present at each, and as the majority did not comprise so large a proportion, the motion was not carried. A new Committee was appointed at the same meeting, in order to consider the matter further, and report to the College.

The new Committee presented their Report on 6th April 1886. It was substantially the same as, but more definite than, that submitted by the previous Committee, and recommended the College to found and maintain a Laboratory for the purpose of providing facilities for

Marginal notes:

General desire to further Scientific Work.

Proposal to found Research Laboratory.

Proposal defeated.

Proposal again brought forward.

carrying on scientific investigations. A motion for the adoption of the Report was supported by more than three-fourths of the Fellows present at this meeting, and

was therefore read for a first time. The Report, however, when submitted for its second reading, on 15th May 1886, was not carried, as, although supported by a majority, the number of Fellows in favour of it was not large enough to secure its adoption.

The strong feeling which prevailed in the College in favour of such a scheme was not extinguished by the lack of success which had hitherto attended the efforts of its supporters, and it found expression in a Petition to the Council, calling attention to the want of a Laboratory, influentially signed by Fellows of the College. The Petition was remitted to the College, and was read 3rd August 1886. As a result of this movement, a new Committee was appointed to draw up a Report on the subject.

The Report of the Committee, which was laid before the College on 2nd November, was in similar terms to those previously submitted. The motion for its adoption was carried unanimously, and declared to be read for a first time. The same result was obtained when the motion for its adoption was submitted for its second reading on 28th December 1886, and for its third reading on 15th February 1887, when it was declared to be finally approved of and adopted by the College.

The Report of the Committee, as adopted by the College, recommended :—

1. That the College shall establish and maintain a Laboratory for the prosecution of Original Research.
2. That the President and Council of the College shall appoint a Curator and Committee, whose duty shall be to superintend the establishment and

equipment of the Laboratory, and to supervise its work and control its expenditure. In the opinion of your Committee the Laboratory Committee should discharge duties analogous to those of the Library Committee, should bear the same relations to the Council, and should be appointed annually in the same manner.

3. That the Council of the College shall also be empowered to appoint a scientific man as Superintendent of the Laboratory.

This officer shall be held responsible for the maintenance of order in the establishment, and for the safe-keeping of all instruments and apparatus. He shall devote such portion of his time as may be determined by the Council to the work of the Laboratory; where, under the supervision of the Curator and Committee, he shall himself undertake the prosecution of Original Research, and be prepared to assist, if required to do so, in the work of other investigators. Under like supervision, he shall also be prepared to furnish Fellows of the College with Reports upon such matters as the histology of morbid specimens, and of the chemical and microscopic characters of urines.

For the first three years after the establishment of the Laboratory, the salary of the Superintendent shall be £200 per annum. After the expiry of that period the amount of the salary shall be determined by the Council.

The Superintendent shall be elected annually by the Council at the meeting for the election of Office-bearers.

4. That the Laboratory should be open, without Fee—

(1.) To Fellows of the College.

(2.) To Members.

(3.) To any Licentiate who shall obtain the sanction of the Curator and Committee to use the Laboratory for purposes of Scientific Research.

(4.) To any Medical Man or Investigator who shall obtain the sanction of the Council of the College, as well as of the Curator and Committee, to use the Laboratory for purposes of Scientific Research.

5. That the College shall vote from its capital funds, for the establishment of this Laboratory, the principal sum of £1000, and shall empower the Curator and Committee to draw every year upon the Treasurer for such sums as may be required for its maintenance and current expenses; it being provided that the whole yearly expenditure, including the rent of the premises and the salary of the Superintendent, shall not exceed the sum of £650.

6. It is suggested that the fitting-up of the Laboratory should be proceeded with cautiously, and that apparatus should be procured only as occasion requires. Although £1000 is asked as probably necessary for the full equipment of a Laboratory, it is suggested that only the essentials of a Laboratory should be at first procured, and that the balance should remain at the disposal of the Laboratory Committee, to be employed, if necessary, for its further development.

7. That every year, before the Quarterly Meeting of the College in February, the Curator shall submit to the Council a written Report regarding the year's work done in the Laboratory, and the Expenditure incurred. This Report, along with the Report of the Council upon it, shall thereafter be submitted to the College at the Quarterly Meeting in February.

8. That the College shall vote annually a sum of £100, which may be employed by the Council, as it deems fit, in making grants to investigators, in furthering the publication of Researches made in the Laboratory or elsewhere, in offering prizes for original work, or for any other allied purpose.

Nature of Scheme.

No time was lost in executing the scheme after its adoption. The Council appointed Dr. Tuke as Curator, and Dr. Woodhead as Superintendent of the Laboratory. A house, situated in the immediate vicinity of the Royal Infirmary, was rented and fitted up with the instruments and apparatus necessary for scientific research, and the work of investigation was forthwith entered upon.[1] In honour of the opening of the Laboratory, the College entertained a distinguished gathering at a Conversazione within the Hall, on 21st February 1889.

Execution of Scheme.

Laboratory opened.

The good results which have flowed from the institution of the Laboratory have exceeded the most sanguine hopes of those most ardent in the prosecution of the scheme. The Laboratory has not only been taken advantage of by many Fellows, Members, and Licentiates of the College, but a considerable number of scientific men unconnected with it have found in the Laboratory a means of making observations which would have been difficult to carry out but for the provision thus afforded. So much good work was produced that the College, desirous of fostering in every way the pursuit of Medical Science, resolved to publish an annual volume of Reports of the work done. Three volumes have already

Success of Laboratory.

" Laboratory Reports."

[1] A full description of the Laboratory, by Dr. G. Sims Woodhead, will be found in *Reports from the Laboratory of the Royal College of Physicians, Edinburgh*, vol. i. p. 3, 1889.

appeared, each containing a large number of valuable contributions by workers in the Laboratory.

In order to stimulate a spirit of research, Dr. Barbour, a Fellow of the College, has generously presented a sum of money to be held in trust by the College for the purpose of endowing " The Freeland - Barbour Fellowship " in connection with the Laboratory, and awarded for distinction in original investigation.

It is very gratifying to be able to record that the example of the College was soon afterwards followed by the sister College in London, which, in conjunction with the Royal College of Surgeons of England, now possesses a similar Laboratory devoted to scientific investigation.

During recent years the College has on several occasions been appointed Trustee for funds destined to encourage the study of Medicine.

Sir Alexander Morison, a Fellow and former President of the College, on 2nd August 1864 handed to the College the house and lands of Larchgrove, Midlothian, for the purpose of founding and endowing the " Morison Lectureship " on Insanity. The Lectureship has since been held by several distinguished Fellows of the College, as well as by eminent members of the Medical Profession unconnected with the College, among whom may be mentioned Dr. William Sellar, Sir Arthur Mitchell, Dr. Skae, Dr. W. T. Gairdner, Dr. J. B. Tuke, Dr. D. J. Hamilton, Dr. A. Keiller, and Dr. T. S. Clouston.

On 2nd May 1876 it was announced that Dr. Thomas Hill Pattison, a Fellow of the College, had assigned two Policies of Assurance on his life, for £850, to the College, for the purpose of founding and endowing a Bursary to be awarded to Male Students

of Medicine studying in Edinburgh. On the decease of
Dr. Pattison in 1885 the arrangement took practical
effect, and on the 1st May 1888 the College adopted a
scheme for the administration of the "Pattison Bursary."
The Bursary has been awarded by competition on three
occasions.

It was announced, on 2nd November 1886, that His
Excellency Dr. Robert Halliday Gunning, Grand Digni-
tary of the Empire of Brazil, had resolved to found a
Triennial Prize, to be awarded for the greatest benefit
done to Practical Medicine by any Fellow, Member, or
Licentiate of the College, in commemoration of the
Jubilee of Her Majesty Queen Victoria, to be known as
the "Victoria Jubilee Cullen Prize," in memory of the
celebrated Dr. William Cullen. The sum set apart
by Dr. Gunning for this purpose amounted to £1000.
The College, in accepting the generous gift, adopted a
Scheme which was approved of by Dr. Gunning, and
the first award took place in 1890.

The late Dr. John Parkin, a Fellow of the College,
bequeathed £1500 for the purpose of founding and
endowing Prizes for Original Research, upon certain
subjects, open to the entire Medical Profession. This
Bequest, with the conditions attached to it, was intimated to the College on 7th May 1889. The first
award will be made next year.

On 5th November 1889, as already mentioned in
connection with the Laboratory, it was announced
that Dr. Alexander Hugh Freeland Barbour, a Fellow
of the College, had resolved to hand over the sum of
£1250, in order to endow a Prize for Original Research,
to be called, in memory of his father, the "Freeland-
Barbour Fellowship." This Fellowship has been already
awarded.

Cullen Prize.

Parkin Prizes.

Freeland-
Barbour
Fellowship.

Request by
Dr. Struthers.

Finally, on 4th August 1891 it was announced that
Dr. James Struthers, a Fellow of the College, had
bequeathed a sum of £1000 to the College, "to be
added by the College so as to form part of, and be
administered in the same manner as, the Bequest to
the College by the deceased Dr. Pattison of Edinburgh."

Morison Prizes.

Sir Alexander Morison, in addition to founding the
Lectureship, bequeathed a sum of money for the pur-
pose of founding Prizes, which are annually awarded for
Meritorious Attendance on the Insane.

It has been thought advisable to conclude this short
sketch of the History of the College, by a brief summary
of some of the more interesting or more important
Minutes of the College.

First Meetings,
7th, 8th, and 9th
December 1681.

Bye-Laws.

The first two Meetings of the College (*7th and 8th December
1681*) were occupied with the election of Office-Bearers. Immediately thereafter they proceeded (*9th December 1681*),
under the powers vested in them by the Charter, "to enact
Laws for its due government and welfare." It is exceedingly
interesting to find, that, in addition to fixing the number
necessary to constitute a quorum, the two Laws then enacted
have continued in force to the present time. The one pro-
vides that every new Law shall be considered at two separate
Meetings of the College before being enacted, and that every
proposal to abrogate a Law shall be considered at three
several Meetings before a decision is come to; the other,
that every proposal before being laid before the College,
"shall be represented to the President and Council, who
shall take it into consideration, and report the same at the
next Meeting of the College, with the sense of the Council
thereupon."

Period of Elec-
tion of Office-
Bearers.

4th and 18th January 1682.—Nearly as early in the history
of the College, the day for the election of the Office-Bearers,
and the periods at which the Quarterly Meetings were to be

held, were fixed, and these, too, have continued unaltered to the present time.

10*th February* 1682.—At these Meetings, fines of "*seri*" (coming one quarter after the hour of meeting) and "*absentes*," are first mentioned, although, as the time for collecting them only is fixed, it seems probable that they had been inflicted previously. Fines.

21*st March* 1682.—The draught of the promissory engagement, to be signed by Fellows on taking their seats, was agreed to. Promissory Engagement.

3*rd November* 1684.—A Committee was appointed "to revise all former Acts, and to order the booking of such of them as they shall think fit in the Great Register." Revisal of Laws.

6*th January* 1685.—The Committee appointed to revise the Laws reported. They first proposed a regulation for the minimum course of study for the Licence; next for the trial of Apothecaries, suggesting that none should be permitted to officiate as Apothecaries until they had been examined "upon their skill in the Simples, in the Latin tongue, reading of receipts, and what else shall be found needful." Rules for Examination of Licentiates and Apothecaries.

From 22*nd November* 1684 to 21*st March* 1693, a blank occurs in the Minutes; and during that period, and for some time thereafter, the College would appear to have been chiefly occupied with the discussions between it and the Chirurgeon Apothecaries, and the legal proceedings consequent upon them. Blank in Minutes from 22nd December 1684 to 21st March 1693.

9*th November* 1693.—The Fees to be paid by Fellows and Licentiates were fixed. Fees.

It would appear that a custom had prevailed of the whole College electing the President. It was, however, proposed and discussed at two Meetings, and passed into an Act (14*th November* 1695), that the seven Councillors chosen by the College should elect one of their number to be President, and this notwithstanding any custom to the contrary; and this Law, which indeed seems to have been compulsory by the Charter, continued in force until the first Bye-Laws under the new Charter of 1860 were passed. Election of President.

G

26th August 1701.—The Fees of admission of Fellows and Licentiates were again altered.

12th January 1704.—A Committee was named to revise the Laws.

6th May 1707.—An Act was passed to render more effectual the separation between the Physician and Surgeon. It was ordained that this Act should be signed by all the Fellows. This would appear to have been done; and, subsequently, each Fellow at his entrance would seem to have signed it up to 1756, when the practice was discontinued, but without any notice of its discontinuance in the Minutes.

For some time subsequently to this, various Acts were passed regulating the "dues of Entrants and Licentiates," but nothing of particular interest occurs until—

6th November 1750.—When an Act was unanimously passed, prohibiting the admission of any one as a Fellow of the College who was a Member of the Corporation of Surgeons or Apothecaries, or who kept a shop for the dispensing of Medicine, and declaring that any one doing so after his admission "shall, *ipso facto*, forfeit all privileges which he did, or might, enjoy as a Fellow of the College, and his name shall be expunged out of the Roll of Fellows."

11th April 1754.—A further Act to prevent the same person from conjoining the professions of Medicine and Pharmacy was read a third time, and passed unanimously.

1st November 1763.—An Act was read a third time, and passed, "that in all time coming every Doctor of Medicine should remain a Licentiate one whole year before becoming a Fellow; that no Member of the Corporation of Surgeons should be admitted a Fellow or Licentiate, and that any Licentiate or Fellow becoming a Member of the said Corporation should forfeit his Licence or Fellowship."

1st May 1764.—On the Report of a Committee, the College confirmed its former Act (*11th April* 1754) in regard to Fellows keeping Apothecaries' shops, and extended it to all residing in great Britain and Ireland, declaring that any Fellow of the College practising Pharmacy within the three kingdoms should, *ipso facto*, forfeit his right of Fellowship, and his name should be struck off from the Roll of Fellows.

17th May 1765.—An Act was passed declaring that for the future no person should be admitted to be one of the Fellows, "whose common business it is either to practise Surgery in general, or Midwifery, Lithotomy, Inoculation, or any other branch of it in particular ; and further, that if any Member of the College shall, after his being received a Fellow, practise any of these lower acts in the manner above mentioned, and shall thereof be lawfully convicted, he shall be degraded from the honour conferred upon him when he was admitted a Fellow, and his name shall be struck out of the Roll." *(margin: No Fellow to practise Surgery or Midwifery.)*

7th February 1769.—After full consideration by a Committee, and repeated discussion in the College, an Act was passed providing that no Fellow or Licentiate of the College should exercise the business or profession of Midwifery, Lithotomy, or any of the other manual operations of Surgery ; and providing that, if lawfully convicted, he should be fined 40 pounds Scots for the first offence, and for the second, if convicted, he should forfeit his right of Fellowship, if a Fellow of the College, or his right of Licence, if a Licentiate, and all right and title whatever to practise physic within the city of Edinburgh and Liberties thereof. *(margin: No Fellow to practise Midwifery or Surgery.)*

7th November 1769.—The Act of *7th February* was rescinded. *(margin: Subsequent Discussions on the above.)*

5th May 1770.—A motion to rescind the Act *17th May* 1765 was rejected.

5th February 1771.—An Act was passed for henceforth balloting for Candidates for the Fellowship. *(margin: Candidates to be balloted for.)*

6th August 1772.—The Act of *17th May* 1765 was amended on the Report of a Committee to whom it had been remitted for consideration.

4th August 1772.—The Act prohibiting Fellows from practising Surgery or Midwifery was renewed, and it was ordained that all Fellows doing so, and against whom it *(margin: Renewal of Act prohibiting the practice of Surgery and Midwifery.)*

should be fully proved, should forfeit their Fellowship, and
their name should be struck out of the Roll.

3rd November 1773.—The number of Honorary Fellows
was restricted to ten.

Honorary Fellows ex officio to be distinguished.

24th February 1784.—Professors of Universities having by
the Charter a right to be admitted Honorary Fellows, it was
resolved that in any lists of Fellows thereafter published, such
Honorary Fellows, *ex officio*, "shall be distinguished by some
proper mark from those admitted by the voluntary act of the
College."

4th November 1783.—The form of petition for Non-
Resident Fellows was altered.

Graduates of Foreign Universities.

8th June 1784.—An Act was passed permitting the Graduates
of Foreign Universities to be admitted Fellows without examination, on a motion to that effect being proposed at one Quarterly
Meeting, and duly determined by ballot at the next.

Hitherto the Laws and Regulations of the College are
to be gathered only from the Minute-Books. It is apparent,
however, that a growing desire began to be felt that these
Laws should be digested into one body or code, and printed.
In this matter the College appears to have acted with
becoming caution and consideration, for on the

Abstract of Laws to be prepared.

2nd November 1784, a Committee was appointed for the
purpose of preparing an Abstract of the Laws enacted from *7th
December* 1681 to *3rd August* 1784. This Committee reported
on the *2nd May* 1786, when the matter was re-committed to be
further considered and completed.

1st August and 7th November 1786. — From statements
made at these Meetings, it would appear that the Committee
was not yet prepared finally to report.

6th February 1787.—The Report of the Committee was
laid on the table, ordered to be printed, and circulated among
the Fellows.

1st May 1787.—A motion approving of the Report was
read a first and a second time.

6th November 1787.—Some delay was now interposed,

until the question of the repeal of the Law preventing Fellows from practising Midwifery was settled. This Law having been repealed on the 5*th August* 1788, the College, at the first Quarterly Meeting thereafter (4*th November* 1788), unanimously approved of the Laws as proposed, "sanctioned and established the same, and resolved that the Laws should be printed as amended." Thus the first Code of Laws was arranged and printed in the year 1789. Copies of this little volume are still extant.

First Edition of Laws.

6*th May* 1788.—The College repealed the Resolution of 4*th August* 1772, "in so far as it prohibits the Fellows of the College from the practice of Midwifery."

Repeal of Act against Fellows practising Midwifery.

Soon after the changes were introduced, and, on the 2*nd February* 1790, it was enacted—

First, That when two or more Licentiates were elected Fellows at the same Meeting, they should be marked on the Roll according to the date of their admission; and if they were of the same date as Licentiates, they should be enrolled according to the date of their Diplomas; and if their Diplomas were of the same date, they should be enrolled according to their age.

Order of Seniority.

Second, That any Law of the College might be suspended for a limited time, provided said suspension was agreed to by two-thirds of the Fellows present, and that due intimation of the proposal was made in the Billets by which the Fellows were summoned.

Suspension of a Law.

3*rd August* 1790.—To secure the strict enforcement of the payment of fines, it was ordered that absentees at the last Meeting should be called on to pay their fines immediately after the roll-call, and Fellows who were late, to pay the fines as they came in.

Payment of Fines.

6*th August* 1793.—The Entrance-Fee of Resident Fellows was fixed at £100 *net.*

Entrance Fee.

2*nd February* 1796.—A proposal was made to repeal the Act dated 11*th April* 1754, in so far that every Fellow or Licentiate of the College might have it in his power to supply

Discussions in regard to Fellows supplying Medicine.

his own patients with medicines, or the patients of those with whom he might be conjoined in practice. This motion was read a second time *3rd May* 1796, and a third time *2nd August* 1796, when the discussion was adjourned, to be resumed *1st November* 1796, and again adjourned.

The proceedings connected with this gave rise to a most painful personal dissension between some of the most eminent Fellows, the discussions on which appear to have occupied much of the Minutes at that time. All these Minutes were, however, erased by an order of the College, dated *4th May* 1830. Enough, however, is still to be found in the volumes printed on the subject: Dr. James Gregory's Censorial Letter; Dr. Andrew Duncan's Opinion on a Charge against Dr. James Gregory, 4to, Ed. 1808; Dr. Andrew Duncan's Letter to Dr. Gregory, 8vo, Ed. 1811; Narrative of the Conduct of Dr. James Gregory, published by authority of the Royal College of Physicians, 4to, Edin. 1809.

Contributions from Fellows.

On the *4th August* 1795, another attempt to enforce the rigid collection of the fines was made, and the reason of this became apparent on *2nd May* 1797, when, the contributions and fines not being sufficient to defray the expenses of the entertainments, the College resolved that in future £5 be paid by each Fellow towards them.

Revision of Laws.

7th February 1804.—A Committee was appointed to revise the Laws with a view to a new edition being issued. This Committee reported progress *1st May* 1804, and laid a copy of their Report before the College *7th August* 1804.

The Report was considered in *November*, and again in *February*, when, in consequence of much difference of opinion, it was (*5th February* 1805) re-committed. The amended Report having been brought up (*7th May* 1805), the first reading engaged the attention of the College at no fewer than four Meetings. The Laws, however, were finally read a third

Second Edition of Laws adopted.

time and adopted (*2nd September* 1805), not however, without a protest.

5th November 1805.—It having been stated that the copy

of the promissory engagement signed by each Fellow on taking his seat was irretrievably lost, the Clerk was directed to prepare a new one.

4th February 1806.—The new edition of the Laws in print was laid on the table. A new promissory engagement was produced and signed by those present.

6th May 1823.—The Council of the College was appointed a Committee for the purpose of revising the Laws of the College, with a view to the printing of a new edition.

6th May 1823.—The Act of 1754, as far as it regarded the practice of Surgery, was totally repealed, and that part of it relating to the practice of Pharmacy altered as follows :—" If any Fellow or Licentiate of the College shall, by himself, copartner, or servants, keep a public Apothecary's, Druggist's, or Chemist's shop, he shall, *ipso facto*, forfeit all the rights and privileges which he does, or may, enjoy as a Fellow or Licentiate of the said College, and his name shall be expunged from the List."

3rd August 1824.—The Committee appointed *6th May* 1823 laid on the table proof copies of the Revised Laws ; these were considered at no fewer than eleven Meetings of the College, but were never finally adopted.

5th August 1828.—The President having reported that the edition of the Laws, 1805, was exhausted, it was agreed that the Laws which had been in proof for four years should be again revised, for which purpose a Committee was appointed.

4th November 1828.—The Report of the Committee on the Laws was given in ; it was ordered to be printed and circulated among the Fellows.

4th August 1829.—The Laws and Regulations of the College as amended were finally adopted.

1st February 1831.—It was agreed that any Fellow leaving the room during a meeting of the College should be fined.

3rd May 1831.—A motion was carried, regulating the Fees for the Licence and Fellowship.

1st August 1831.—Dr. W. Moncreiff, Fellow and Librarian of the College, presented a cane to the President and Fellows for the use of the President.

7th August 1832.—It was resolved that the ballot for the admission of Ordinary Resident Fellows might take place at the Quarterly Meeting following the presentation of their petition, in the same way as in the case of Non-Resident Fellows.

5th November 1833.—A Motion for the infliction of Fines upon the Members of the Council of the College for non-attendance was agreed to.

1st August 1837.—A Letter was read from a Fellow of the College, proposing that for the future Candidates for the Licence and Fellowship should not be required to possess Medical Degrees, but that provision should be otherwise made for ascertaining their Qualifications. This subject occupied much of the time of the College, and gave rise to much discussion at many subsequent Meetings. At the succeeding Meeting,

7th November 1837, a Committee was appointed to consider and report upon it.

7th February 1838.—The Report of this Committee was given in, along with the Opinion of Mr. John Hope, Dean of the Faculty of Advocates, and Mr. James Ivory, Advocate, on certain Queries submitted to them regarding it. The remit to the Committee was continued, that they might report further on the matter.

19th May 1838.—In consequence of the death of a gentleman who had been balloted for, and admitted a Fellow of the College, but who died before taking his seat, a question arose as to whether his fees of admission should be returned to his heirs. The College resolved that money so paid was the property of the College, and could not be alienated unless in the manner prescribed by law for the alienation of other property.

18th December 1838.—The Report of the Committee on the admission of Fellows was again considered, and the final decision on it postponed.

20th February 1839.—The Report of a Committee on the admission of Fellows was again considered. Two motions were made :—1st, Motion to approve of the Report. 2nd, Motion to disapprove. The vote being taken, the second Motion was carried by the casting vote of the President.

21st March 1843.—The draught of a proposed new Charter for the College was read and approved of. Owing to the prospect continually held out of some measure of Medical Reform being adopted by the Legislature, by which the Charters of all existing bodies would be altered, no further steps were taken to procure this new Charter for the College.

Draught of New Charter.

1st August 1843.—Resolved that all property belonging to the College should be invested in Trustees to be chosen by the Council with the approval of the College. The Trustees to be five in number, of whom the Treasurer should be one *ex officio*.

Trustees.

7th November 1843.—Certain regulations for the examination of Foreign Graduates, which had been several times under the consideration of the College, were read a third time, and passed.

Foreign Graduates.

4th November 1846.—A motion that an official costume should be worn by the Fellows was read a second time, and negatived.

Proposed Official Costume.

4th May 1847.—Resolved that as full a notice as possible of the business to be transacted at the Meetings of the College be given in the Billets by which the Meeting was summoned.

4th May 1847.—Report of Committee on the examination of Fellows proposing to deliver Lectures on the subjects required by Examining Medical Boards, laid on the table.

Certificate required of Fellows proposing to Lecture.

2nd November 1847.—Regulations in regard to the examination of Fellows proposing to Lecture finally adopted, after being discussed at Meetings held 11*th* and 14*th May* and 3*rd August* 1847.

1st August 1848.—Resolved that the book containing the record of examination of Foreign Graduates should not henceforth be laid on the table, but only a copy of the entry regarding the examination of successful Candidates.

5th November 1850.—Moved that a Committee be appointed
to revise the laws, and to report to the Council such suggestions
for their improvement as might appear to them desirable ; and
that the Council, after full consideration of these suggestions,
should report them to the College, with their opinion thereon.

5th August 1851.—The new Laws, as considered by the
Council, were laid on the table, and the following motion was
unanimously adopted :—" That, as it is extremely desirable that
no Law should be adopted until it has received the fullest
possible consideration, the College do now resolve that all
proposed amendments on the Laws be given in to the Secretary, in writing, within ten days, and be thereafter considered
by the Council and Law Committee conjointly, who shall
Report them, with their opinion thereon, at next Meeting of
the College."

It was further resolved, That the amendments to be
proposed, with the Opinion of the Council and Committee
thereon, should be printed, and circulated among the Fellows
previous to the Meeting at which they are to be discussed.

4th May 1852.—The new Laws were considered for the
third time, and agreed to.

2nd November 1852.—Standard Order regulating the manner
in which Fellows were to take their seats, unanimously adopted.

2nd August 1853.—The College agreed to petition Parliament on behalf of the Assistant Surgeons of the Royal Navy.

Dr. George Paterson presented to the College a Digested
Index of its Proceedings for the first fifty years of its existence,
for which he received the " warm thanks " of the College.

1st November 1855.—Mr. Craig, Surgeon, Ratho, presented
to the College the cane which had belonged to, and had been
used by, the late Dr. Cullen. This cane has since been used
as one of the insignia of the Vice-President.

9th May 1854.—A Committee appointed for the purpose,
presented a Report on the Bill for the Registration of Births,
Deaths, and Marriages. The College adopted the Report,
and petitioned in favour of the Bill.

7th August 1855.—A Committee reported on the expediency of having a Meteorological Society established in Scotland. Meteorological Society.

5th August 1856.—A Committee reported in favour of the College offering a Prize for competition. Motion to that effect read a first time. Prize to be offered.

14th November 1856.—The College resolved that at the Election Meeting Fellows should vote by signed lists instead of *viva voce*, as heretofore. Election of Office-Bearers to be by signed lists.

3rd February 1857.—Resolutions in regard to the position of the Army Medical Service agreed to, and ordered to be transmitted to the Secretary at War. Army Medical Service.

3rd February 1857.—The College agreed to a motion offering a Prize of Twenty-five guineas for an Essay. Prize to be offered.

21st July 1857.—The College considered the Lunacy (Scotland) Bill then before Parliament, and adopted certain resolutions regarding it,—in particular, the College agreed to suggest and recommend the "Emergency Clause," which has since become Law. Lunacy Bill.

3rd November 1857.—Power was granted to the Council to withhold inspection of the Minutes of the Council as to any particular piece of business still in dependence. Minutes of Council to be private in certain circumstances.

2nd February 1858.—The College agreed to have the State of the Accounts and Funds of the College printed and circulated annually. Accounts.

9th April 1858.—The College memorialized the Board of Trade to grant some pecuniary aid to the Meteorological Society of Scotland. Meteorological Society.

20th July 1858.—The College agreed to entertain the Members of the British Medical Association, then about to visit Edinburgh. Entertainment to British Association.

21st September 1858.—The College resolved to publish annually a complete list of the Fellows. List of Fellows to be annually published.

21st December 1858.—The College resolved to apply for a new Charter.

1st February 1859.—The Trustees submitted to the College the Opinion of Mr. Maitland, Advocate (afterwards Legal Opinion as to College Investments.

Lord Barcaple), as to the nature of the Investments which they were warranted in availing themselves of for placing the funds of the College.

Investments.

8th February 1859.—The College resolved that the funds be withdrawn from investments in companies where a liability might exist for sums beyond those invested.

Committee on Library accommodation.

A Committee was appointed to consider the best means of accommodating the rapidly increasing Library.

Election of Office-Bearers to be by unsigned lists.

The College altered the Laws relating to the election of the Council, and decided that the voting papers should not be signed.

An application from certain Non-Resident Fellows was read, desiring to be admitted to participate in the government of the College.

Repeal of Stamp Duties on Diplomas attempted.

18th February 1859.—The College agreed to a Memorial to the Chancellor of the Exchequer, praying for relief from the Stamp Duties on the Licence of the College. It was resolved to join with the London and Dublin Colleges of Physicians in sending a deputation to London on the subject.

New Charter.

1st March 1859.—The draft of the new Charter, with the Opinion of Mr. Roundell Palmer (afterwards Lord Chancellor Selborne), was further considered, and ultimately agreed to.

Petition in favour of " Sale of Poisons Bill."

8th March 1859.—The College, on a Report by the Council, resolved to petition in favour of the "Sale of Poisons Bill;" it also resolved not to interfere in regard to two Lunacy Bills which appeared to refer to England exclusively.

President refuses to allow the business of Extraordinary Meeting to proceed.

29th March 1859.—The President refused to allow the business of an Extraordinary Meeting, called by requisition, to proceed, because the requisitionists had failed to submit their proposed Motion to the Council previously, as required by the Laws of the College.

Establishment of a new class of Licentiates resolved on.

5th April 1859.—The College, by a majority of one, resolved to admit to examination as Candidates for its Licence, gentlemen who had no previous Medical Degree or Qualification.

20th April 1859.—The Regulations for the examination and admission of Candidates for the Licence were finally agreed to, after having been discussed at many previous Meetings of the College.

14th June 1859.—The Council gave in a Report on the Stamp Duties on the Diplomas of Licentiates, which, through the exertions of the President, Dr. Alexander Wood, the Lords of Her Majesty's Treasury had agreed to remit.

The College resolved to revise the Laws, and bring them into conformity with the proposed Charter.

15th June 1859.—The Council announced that by the exertions of the President, Dr. Alexander Wood, the English Poor Law Board had agreed to recognise the Licence of the College as a Medical Qualification.

26th July 1859.—The College agreed to certain Regulations for giving a Double Qualification along with the Royal College of Surgeons, by a single examination, to be submitted for the approval of the next Meeting of the General Council of Medical Education.

27th September 1859.—The College agreed to a Minute recording their sense of the loss the community had sustained by the death of Dr. William Pulteney Alison, and resolved to attend his funeral as a body.

Professor Allen Thomson of Glasgow, with consent of the direct descendants of Dr. Cullen who were in this country, presented to the College the manuscripts left by the late Dr. Cullen, consisting of about fifteen volumes in folio and twenty in quarto, with about an equal number of loose papers.

7th February 1860.—The College resolved to procure for the Hall a marble bust of the late Professor Alison.

It was agreed to send Delegates to a conference with the Colleges of Physicians of London and Dublin, with a view to securing some uniformity in the Charters to be granted to the three Bodies.

29th March 1860.—The College agreed to co-operate with the London and Dublin Colleges in having a Bill introduced

Licence.

Stamp Duties to be remitted.

Revision of Laws.

Recognition of Licence by Poor Law Board.

Regulation as to Double Qualification agreed to.

Funeral of Dr. Alison to be attended.

Donation of Dr. Cullen's MSS.

Bust of Dr. Alison to be procured.

Co-operation with London and Dublin Colleges.

into Parliament to abolish the 47th clause of the Medical Act, and to leave to Bodies obtaining new Charters the privileges they possessed at the time of passing of the Medical Act.

Use of Hall granted for Dinner to the Rt. Hon. W. E. Gladstone.

The College granted the use of the Hall to the Senatus Academicus of the University, for the purpose of entertaining the Chancellor of the Exchequer (The Right Honourable W. E. Gladstone) at dinner, on occasion of his Installation as Rector of the University, but carefully guarded against this being construed into a precedent.

Resolve to present the President with his Portrait.

1st May 1860. — The College unanimously adopted a Report from a Committee appointed on the 1st February, to consider in what manner the College should mark its sense of the services rendered to it by the President, and agreed to the recommendation of the Committee, that the College should present him with his portrait, painted by an Artist of high eminence, and that, on the condition of adequate eminence, the choice of the Artist should be with Dr. Wood himself.

Report on the Ordinances of University Commissioners.

1st May 1860.—The Council, at the request of the University Commissioners, reported on the Ordinances which were proposed in regard to conferring Degrees in Medicine.

Dinner to Lord Brougham.

14th May 1860.—The College resolved to entertain at Dinner, Lord Brougham, Chancellor of the University, Drs. Watson and Sharpey of London, and Dr. Stokes of Dublin, who were to receive the degree of LL.D. from the University.

Licence recalled.

The College recalled a Licence on account of a false statement of age having been made.

Entertainment to Medical Officers of the Channel Fleet.

19th June 1860.—The College agreed to invite the Officers of the Channel Fleet, lying at St. Margaret's Hope, to an entertainment.

Date of Meeting.

3rd August 1860.—The College resolved to alter the day on which the next Quarterly Meeting of the College should have been held to the day following (first Wednesday in August 1860), inasmuch as the former had been fixed upon by Her Majesty to review the Volunteers.

Fees.

6th November 1860.—The College resolved to reduce the fees payable by Fellows on entrance.

5*th February* 1861.—The College presented the President, Dr. Alexander Wood, with his portrait, painted by Sir John Watson Gordon, President of the Royal Academy.

Portrait of himself presented to the President.

The Council reported in regard to the new Charter, and recommended the College to retain the name of the Royal College of Physicians *of Edinburgh*, instead of assuming that of the Royal College of Physicians *of Scotland*, to which it was entitled by the Medical Act. This was agreed to by the College.

Name of College.

7*th May* 1861.—The Council reported a correspondence between the President and the War Office, and also the proceedings at a conference between the President, a Delegate from the Royal College of Surgeons of Edinburgh, and Lord Herbert, Secretary-at-War, in regard to the recognition of the Double Qualification by the Army Medical Board.

Negotiations with War Office.

The Council reported a correspondence between the Secretary of the College, and the Poor Law Board of England, in regard to the recognition by the Board of the Double Qualification as equivalent to a Degree in Medicine and a Degree in Surgery.

Negotiations with Poor Law Board.

5*th November* 1861.—The President laid before the College the new Charter, dated 16th August, and sealed 31st October 1861.

New Charter laid before College.

20*th December* 1861.—The College agreed to an Address of Condolence to the Queen on the death of the Prince Consort.

Address to the Queen on death of Prince Consort.

4*th February* 1862.—The Address to the Queen, and Reply, were reported to the College.

25*th June* 1862.—The College voted twenty-five guineas towards the subscription for a National Memorial to the late Prince Consort.

Vote to Albert Memorial.

The petition of a Lady to be allowed to pass the Preliminary Examination with a view to taking the Licence of the College was, on a division, rejected.

Lady refused to be admitted to Preliminary Examination.

11*th July* 1862.—The College resolved that the Bye-Laws, which had been repeatedly under the consideration of the College, should be the Statutes and Bye-Laws of the College,

New Bye-Laws agreed to.

by which it should be governed and directed,—these Laws were ordered to be printed.

25th October 1862.—The College agreed to a resolution recommending the Medical Council to adopt the Decimal System of Weights and Measures in the forthcoming British Pharmacopœia.

4th November 1862.—The Council reported to the College the neglected state of the Tomb of the late Dr. Cullen, in Kirknewton burial-ground, and recommended the College to erect some memorial to his memory.

27th November 1862.—The College took up the case of a Licentiate accused of advertising in an improper way, and of publishing an indecent quasi-medical book. The Licentiate appeared by his Procurator, who emitted a declaration in presence of a Justice of the Peace, which set forth, *inter alia*, that his name was inserted in the advertisements and on the title page of the publication complained of, without his authority and against his remonstrance. On this the College delayed proceedings.

An Address to the Queen on the Prince of Wales attaining his majority was agreed to, and directed to be forwarded for presentation.

3rd February 1863.—The College resolved to request Mr. Whyte Melville, of Mount Melville, to allow the portrait of his grandfather Dr. Whytt to be copied for the College.

31st March 1863.—The College agreed to present an Address of Congratulation to the Queen on the marriage of the Prince of Wales, and also one to the Prince of Wales.

5th May 1863.—A bust of the late Professor James Gregory was presented by Dr. Keiller to the College.

The Council reported on the state of the grave of the late Dr. Cullen, and the College voted £100 to carry out their recommendations.

7th July 1863.—A motion was made to remove the name of a Licentiate from the Roll for having published an indecent quasi-medical work. The College agreed to entertain it.

4th August 1863.—The College agreed to approve of change, proposed in the duration of the Session of the University.

The College agreed to entertain at Dinner the President and leading Members of the Social Science Congress, about to be held in Edinburgh.

Dinner to Social Science Congress

12th October 1863.—The College entertained at Dinner, in their Hall, His Royal Highness Prince Alfred, attended by Major Cowell; Lord Brougham; The Right Honourable Charles Lawson, Lord Provost; The Right Honourable W. E. Gladstone, Chancellor of the Exchequer; The Right Honourable Joseph Napier, M.P.; Sir Christopher Rawlinson; Sir Harry Young, K.C.B.; Sir J. Kay Shuttleworth, Bart.; Sir Charles Hastings; Judge Longfield; Sir David Brewster; John Pender, M.P.; Nassau Senior, Esq.; John Thomson Gordon, Esq., Sheriff of the County of Edinburgh; Dr. Newbigging, President of the Royal College of Surgeons; Mr. William Brougham; M. Garnier Pages; M. Desmaret; M. Henri Martin; M. Herold; Professors Syme, Maclagan, Lyon Playfair, and Archer; Colonel Torrens; the Rev. Dr. Bell of Goole; Messrs. Whyte Melville, E. Chadwick, Westlake, R. Rawlinson, W. Cookson, Hastings, H. Roberts, A. Kinnear, and Dr. Markham.

Apologies were received from His Grace the Duke of Buccleuch; Earls Russell and Minto; Lord Dunfermline; the Lord Justice-General (M'Neill); the Lord Advocate (Moncreiff); the Lord Justice-Clerk (Inglis); Lords Currichill, Neaves, and Ardmillan; Sir Walter Crofton; Sir John M'Neill, G.C.B.; Sir William Gibson-Craig, Bart.; Hon. M. Waldegrave Leslie; Bishop Morell; Captains Speke and Grant; Adam Black, M.P.

Letters of Apology.

3rd November 1863.—The College resolved to obtain portraits of Drs. Christison and Seller.

Portraits of Drs. Christison and Seller to be procured.

A Licentiate of the College was deprived of his Licence for publishing an indecent quasi-medical work.

Licentiate expelled for indecent publication.

2nd February 1864.—The College agreed to Congratulatory Addresses to the Queen and Prince of Wales on the occasion of the birth of the Prince Royal.

Congratulation on birth of Prince Royal.

The College, on the suggestion of the Council, remitted to the Council to procure a portrait of Sir Alexander Morison, the oldest Fellow of the College.

The College agreed to a series of resolutions explaining to the Fellows, Members, and Licentiates, their duties under the Vaccination (Scotland) Act.

19th February 1864.—The College adopted certain resolutions in regard to the protection of Medical men signing Certificates of Lunacy.

22nd March 1864.—A Report of a Committee on Improvements on Medical Education was read and discussed.

The purchase of No. 8 Queen Street, the house adjoining the College on the east, by the Trustees for £6000 was announced.

3rd May 1864.—The Committee formerly appointed reported the Answers which they recommended the College to send to the Resolutions and Recommendations on General and Professional Education, issued by the General Council of Medical Education and Registration in June 1863.

The College remitted to the Council to consider the present state of the Army Medical Department, and especially the offer made to Civilians to enter for temporary service.

The College approved of a letter dated 26th March 1864, addressed by the President to the Home Secretary, pointing out the prevalence of small-pox in the Western Highlands, and the want of facilities for procuring supplies of vaccine lymph.

2nd August 1864.—A Committee was appointed to consider the extension of accommodation for the Library.

A scheme for the formation of Scholarships, prepared by a Committee in conjunction with the Council of the College, was approved of, and £25 *per annum* was voted from the College funds to carry it on.

A report of conferences with the College of Surgeons and Glasgow Faculty, on the Education Report of the General Medical Council, was approved of.

Sir Alexander Morison made over to the College the house and lands of Larchgrove, in the County of Edinburgh, the proceeds to be devoted to the salary of a Lecturer on Mental Diseases, Sir Alexander naming Dr. William Seller as the first Lecturer.

The College negatived a motion to make the offices of Secretary and Treasurer paid offices; but remitted to the Council to consider the expediency of appointing a Fellow to manage the applications for the Licence of the College, and the conditions on which the office should be established.

18th November 1864.—The College agreed to a plan of Library accommodation, by which the Hall was to be extended to double its present size, and surrounded with low book-cases.

7th February 1865.—The College resolved to have a copy executed of a portrait of a former President, Dr. John Clark, in the possession of Hugh H. Brown, Esquire of Newhall, whose permission for this had been obtained.

The College granted the use of the Hall for an entertainment to be given by the President (Dr. Burt) to the Fellows.

2nd May 1865.—The College on the recommendation of the Council, made in obedience to a remit from the College (1st November 1864), agreed to appoint a Registrar, whose duty should be the management of the applications for the Licence of the College; the Council to elect annually to the office, and to have the power of conjoining it with the office of Secretary, or of separating the two offices at any time, as might seem most expedient.

7th November 1865.—The College, on the recommendation of the Council, agreed to adopt a Collegiate costume, and remitted to the Council to determine what the costume should be.

6th March 1866.—The College expressed its approval of the action of the Municipal Authorities in inaugurating a comprehensive scheme of Sanitary Reform.

10th April 1866.—The College approved of the Report of the Council on the Lunacy Acts (Scotland) Bill then before Parliament.

21*st May* 1866.—The College agreed to petition Parliament, to the effect that two Representatives in Parliament at
least be granted to the Scottish Universities.

7*th May* 1867.—College resolved to petition in favour of
the Public Health (Scotland) Bill, which had been introduced
into Parliament.

4*th February* 1868.—The College approved of the Report
of the Council, on the recommendations of the General
Medical Council, on the subjects of Preliminary Examinations
of Medical Students, and on the Report of the Committee on
the Visitation of Examinations.

A copy of a portrait of Dr. Arbuthnot was presented to the
College by Dr. Seller.

18*th February* 1868.—The College voted the sum of
£1000 in aid of the fund for the buildings of the New Royal
Infirmary.

5*th May* 1868.—The College agreed to present an Address
to the Queen with reference to the attempted assassination of
the Duke of Edinburgh; also to His Royal Highness, con-
gratulating him on his providential escape.

The College agreed to purchase, for the sum of £100,
a bust, by Maccallum, of the deceased Dr. John Graham
Macdonald Burt, lately President of the College.

The College recommended that the Maternity Hospital
should be combined with the Royal Infirmary, and that it
should be placed in a separate building of the New Hospital.

4*th August* 1868.—The College met for the first time in
their new Hall, the old one having been altered and enlarged.

Answers from the Queen and the Duke of Edinburgh to
the Addresses presented to them were reported to the College.

Intimation was made that a marble bust, by Joseph, of
the late Dr. James Hamilton, senior, of Edinburgh, had been
presented to the College by Dr. George Bell. The thanks of
the College were voted to Dr. Bell.

The College resolved that in future all candidates for the
Licence should be required to produce, prior to the final

examination, a certificate of having studied Vaccination under a competent and recognised teacher.

3rd November 1868.—A Licentiate of the College was deprived of his Licence for having circulated an indecent publication, and for having caused to be inserted in the newspapers advertisements of an unprofessional character.

4th May 1869.—A Honorarium of one hundred and fifty guineas was voted to Dr. Samuel Somerville, Treasurer of the College, in recognition of his valuable services.

1st February 1870.—The College resolved that every candidate for the Licence should be required to pass an examination in Clinical Medicine, and agreed to a plan under which the examinations were to be carried out.

The College directed that a Supplemental Catalogue to the Library should be prepared and printed.

22nd February 1870.—The College agreed to a Report by the Council of the College to the General Medical Council, as to the formation of a Joint Board for Medical Examination in Scotland.

8th March 1870.—The College agreed to a Report of the Council, on the Report of State Medicine, prepared by a Committee of the General Medical Council.

31st May 1870.—The College approved of the Report of the Medical Reform Committee on the Medical Act (1858) Amendment Bill.

7th February 1871.—The College subscribed fifty guineas to the local fund instituted to defray the expenses of the reception of the British Association for the Advancement of Science in Edinburgh in August next.

A portrait of the late Dr. James Begbie was presented to the College by his son, Dr. James Warburton Begbie.

2nd May 1871.—The College resolved to petition in favour of the Anatomy Act (1832) Amendment Bill, and the Habitual Drunkards Bill.

The College agreed to procure a marble bust, by Brodie, of the late Sir James Young Simpson, Bart.

6th February 1872.—The College agreed to send Addresses of Congratulation to the Queen and Prince of Wales, on the recovery of the Prince from a severe attack of enteric fever.

Resolutions adopted at a Conference held at Glasgow, of Delegates from this College, the Royal College of Surgeons of Edinburgh, and the Faculty of Physicians and Surgeons of Glasgow, in reference to a remit from the General Medical Council as to the establishment of a Conjoint Examining Board for Scotland, were submitted to the College, and after discussion were approved of.

7th May 1872.—Answers to the Congratulatory Addresses to the Queen and Prince of Wales were reported to the College.

The Scheme for a Conjoint Board for Medical Examinations in Scotland, drawn up by the Scottish Branch of the General Council of Medical Education and Registration, was laid before the College, and a Delegate was appointed to attend a Meeting of the Branch Council to express the opinion of the College on the Scheme.

10th June 1872.—The Delegate appointed at last meeting of the College to meet the Scottish Branch Council, laid the Scheme, as amended, before the College, to which the College gave its assent.

6th May 1873.—The College voted a sum of one thousand guineas in aid of a scheme for extending the scientific and educational buildings of the University of Edinburgh.

5th August 1873.—Read letter from Sir Alexander Grant, Principal of the University of Edinburgh, acknowledging with thanks on the part of the Senatus the liberality of the College in voting a donation to the Building Scheme.

4th November 1873.—The thanks of the College were voted to Dr. Alexander Wood, on his retirement from the office of Representative of the College at the General Medical Council, which he had held for fifteen years, for his able and valuable services.

3rd February 1874.—The College agreed that Addresses of Congratulation be presented to Her Majesty the Queen and

His Royal Highness the Duke of Edinburgh, on the occasion of the marriage of the latter on the 23rd of January.

5th May 1874.—Answers to the Congratulatory Addresses to the Queen and the Duke of Edinburgh were reported.

The College agreed that in future all candidates for the Licence of the College should be required to pass an examination in Surgery before the Examiners of the College, unless they had already done so before some other Qualifying Body.

All Candidates for the Licence of the College to pass an Examination in Surgery.

The College voted the sum of one hundred guineas in aid of the Building Fund of the Royal Maternity Hospital.

The College voted the sum of twenty-five guineas as a subscription to the fund for erecting a statue to the late Dr. David Livingstone, African explorer.

£105 voted to new Royal Maternity Hospital. £26, 5s. voted towards Statue of Dr. David Livingstone.

29th December 1874.—The College approved of a suggestion by the Chairman of the Board of Supervision, that, in the interests of public health, members of the medical profession in Scotland be requested to make Returns to the Local Authority of all cases of infectious or contagious disease which may occur in their practice. At the same Meeting the College expressed its strong objection to a proposal by the Convener of the Public Health Committee of the Town Council of Edinburgh, that a clause should be introduced into the Public Health Act, rendering it compulsory on medical practitioners to report to the Local Authority all cases of infectious disease occurring in their practice.

Medical Practitioners recommended to report cases of infectious disease, but College objected to such report being made compulsory.

29th December 1874.—The College resolved to establish a certificate of Qualification in State Medicine, and remitted to the Council to consider and report upon the details of the Examination which should be instituted.

Agreed to establish a qualification in State Medicine.

The College voted the sum of three hundred guineas, to be expended in the purchase of a service of plate, to be presented to Dr. D. R. Haldane on his retirement from the office of Secretary, which he had held for upwards of fifteen years.

Service of Plate voted to Dr. Haldane in resigning office of Secretary.

The use of the Hall was granted to the President (Dr. Lowe) for the purpose of giving an entertainment to the Fellows of the College.

Entertainment by President to Fellows.

5th March 1875.—The plate voted to Dr. Haldane was presented to him at an Extraordinary Meeting of the College.

4th May 1875.—The College voted fifty guineas in aid of the Building Fund of the Livingstone Medical Missionary Memorial Dispensary.

The Regulations proposed by the Council to be observed by candidates for the certificate in State Medicine were approved of by the College, and were adopted as temporary regulations.

The College voted a donation of ten guineas in aid of the funds of the Scottish Meteorological Society.

The Secretary stated that the President and Council of the College had had under consideration a Bill to amend the Medical Act 1858, so far as relates to the Registration of Women who have taken the Degree of Doctor of Medicine in a Foreign University, and that, as the matter was urgent, they had petitioned against it. The diligence of the Council in forwarding the petition was approved of by the College.

8th June 1875.—The College agreed to entertain the Members of the British Medical Association at their approaching visit to Edinburgh, the entertainment to consist of a promenade, with music and refreshments, in the Hall of the Museum of Science and Art.

3rd August 1875.—Two Licentiates of the College whose names had been removed by the General Medical Council from the Medical Register, in consequence of having been connected with a conspiracy to defraud, were declared to be no longer Licentiates of the College, and the Registrar was instructed to delete their names from the College Register.

28th December 1875.—Plans for additional Library accommodation, involving a probable cost of £3300, were approved of by the College.

2nd May 1876.—The recommendations of a Conference of Representatives of the Royal Colleges of Physicians and Surgeons of Edinburgh, and of the Faculty of Physicians and Surgeons of Glasgow, in regard to improvements in the examinations for their Diplomas, were approved of by the College.

It was decided that no Fellow resident upwards of ten miles from Edinburgh should be permitted to borrow books from the Library without the special permission of the Council.

The College agreed to petition against the Bill introduced into Parliament by Mr. Cowper Temple to amend the Medical Act 1858, as far as relates to the Registration of Women who have taken the Degree of Doctor of Medicine in a Foreign University. *[margin: College to petition against Bill for Registration of Women with Foreign Degrees.]*

The Treasurer announced that Dr. Thomas Hill Pattison, a Fellow of the College, had assigned two policies of insurance on his life, amounting to £850, for founding a Bursary towards the education of a male medical student in Edinburgh, under the direction and nomination of the Council of the College. The College accepted the assignation, voted its thanks to Dr. Pattison, and agreed that the Bursary be named the Pattison Bursary. *[margin: Bursary founded by Dr. T. H. Pattison.]*

1st August 1876.—The fee for the Licence of the College was raised to £15, 15s. *[margin: Fee for Licence raised to Fifteen Guineas.]*

7th August 1877.—Two persons who had been deprived of the Licence of the College in consequence of their names having been removed from the Medical Register, but which had since been reponed by the General Medical Council, were restored to their position as Licentiates of the College. *[margin: Names of two Licentiates, restored to College Registrar.]*

A donation of ten guineas was voted to the Scottish Meteorological Society. *[margin: Ten Guineas voted to Scottish Meteorological Society.]*

5th February 1878.—The College agreed to a reply to be made to the General Medical Council on the subject of Preliminary Examination. *[margin: Reply to Medical Council on Preliminary Education.]*

29th March 1878.—The College agreed to support a Bill introduced into Parliament by the Duke of Richmond and Gordon, entituled the Medical Act (1858) Amendment Bill. *[margin: College agreed to support Medical Act Amendment Bill.]*

6th August 1878.—A Licentiate of the College whose name had been removed by the General Medical Council from the

Medical Register, in consequence of his having been convicted
of feloniously using instruments to procure miscarriage, was
declared to be no longer a Licentiate of the College, and the
Registrar was instructed to delete his name from the College
Register.

24th December 1878.—The College voted two hundred and
fifty guineas in aid of the subscription for the relief of the
sufferers by the failure of the City of Glasgow Bank.

A letter was read from the Rev. Sir W. G. Carmichael,
Bart., requesting the College's acceptance of a marble bust,
by Sir John Steell, of the late Dr. James Warburton Begbie.
The College accepted the offer, and voted thanks to the
donor.

4th February 1879.—The President reported that he and
the Council, as representing the College, had by invitation
attended the Special Services in St. Giles' Cathedral Church
on 22nd December last, on the occasion of the death of the
Princess Alice of Hesse.

14th March 1879.—The College having considered the
Medical Act (1858) Amendment Bill introduced into the House
of Lords by the President of the Council, concluded that it
was not expedient that a Conjoint Board be established for
each division of the United Kingdom, and that previous to
legislation taking place, the whole subject of Medical Reform
should be submitted to a Select Committee of Parliament, and
instructed the Council to take such steps as they might consider necessary to carry out the wishes of the College.

3rd May 1879.—The College agreed to contribute a sufficient
sum to furnish two Medical Wards in the new Royal Infirmary.
(The sum required amounted to £630.)

The Council reported that in accordance with the instructions of the College, they had forwarded a petition against the
Medical Acts Amendment Bill to both Houses of Parliament.

5th August 1879.—It was reported to the College that the
Medical Act Amendment Bill, having passed the House of
Lords and been introduced into the House of Commons, had

been referred to a Select Committee, and that evidence to a certain extent had already been taken.

16th December 1879.—The College voted a retiring allowance of £75 per annum to their late Officer.

Retiring Allowance voted to late Officer.

A communication was made from the Presidents of the Royal Colleges of Physicians and Surgeons of London, intimating that it was proposed to hold the next meeting of the International Medical Congress in London in 1881, and requesting to be informed how far the holding of the proposed Congress would meet with the approval and co-operation of this College. The College approved of the proposal, and gave power to the Council to send a Delegate to be present at a Preliminary Meeting, which it was proposed to hold.

College approved of proposal to hold next Meeting of International Medical Congress in London.

24th February 1880.—A Committee was appointed to consider the Laws relative to admission to the Membership and Fellowship of the College, and to report at the next Quarterly Meeting of the College.

Consideration of Laws as to Membership and Fellowship of the College.

The College, by a majority, voted the sum of one hundred guineas towards the fund for the Restoration of St. Giles' Cathedral.

100 Guineas voted towards Restoration of St. Giles.

3rd May 1880.—The Committee appointed to consider the Laws relative to admission by Examination to the Membership of the College, laid a Report before the College, which was approved of, and read for a first time.

3rd August 1880.—Further consideration of the Report as to the Laws relative to admission to the Membership and Fellowship of the College was postponed till the November Quarterly Meeting.

The College voted the sum of fifty guineas in aid of the fund required to meet the expenses consequent on the Meeting of the Congress of the National Association for the promotion of Social Science, to be held in Edinburgh in October next.

Fifty Guineas voted towards defraying expenses of Social Science Congress.

2nd November 1880.—The Report of the Committee on the Laws relative to admission to the Membership and Fellowship of the College was approved of, and read for a second time.

Five Guineas
voted to aid in
defraying
expenses of
Library
Association of
United
Kingdom.

The Treasurer reported that, under authority of the Council, he had on behalf of the College subscribed and paid five guineas towards defraying the expenses of the Library Association of the United Kingdom, which had met in Edinburgh last month. The College approved of and confirmed the subscription made.

New Laws as to
admission to
Membership
and Fellowship
of the College
approved of.

1st February 1881.—The Report of the Committee on the Laws relative to admission to the Membership and Fellowship of the College, which had been somewhat modified, was approved of, and read for a third time, and the Laws proposed in the Report were declared to be the Laws of the College.

College voted
that £50 be
paid annually to
Clinical Tutor
in ordinary
Medical Wards
of Infirmary.

2nd August 1881.—The College voted that a sum of fifty pounds be paid annually, during the pleasure of the College, to the Clinical Tutor attached to the Wards of the Ordinary Physicians to the Royal Infirmary.

£50 voted to aid
in defraying
expenses of
International
Medical
Congress.

The College voted that a sum of fifty pounds be paid towards defraying the expenses of the Meeting of the International Medical Congress to be held in London this month.

The Council reported to the College certain queries addressed by the Medical Acts Commission to the several Licensing Bodies, and submitted the reply which they proposed to make on behalf of the College. The College approved of the reply, and authorized the same to be transmitted as the reply of the College.

Celebration of
Bicentenary
of Incorporation
of the College.

7th February 1882.—The Vice-President, in the absence of the President, reported that the Bicentenary of the Incorporation of the College had been celebrated at the Annual Dinner, held on 8th December last, which was attended by not only most of the Resident Fellows of the College, but also by Representatives of both Houses of Parliament, Her Majesty's Navy and Army, the Magistracy of Edinburgh, the College of Justice, and other eminent citizens, and by Representatives of the Medical Profession from Glasgow, and other Cities and Towns in Scotland.

Donation to
Meteorological
Society.

2nd May 1882.—The College voted a sum of ten guineas in aid of the funds of the Scottish Meteorological Society.

1st August 1882.—Certain alterations on the Laws, affecting the rights and privileges of Fellows, Members, and Licentiates, were read for a first time.

7th November 1882.—The alterations on the Laws of the College proposed at the previous meeting were read for a second time.

26th December 1882.—The alterations on the Laws of the College were read for a third time, and unanimously adopted.

1st May 1883.—The College remitted to the Council to watch the progress of the Medical Act Amendment Bill, and granted powers to take all needful steps to safeguard the interests of the College.

The College appointed a Committee to consider and report on an application by the Extra-mural Lecturers in Edinburgh, addressed to the Royal Colleges of Physicians and Surgeons, praying to be associated under the name of 'The Medical School of the Royal Colleges of Physicians and Surgeons.'

The College unanimously voted a Honorarium of two hundred guineas to Dr. John Alexander Smith, in consideration of his valuable services as Treasurer to the College.

16th May 1883.—The College considered the Medical Act Amendment Bill then before Parliament.

13th June 1883.—The College again considered the Medical Act Amendment Bill.

7th August 1883.—The Committee appointed to consider and report upon the proposal to associate the Extra-mural School of Edinburgh with the Colleges, reported that in the existing position of Medical Legislation it would not, in their opinion, be expedient for the College to take any immediate steps in the matter. The report of the Committee was unanimously agreed to.

6th November 1883.—The College unanimously resolved that it was expedient to entertain motions that three Licentiates be deprived of all their rights and privileges as Licentiates of the College, for conduct unbecoming the character of a Physician.

Marginal notes:
Changes in Laws.
Medical Bill.
Petition of Extra-mural School.
Honorarium to late Treasurer.
Medical Bill.
Petition of Extra-mural School.
Motion for Expulsion of Licentiates.

It was reported to the College that the Medical Act Amendment Bill had been withdrawn.

A motion was read for the first time, that from 18th October 1884 the College cease to give the Licence as a Single Qualification to practise except to Candidates who have already passed such an Examination in Surgery as shall entitle them to have their names inserted in the Medical Register.

28th December 1883.—The proposed alterations on the Regulations for the Licence were read for a second time.

5th February 1884.—The proposed alterations on the Regulations for the Licence were read for a third time, and adopted.

18th March 1884.—The College considered and approved of the Scheme for Conjoint Examination and Qualification by the three Scottish Medical Corporations.

A Committee appointed by the Council to consider the proposed New British Pharmacopœia handed in their report.

The College agreed to entertain to Luncheon a number of the distinguished medical guests of the University of Edinburgh, on the occasion of the Tercentenary of the University.

The College adopted a joint petition from the Scottish Corporations to the House of Lords against the Medical Act Amendment Bill, which had been re-introduced.

6th May 1884.—The College agreed to forward an illuminated congratulatory Address to the University of Edinburgh on the attainment of the Tercentenary.

5th August 1884.—The College departed from a motion to deprive a Licentiate of his rights and privileges as a Licentiate, but severely censured him for his conduct.

It was reported that the Medical Act Amendment Bill had again been abandoned.

4th November 1884.—Two Licentiates were deprived of their rights and privileges as Licentiates.

26th December 1884.—The College considered the recommendation of the General Council in regard to Professional Education and Examination.

4th February 1885.—The College voted a sum of five hundred guineas in aid of the new buildings of the University of Edinburgh, and a sum of fifty guineas in aid of the Marine Station at Granton.

The College appointed a Committee, on the motion of Dr. Batty Tuke, to consider what means might be devised for the prosecution of Scientific Work.

5th May 1885.—The College voted a sum of two hundred guineas to Dr. John Wyllie in recognition of his valuable services as Secretary to the College.

The College guaranteed a sum not exceeding £400 to enable Dr. Hamilton, of Aberdeen, to publish an illustrated work on the Nervous System.

The College agreed to discontinue the Preliminary Examination conducted by the Edinburgh Colleges in the event of the General Council recognising the Examinations of the Educational Institute of Scotland as a qualifying Preliminary Examination.

7th July 1885.—The Committee appointed to consider the best means of promoting Scientific Work in connection with the College, recommended the College to establish and maintain a Laboratory for Physiological and Pathological Investigation. A formal motion for the adoption of the Report was carried by a majority, but inasmuch as it was not supported by a majority of three-fourths of the Fellows present, it could not be adopted. A new Committee was thereafter appointed.

4th August 1885.—The name of a Licentiate of the College which had been removed by the General Council from the Medical Register was removed from the College List.

The College resolved to present a loyal Address to Her Majesty the Queen on the marriage of the Princess Beatrice.

18th December 1885.—The name of a Licentiate of the College which had been removed by the General Council from the Medical Register was removed from the College List.

Marginal notes:

Vote to Edinburgh University and Marine Station.

Committee on Original Research.

Honorarium to late Secretary.

Guarantee towards Dr. Hamilton's Work.

Preliminary Examination.

Proposal to found Laboratory.

Defeated.

New Committee.

Licentiate removed from List.

Loyal Address to Queen.

Licentiate removed from List.

2nd February 1886.—The College resolved to give its consent to the Admission of Women to the Examinations for the Conjoint Qualification.

6th April 1886.—The Committee appointed to consider and report on the prosecution of Original Research in connection with the College, handed in a Report recommending the College to establish and maintain a Laboratory for the prosecution of Original Research. A formal motion for the adoption of the Report was carried by a majority of three-fourths of the Fellows present, and declared to have been read for a first time.

4th May 1886.—The College voted a donation of twenty-five guineas to the Ben Nevis Observatory.

15th May 1886.—The Report of the Committee appointed to consider and report on the prosecution of Original Research in connection with the College came up for second reading, but the motion for its adoption was lost, because the majority voting for it did not comprise three-fourths of the Fellows present.

3rd August 1886.—A petition was presented, signed by certain Fellows of the College, calling attention to the great need for the establishment of a Laboratory. On the motion of Dr. Batty Tuke a new Committee was appointed to consider the prosecution of Original Research by the College.

2nd November 1886.—The College voted an annuity of twenty-five guineas to Mrs. Small, wife of the former and mother of the late Sub-Librarian of the College.

It was announced that His Excellency Dr. Gunning had endowed a triennial prize, to be called "The Victoria Jubilee Cullen Prize," in commemoration of the approaching Jubilee of Her Majesty the Queen, and in memory of Dr. William Cullen,—the prize to be awarded for the greatest benefit done to Practical Medicine by any one connected with the College.

The Committee appointed to consider and report on the prosecution of Original Research in connection with the College reported in favour of the establishment of a Labora-

---

Marginal notes:

Women admitted to Licence

Proposal to found Laboratory read for first time.

Donation to Ben Nevis Observatory.

Proposal to found Laboratory defeated.

Petition in favour of Laboratory.

New Committee.

Annuity to Sub-Librarian's Mother.

Cullen Prize.

Laboratory Scheme read for first time.

tory. A formal motion for the adoption of the Report was unanimously carried, and declared as read for the first time.

28th December 1886.—The Report of the Committee on the prosecution of Original Research in connection with the College was read a second time.

Read for second time.

1st February 1887.—The College voted a piece of plate of the value of one hundred guineas to Mr. Christopher Douglas, W.S., in acknowledgment of his valuable services as Clerk to the College for above thirty years.

Vote of Plate to the Clerk.

15th February 1887.—The Report of the Committee on the prosecution of Original Research was read for a third time, and was declared to be finally approved of and adopted by the College.

Laboratory Scheme read for third time and adopted.

The College resolved that it was expedient that a motion should be entertained for the expulsion of a Member of the College, for having published and exposed for sale an indecent publication.

Motion for Expulsion of a Member.

3rd May 1887.—The College unanimously resolved to present a loyal Address to Her Majesty the Queen, on the occasion of her Jubilee, and remitted the preparation of such an Address to the Council.

Loyal Address to Queen proposed

7th June 1887.—The College adopted the loyal Address to Her Majesty, prepared by the Council, and authorized the Council to make arrangements for its presentation.

and adopted.

21st June 1887.—The College was represented at the Commemoration of the Jubilee of Her Majesty in Westminster Abbey.

Her Majesty's Jubilee.

27th June 1887.—The Loyal Address was presented at Windsor Castle to Her Majesty by a Deputation from the College.

Loyal Address presented.

2nd August 1887.—The College voted a sum of one hundred guineas to the Imperial Institute.

Donation to Imperial Institute.

1st November 1887.—A resolution was adopted that the Oral Examinations of the Conjoint Qualification be open to the inspection of the Fellows of any Scottish Corporation, or of any registered Medical Practitioner introduced by them.

Examinations to be open.

Removal of Names of a Member

23*rd December* 1887.—The name of the Member of the College, for whose expulsion the College resolved on 15th February 1887 that it was expedient to entertain a motion, having been removed from the Medical Register by the General Council, was formally removed from the College List.

and of a Licentiate.

The name of a Licentiate which had also been removed from the Medical Register was also removed from the College List.

Action of English Colleges,

The College considered the action of the English Medical Colleges in proposing to obtain a Charter from Her Majesty the Queen in Council granting powers to confer degrees in Medicine and Surgery.

and

3*rd January* 1888.—The College further considered the action of the English Medical Colleges, and appointed a Committee to confer with Committees of the other Corporations on the subject.

consequent action of Scottish Corporations;

9*th January* 1888.—The College further considered the action of the English Medical Colleges, and the report of the delegates appointed to confer with representatives of the other Corporations, and resolved to hold a Conference of the Fellows of the College with the Fellows of the other two Scottish Corporations.

Conference,

10*th January* 1888.—The proposed Conference of the Fellows of the Scottish Corporations took place.

and Result.

11*th January* 1888.—The College resolved, in consequence of the action of the English Medical Colleges, to present to the Queen in Council a joint petition by the three Scottish Corporations, requesting powers to confer degrees in Medicine and Surgery.

Pattison Bursary.

1*st May* 1888.—The College adopted a scheme for the management of the Pattison Bursary, founded by the late Dr. Thomas Hill Pattison, a Fellow of the College.

Royal Commission on Medical Degrees.

It was reported that the Petition of the Scottish Corporations for powers to confer degrees in Medicine and Surgery had, along with that of the English Colleges, been referred to a Royal Commission.

7th August 1888.—The College resolved to obtain a bust of the late Dr. Daniel Rutherford Haldane. *[margin: Bust of late Dr. D. R. Haldane.]*

The College voted a donation of twenty-five guineas to the Ben Nevis Observatory. *[margin: Ben Nevis Observatory.]*

A Report by the Council on an application by University College and King's College, London, to be erected by Royal Charter as the Albert University, was laid before the College. *[margin: Proposed Albert University.]*

27th December 1888.—The College resolved to hold a Conversazione in connection with the foundation of the Research Laboratory. *[margin: Conversazione.]*

5th February 1889.—The College resolved that it was expedient to entertain a motion for the expulsion of a Licentiate who had been convicted of, and imprisoned for, conspiring to cheat and defraud a Life Assurance Society. *[margin: Motion for expulsion of Licentiate.]*

7th May 1889.—It was announced that the Oral Examinations under the Conjoint Scheme would for the future be open to the inspection of the Fellows of the Scottish Corporations, and to any registered Medical Practitioner introduced by them. *[margin: Examinations open to Inspection.]*

A Bequest of £1500 by the late Dr. John Parkin, a Fellow of the College, was intimated, for the purpose of founding Prizes for Original Research. *[margin: Parkin Prizes.]*

24th May 1889.—The College considered the motion entertained 5th February 1889, for the expulsion of the Licentiate convicted of conspiring to cheat and defraud a Life Assurance Society, and heard his solicitor in his defence. *[margin: College departs from Motion for expulsion of Licentiate.]*

Having heard what had been stated for the defence, and having considered the same, and a petition in his favour presented to the College by Practitioners in the district where the Licentiate practised, the College unanimously resolved to depart from the motion.

1st July 1889.—The College voted a donation of two hundred and fifty guineas to the Scottish Branch of the Queen Victoria's Jubilee Institute for Nurses. *[margin: Donation; Jubilee Institute for Nurses.]*

6th August 1889.—The College resolved to invite the Physiological Society to hold a meeting, during July 1890, within the College Hall and Laboratory. *[margin: Invitation to Physiological Society.]*

22nd October 1889.—The College resolved to appoint a Committee to consider the expediency of establishing a Fund for the benefit of the Widows and Orphans of the Fellows, Members, and Licentiates of the College.

5th November 1889.—The College resolved to obtain a copy of the portrait of the late Dr. John Rutherford, a former President of the College.

It was intimated that Dr. A. H. Freeland Barbour, a Fellow of the College, had determined to hand over the sum of £1250 to the College, in trust for the purpose of constituting and endowing a Fellowship in connection with the Laboratory, to be named "The Freeland-Barbour Fellowship," in memory of the late George Freeland Barbour, Esq. of Bonskeid.

The College resolved to publish an Annual Volume of Reports of the Work done in the Laboratory of the College.

21st November 1889.—The College revised the Regulations regarding the Diploma in Public Health.

A Committtee was appointed to consider and report on the nature of the evidence to be laid before the Scottish University Commissioners.

27th December 1889.—A Committee was appointed to report on new remedies to be introduced into the addendum of the British Pharmacopœia.

7th March 1890.—The College considered and adopted a statement to be laid before the Scottish Universities Commission, and remitted to the Council to arrange with regard to the appointment of representatives of the College to give evidence before the Commissioners.

The Committee appointed to consider the addendum to the British Pharmacopeia handed in their Report.

6th May 1890.—The College voted a service of plate of the value of one hundred guineas to Dr. R. Peel Ritchie, in acknowledgment of his valuable services as Treasurer to the College.

3rd June 1890.—The Laws of the College as revised and amended by the Council were read for a first time.

12th June 1890.—The Committee appointed to consider the expediency of instituting a fund for the benefit of the Widows and Orphans of the Fellows, Members, and Licentiates of the College, submitted their Report, and a new Committee was appointed to reconsider the whole question. Proposed Widows' Fund.

It was resolved to entertain the Members of the Physiological Society to dinner on the occasion of their visit to Edinburgh. Dinner to Physiological Society.

It having been ascertained that the portrait copied for the College was not that of Dr. John Rutherford, but of his son, Dr. Daniel Rutherford, also a former President of the College, the College resolved to secure a copy of the portrait of Dr. John Rutherford. Portrait of late Dr. Daniel Rutherford.

The College also resolved to obtain a copy of the portrait of the late Dr. John Abercromby. Portrait of late Dr. Abercromby.

The Laws as revised and amended by the Council were read a second time. Revised Laws.

29th July 1890. — The College resolved that it was expedient to entertain a motion for the expulsion of a Licentiate for having acted as cover to an unqualified practitioner engaged in an unprofessional if not indecent practice. Motion for expulsion of Licentiate.

30th October 1890.—The College considered the Laws as revised and amended by the Council, along with amendments thereon proposed by Fellows of the College, and the Laws were read for a third time, and adopted. Revised Laws.

4th November 1890.—It was intimated that the Licentiate for whose expulsion the College, on 29th July 1890, had entertained a motion, had died during the interval. Death of Licentiate proposed to be expelled.

12th December 1890.—The Committee of the College appointed to consider the expediency of instituting a fund for the benefit of the Widows and Orphans of the Fellows, Members, and Licentiates of the College, handed in their report, which was generally approved of, and referred to the Council for further consideration and report. Proposed Widows' Fund.

5th May 1891.—One or two minor additions to the Laws were read for the first time. Additions to Laws.

22nd May 1891.—The additions to the Laws were read for a second time.

12th June 1891.—The additions to the Laws were read for a third time, and adopted by the College.

Proposed Sale of Larchgrove.

The College resolved that it was expedient, in order to obtain a more steady source of endowment for the "Morison Lectureship," to sell Larchgrove, at a price not under £1100.

Vote towards Congress of Hygiene.

The College voted a sum of twenty-five guineas towards the International Congress of Hygiene and Demography, to be held in London during August 1891.

Bequest by late Dr. Struthers.

4th August 1891.—It was intimated that the late Dr. Struthers, a Fellow of the College, had bequeathed a sum of one thousand pounds "to be added by the College so as to form part of, and be administered in the same manner as, the bequest to the College by the deceased Dr. Pattison of Edinburgh."

LAWS.

CHAPTER I.

Of the College and Common Seal.

1. THE College shall consist of Fellows and Members.

2. The business of the College shall be managed by the Fellows on the Roll of Attendance.

3. The Seal, whereof the above is an engraving, is the Seal of this College; and shall be affixed to all Diplomas, Certificates, and other Public Acts of the College.

To be kept by Secretary.

4. The Common Seal shall be kept in the custody of the Secretary, and shall be affixed by him to such Documents as the College, Council, or President shall direct.

College shall grant Licences

5. The College shall grant Licences to practise Medicine and Midwifery, the holders of which shall be entitled Licentiates of the College. (See Chapter IV.)

and Diplomas in Public Health.

6. The College shall grant Diplomas of qualification in Public Health, the holders of which shall be designated Diplomates in Public Health of the College.

CHAPTER II.

Of Fellows.

Powers of the Fellows.

1. The Fellows of the College on the Roll of Attendance shall administer the property and affairs of the College, enact its Laws, elect Fellows and Members, admit Licentiates, and elect the President and Council.

Who are eligible.

2. No one shall be elected a Fellow of the College until he has been at least one year a Member thereof, and has attained the age of twenty-five years.

Ordinary mode of election.

3. Every motion for the election of a Fellow shall be made at a Quarterly Meeting of Fellows by one of the Fellows present, and seconded by another ; and this motion shall be determined by ballot at the next Quarterly Meeting of Fellows,—a majority of three-fourths being necessary to carry it in the affirmative.

4. The names and addresses of Candidates for admission as Fellows, with the names of their proposers

and seconders, shall be announced by Billet to the Fellows on the Roll of Attendance, within one week from the date of the Meeting at which the motion for their election has been made. The names and addresses here referred to shall be repeated in the Billet (Chapter X., Law 9) summoning the Meeting at which the motion for election is to be determined.

Names of Candidates to be announced to Fellows.

5. If an urgent reason, satisfactory to the Council, be assigned, a Candidate may be proposed at an Extraordinary Meeting of the Fellows summoned for the purpose, and his petition may be balloted for at an Extraordinary Meeting of the Fellows summoned for the purpose; provided that the holding of this Special Meeting be agreed to by a majority of five-sixths of the Fellows present at the Meeting at which the Candidate was proposed; provided also that not less than one week intervene between the two Meetings, and that due notice of the intended ballot be given in the Billets summoning the second Meeting. The Candidate shall in this case pay to the Treasurer a sum of ten guineas in addition to the ordinary Fees.

Election in cases of urgency.

6. No Fellow shall take his seat in the College until the next Quarterly Meeting after his election,—intimation to attend being sent to him by the Clerk.

Taking of seat.

7. The Fellows shall be placed on the Roll according to the date of their election. When two or more Fellows are elected on the same day, they shall be entered on the Roll according to the date of their Membership; and if their election as Members be of the same date, they shall be enrolled according to seniority of original qualification.

Order on Roll.

8. Every Fellow resident within five miles from the General Post Office of Edinburgh shall, on his admission, have his name placed on the Roll of Attendance, and

Roll of Attendance.

shall pay the annual contribution, and be subject to all the Laws of the College regarding fines. Fellows resident beyond five miles shall have the option of having their names on the Roll of Attendance or not ; but if their names be on the Roll of Attendance, they shall pay the Annual Contribution, and be subject to fines.

Removal of Names from Roll.

9. Any Fellow may petition that his name be taken off the Roll of Attendance ; which petition shall be determined by ballot at next Quarterly Meeting.

Placing of Name on Roll of Attendance.

10. Any Fellow whose name is not on the Roll of Attendance may petition that his name be placed on the Roll of Attendance; which petition shall be determined by ballot at next Quarterly Meeting.

Fellows leaving Edinburgh may have their Names taken off the Roll.

11. Any Fellow leaving Edinburgh for a length of time, and omitting to petition to have his name taken off the Roll of Attendance, or wishing the same to be continued on it during his absence, shall be charged with his Annual Contribution and fines.

Fellows not on Roll not to have use of Library :

12. Fellows whose names are not on the Roll of Attendance shall not have the use of the Library and Reading-room, except in the cases specified in Laws 13 and 14 of this chapter.

except with consent of Council.

13. Fellows whose names are not on the Roll of Attendance, on coming to reside in Edinburgh, or within five miles thereof, for a period not exceeding six months, may, with consent of the Council, be allowed the use of the Library and Reading-room.

Fellows not on Roll of Attendance may use Library.

14. Fellows not on the Roll of Attendance, who reside permanently in Edinburgh, or within five miles thereof, but are not engaged in practice, may, with the consent of the Council, be allowed the use of the Library and Reading-room on payment of the Annual Contribution.

15. Each Fellow, before taking his seat, shall be introduced by the Secretary to the President and Fellows, who shall receive him standing. After the promissory obligation (Appendix No. I.) has been read aloud to him by the Secretary or Clerk (the President and Fellows still standing), he shall affix his name to it in presence of the College, and he shall then receive the right hand of Fellowship from the President and Fellows present.

Mode of reception of new Fellows.

16. Petitions for admission as Fellows shall be in the form given in the Appendix No. II. The further proceedings upon such petitions shall be in the form prescribed in Laws 3 and 4 of this chapter.

Form of Petition.

17. The Diploma presented by the College to its Ordinary Fellows shall be in the terms given in Appendix No. III.

Form of Diploma.

CHAPTER III.

Of Members.

1. Any Licentiate of a College of Physicians, or Graduate in Medicine of a British or Irish University, may be admitted a Member of the College, provided he has attained the age of twenty-four years, produced satisfactory testimonials as to his professional and social status, and satisfied the College as to his proficiency in Medical Science.

Who are eligible.

2. The Council shall, at the Annual Meeting of the College for the election of Office-Bearers, appoint a Board of Examiners to conduct the Examination of Candidates.

Board of Examiners.

3. Every Candidate for the Membership (except such as shall be admissible under the provisions of Law 7 of this chapter) shall be examined—

Subjects of Examination.

(1.) On the Principles and Practice of Medicine, including Therapeutics.

(2.) Also on one of the following subjects, to be selected by the Candidate :—

    (*a*) One or more departments of Medicine specially professed ;

    (*b*) Psychological Medicine ;

    (*c*) General Pathology and Morbid Anatomy ;

    (*d*) Medical Jurisprudence ;

    (*e*) Public Health;

    (*f*) Midwifery ;

    (*g*) Diseases of Women.

Council to prepare Plan of Examination.

4. The Council shall annually, at the Quarterly Meeting of the College in August, submit to the College the Plan of Examination for the Membership, and the dates at which it is proposed that the Examinations shall be held.

Mode of Application.

5. Application for the Membership shall be made through the Secretary, who shall transmit to the Candidate a copy of the Regulations and Plan of Examination, together with a Petition in terms of the Form in the Appendix No. IV.

6. The Candidate shall return the Petition duly filled up to the Secretary, and shall at the same time

Must produce Testimonials.

transmit testimonials of recent date from well-known members of the profession, certifying as to his professional and social standing. These documents shall be submitted to the Council, who shall also employ such other methods of scrutiny as they may deem necessary. If satisfied as to the eligibility of the

Candidate, the Council shall authorize his examination by the Board of Examiners, who shall report the result of the Examination to the Council. If the report of the Examiners be satisfactory, the Council shall report the same to the College at the next Quarterly Meeting, when it shall be competent for a motion to be made for the election of such Candidate to the Membership of the College.

7. If any Candidate who has attained the age of forty years, and has been a Registered Practitioner for not less than ten years, shall produce Testimonials showing that he has been distinguished for his scientific attainments, or eminence as a Medical Practitioner, the Council may, if they see fit, exempt him from the whole or any part of the prescribed Examination.

Certain Applicants to be exempted from Examination in whole or part.

8. Every motion for the election of a Member shall be made at a Quarterly Meeting of the College by one of the Fellows present, and seconded by another, and the motion shall be determined by ballot at the next Quarterly Meeting; a majority of three-fourths of the Fellows present being necessary to carry it in the affirmative.

Mode of Election.

9. The names, qualifications, and addresses of Candidates, along with the names of their proposers and seconders, shall be announced by Billet to the Fellows on the Roll of Attendance, within one week from the date of the Meeting at which the motion for election has been made. The names, qualifications, and addresses here referred to shall be repeated in the Billet summoning the Meeting at which the motion for election is to be determined.

Names of Candidates to be announced to Fellows.

10. The Members shall be placed on the Roll of Members according to the date of their Diplomas of Membership; and when two or more Members are

Order on Roll.

admitted on the same day, they shall be enrolled according to professional seniority.

Use of Library.   11. Members who reside permanently in Edinburgh, or within five miles thereof, may, with consent of the Council, be allowed the use of the Library and Reading-room on payment of the Annual Contribution of one guinea at the Quarterly Meeting in November.

Form of Diploma.   12. The Diploma presented by the College to its Members shall be in terms of the Form given in the Appendix No. V.

CHAPTER IV.

Of Licentiates.

Mode of Application.   1. Application for the Licence to practise Medicine shall be made through the Registrar, or, in the case of the Triple Qualification, through the Inspector of Certificates.

Who are eligible.   2. Every Applicant, before receiving the Licence of the College, shall satisfy the Council that he is twenty-one years of age, that he is of good moral character, that he is not under articles of apprenticeship, and that he has fulfilled all the requirements as to Medical Education that were in force at the date when he commenced his Medical studies.

Declaration to be signed.   3. Every Applicant, before receiving the Licence, must sign the Declaration in terms of Appendix No. VI.

Council to prepare Curriculum of Study.   4. The Council of the College shall annually, at the Quarterly Meeting in August, submit to the College the Curriculum of Study, and Plan of Examination for the Licence of the College.

5. Copies of the existing Curriculum and Plan of Examination shall be printed and furnished to all applicants for the Licence.

Copies of Curriculum to be printed.

6. The College shall admit to examination for its Single Qualification in Medicine any Candidate who possesses a registrable Surgical Qualification.

7. The Licence of the College may also be obtained in conjunction with that of the Royal College of Surgeons of Edinburgh, and of the Faculty of Physicians and Surgeons of Glasgow, under Regulations to be from time to time arranged between the College and these Bodies.

Double Qualification.

8. The Diploma granted by the College to its Licentiates shall be in terms of the Form given in the Appendix No. VII.

Form of Diploma.

CHAPTER V.

Of Diplomates in Public Health.

1. Application for the Diploma in Public Health must be made through the Registrar.

Mode of Application.

2. Every applicant before being admitted to examination for the Diploma must produce evidence that he is already on the Medical Register, and that he has satisfied all the conditions named in the Regulations of the College.

Who are eligible.

3. The Council of the College shall annually, at the

Council to prepare Curriculum of Study.

Quarterly Meeting in August, submit to the College the Curriculum of Study, and Plan of Examination for the Diploma in Public Health of the College.

Copies of Curriculum to be printed.

4. Copies of the existing Curriculum and Plan of Examination shall be printed and furnished to all applicants for the Diploma.

Form of Diploma.

5. The Diploma granted by the College in Public Health shall be in terms of the Form given in the Appendix No. VIII.

CHAPTER VI.

Of the Fees.

Fee of Licentiate.

1. The Fee to be paid by a Licentiate shall be fifteen guineas.

Fee of Members.

2. The Fee to be paid by a Member shall be thirty guineas.

Fee when a Licentiate becomes a Member.

3. When a Licentiate shall be raised to the rank of Member, he shall pay fifteen guineas.

Fee when a Member becomes a Fellow.

4. When a Member shall be raised to the rank of Fellow, he shall pay thirty guineas, exclusive of Stamp-duty.

Fee of Diplomate in Public Health.

5. The Fee to be paid by a Diplomate in Public Health shall be ten guineas.

Fees to be lodged with Treasurer before Petitions presented.

6. All Applicants for Licence or Diploma, and all Candidates for Membership or Fellowship, must lodge their Fees, and the amount of Stamp-duty payable at the time to Government, with the Treasurer, previously to presenting their petitions.

CHAPTER VII.

Of Forfeiture of Fellowships, Memberships, and Licences.

1. No Fellow or Member of the College shall by himself, co-partners, or servants, keep a public Apothecary's, Druggist's, or Chemist's shop. If any Fellow or Member of the College shall by himself, co-partners, or servants keep a public Apothecary's, Druggist's, or Chemist's shop, he shall, *ipso facto*, forfeit all the rights and privileges which he does or may enjoy as a Fellow or Member of the College, and his name shall be expunged from the College List.

Keeping a public shop involves forfeiture of Fellowship or Membership.

2. Any Fellow, Member, or Licentiate of the College who shall, in accordance with the provisions of the Medical Act, Section XXIX., have his name removed from the Medical Register, shall be deprived, *ipso facto*, of his Fellowship, Membership, or Licence to practise, as given by the College.

Removal from the Register involves forfeiture of Fellowship, Membership, or Licence.

3. If any Fellow, Member, Licentiate, or Diplomate in Public Health shall have been convicted by the Law Courts of the country in which he resides of any felony, misdemeanour, crime, or offence, or shall, after due inquiry, be judged by the College to have been guilty of infamous conduct in any professional respect, the College may, if they see fit, expel him from the College, and deprive him of his Fellowship, Membership, Licence, or Diploma in Public Health, and of all the rights and privileges which as Fellow, Member, Licentiate, or Diplomate in Public Health he does or may enjoy.

Unbecoming conduct involves forfeiture of Fellowship, Membership, Licence, or Diploma in Public Health.

Censure or
Suspension.

4. Every Fellow, Member, Licentiate, and Diplomate in Public Health shall at all times conduct himself in a becoming and professional manner. Any Fellow, Member, Licentiate, or Diplomate in Public Health who shall, after due inquiry, be judged by the Fellows to have acted in an unbecoming or unprofessional manner, may be censured, or may be deprived, for such time as the Fellows may determine, of all the rights and privileges which as Fellow, Member, Licentiate, or Diplomate in Public Health he does or may enjoy.

Mode of
Procedure.

5. The proceedings for censure, suspension, or expulsion shall be the following:—The motion for the censure, suspension, or expulsion of the Fellow, Member, Licentiate, or Diplomate in Public Health shall contain a statement of the offence of which the Fellow, Member, Licentiate, or Diplomate in Public Health is accused. This motion shall be submitted to the Council, and shall be laid by them, with their opinion thereon, before a Meeting of the Fellows, at which it shall be proposed and seconded. A vote of the Fellows shall then be taken, as to whether it is expedient to entertain the motion ; and in the event of its being decided by a Majority that the motion shall be entertained, the further proceedings shall be the following :—The motion shall be determined at another Meeting of the Fellows, summoned at an interval of not less than three months after the first. The object of both these Meetings shall be announced in the Billets summoning the Meetings ; and the Billets shall be issued one week previous to each Meeting. A majority of not less than three-fourths of the Fellows present shall be required to carry the motion.

Clerk to send
notice to
accused.

6. The Clerk shall, within three clear days after the Meeting at which the motion has been proposed,

transmit a copy of it to the Fellow, Member, Licentiate, or Diplomate in Public Health accused. It shall be held sufficient evidence of this Law having been complied with, if the notice has been posted in registered envelope with the address of the Fellow, Member, Licentiate, or Diplomate in Public Health as given in the latest issue of the Medical Register.

7. The Fellow, Member, Licentiate, or Diplomate in Public Health accused may appear and plead either personally, or by a Representative, at the Meeting at which the motion is to be considered.

The accused to appear by himself or Representative.

8. It shall be in the power of the Council to shorten the period of three months between the tabling and determining of the motion, should the Fellow, Member, Licentiate, or Diplomate in Public Health accused petition to that effect.

Council may shorten period of three months.

CHAPTER VIII.

Of the Election of Office-Bearers.

1. At the Annual Meeting for the Election of Office-Bearers (*vide* Chapter X., Law 1), it shall be competent for any Fellow to propose one of the Fellows present, as President : and on his motion being seconded by another Fellow, the Fellow so nominated shall be elected President, if no other name be proposed. If, however, another name or names be duly proposed and seconded, a vote shall be taken, and the Fellow having the greatest number of votes shall be President of the College for the ensuing year.

Election of President.

Nomination of
Vice-President.

2. The newly-elected President shall take the Chair, and nominate a Vice-President.

Election of the
Members of
Council.

3. The President shall then nominate three of the Fellows present, not being in the Council, as Scrutineers. Thereupon the roll of the Fellows shall be called by the Clerk. Each Fellow present, as his name is called, shall then place on the table before the President a paper signed with his name, containing the names of six Fellows on the Roll of Attendance whom he may desire to elect to be, with the President, the Council of the College for the ensuing year. The Scrutineers shall, without leaving the room, arrange these Lists, and report to the College what names have received the greatest number of votes. Should any List be found incorrect, it shall be returned for correction to the Fellow who signed it; or if he should have left the meeting, it shall be destroyed.

Council to choose
Office-Bearers.

4. The Council of the College, who shall be Electors of the other Office-Bearers, shall within seven days make choice of a Treasurer, a Secretary, a Librarian, a Curator of Museum, a Curator of Laboratory, and a Registrar of Licentiates, all of whom must be Fellows of the College; and of Examiners, a Clerk, an Auditor, a Superintendent of Laboratory, a Sub-Librarian, and an Officer. These Office-Bearers shall continue in office for one year.

Announcement
of Office-Bearers.

5. The Clerk shall announce by billet the names of the Office-Bearers.

President not to
hold office for
more than two
years consecu-
tively.

6. The same Fellow may be elected President for two years successively, but not for any longer consecutive period, unless by the consent of three-fourths of the Fellows present. But the same Fellow may be re-elected after having been out of office for two years.

7. In the event of the outgoing President having a majority of votes, but not a sufficient number to entitle him to re-election, the Fellow having the next highest number of votes shall not be declared President, but a new nomination (from which the retiring President shall be excluded) shall be made, and a new vote be taken, and the Fellow having the greatest number of votes shall be declared President for the ensuing year.

If retiring President have not enough of votes, another election necessary.

8. The other Office-Bearers may be re-elected for an unlimited number of years.

No restriction on other Office-Bearers.

9. In the event of the death or resignation of any Office-Bearer, with the exception of the President or a Member of Council, during the currency of the year, the Council, in accordance with other Laws, shall have power to fill up the vacancy, such appointment to continue in force until the next Election Meeting.

Council to have power to fill up vacancies.

CHAPTER IX.

Of the Powers and Duties of the Office-Bearers.

§ 1. THE PRESIDENT.

1. The President shall keep order, regulate the debates, call the votes when necessary, and declare in what manner the question is determined.

To regulate the Debates.

2. He shall have one vote as Fellow, and a casting vote in case of an equal division.

To have an ordinary and casting vote.

3. He shall not originate or second any motion while acting as Chairman.

Cannot originate or second a Motion.

4. He shall appoint all Committees, and shall be *ex officio* a member of every Committee.

To appoint Committees.

To sign Diplomas.

5. He shall sign all Diplomas issued by the College.

Duties of Vice-President.

6. In the absence of the President, his duties and powers shall devolve upon the Vice-President.

§ 2. THE COUNCIL.

Members of Council.

1. The word Council shall mean the Council of the College for the time being. The Council shall consist of the President and six of the Fellows resident within seven miles of the General Post Office in Edinburgh, and shall be elected annually, at the Election Meeting fixed by the Bye-Laws; but the acts of the Council shall not be invalidated by the existence of any vacancy in the offices of President, or Member of Council, or by any informality, afterwards discovered, in the election or appointment of any such President or Member of Council. Four Members shall be a quorum.

Council to elect Office-Bearers.

2. The Council shall elect the Examiners of the College, and shall also elect a Treasurer, Secretary, Clerk, and such other Office-Bearers as may be deemed necessary, annually, and as often as occasion may require or vacancies occur by death, resignation, or otherwise, in accordance with the Bye-Laws.

Council to appoint Trustees.

3. The Council shall, with the approval of the Fellows, nominate four Fellows, who, along with the Treasurer, shall be Trustees of the College, and shall fill up vacancies as they arise by death, resignation, or otherwise.

Previous Occupants to remain in Office until Successors appointed.

4. In the event of an Office-Bearer not being elected on the day appointed for the election of such, or if the person elected does not accept office, the previous occupant of such office shall continue to fill the same until his successor is appointed.

5. If any Member of Council die or resign before the expiration of the year or other time for which he shall have been elected, the Fellows present at an Ordinary Meeting of the College, or at an Extraordinary one called as provided, may elect a Member of Council, who shall serve for the remainder of the year of office or other time for which the Member dying or resigning was elected.

Vacancies in Council.

6. The Council may call Extraordinary Meetings of the Fellows for the consideration and disposal of any special business of the College at any time when the same shall be deemed necessary.

Council may summon Fellows,

7. The Council may call Extraordinary Meetings of the Fellows and Members at any time when the same shall be deemed necessary.

or Fellows and Members.

8. The Council shall prepare all business for the Meetings of the Fellows, and shall generally manage and administer the affairs and property of the College in such manner and under such regulations as may from time to time be directed by the Fellows in terms of the Bye-Laws.

Council to prepare Business and manage affairs.

9. The Council shall also arrange the various Examinations for the Licences and Diplomas of the College, and take the general supervision thereof.

Council to arrange Examinations

10. The Council shall take the general supervision of the conduct of the Fellows, Members, Licentiates, and Diplomates in Public Health of the College ; and in the event of its being deemed necessary to take steps for the censure, suspension, or expulsion of a Fellow, Member, Licentiate, or Diplomate in Public Health, shall prepare the motion for such censure, suspension, or expulsion, and make the necessary arrangements for the case being submitted to the College.

Council to exercise supervision over College.

§ 3. COMMITTEES.

To be restricted as to time.

1. At the appointment of every Committee (except standing Committees), a time shall be fixed for the business being finished which the College entrusts to it.

Not to incur expense without a special vote of the College.

2. No expenses shall be incurred by Committees without a special vote of the College, and a limitation of the sum to be expended.

When to report.

3. Committees appointed at one Quarterly Meeting shall bring up written Reports to the next Quarterly Meeting, unless it has been otherwise determined.

When discharged.

4. A Committee shall be held as discharged when its final Report has been laid before the College.

§ 4. THE TREASURER.

Accountable for the Funds.

1. The Treasurer shall receive, disburse, and be accountable, for the Funds of the College.

May defray ordinary expenses without a special order.

2. He may pay, without any special order, the ordinary expenses of the College, but shall not pay or disburse any other sum without previous direction to that effect from the Council.

Accounts to be balanced and audited.

3. He shall balance his Accounts every year on the 20th day of January, or, if that day shall happen to be Sunday, on the 19th January, and shall deliver, or cause to be delivered, to the Quarterly Meeting in February, the Auditor's Abstract and Statement of Accounts, containing his Charge and Discharge of the money belonging to the College, with a true state of his Accounts.

Book of Annual Expenditure.

4. He shall keep a Regular Book of Accounts, containing the various items of Income and Expenditure

for the year, which Book shall be produced yearly at the February Meeting.

5. He shall keep a Book containing a statement of the Capital Account, which Book shall also be produced yearly at the February Meeting.

Book of Capital Account.

6. He may retain £20 in his hands; but any surplus above that shall be lodged in the Banking-house where the cash account of the College is kept; and when the funds so lodged shall exceed £500, as ascertained at the next Meeting of the Trustees of the College, such sum shall be placed on deposit receipt, in name of the Trustees, till an available security is found.

Must lodge all Funds above £20 in Bank.

7. If at any time he shall have occasion to overdraw the cash account of the College, he shall on no account do so without the direct authority of the Council.

Cannot overdraw Bank Account without authority of Council.

8. He may expend the sum of £5 on such repairs on the buildings as may be necessary; but when the expense exceeds that sum, he shall previously obtain the authority of the Council.

Latitude as to repairs.

9. All papers and vouchers relating to the property of the College shall be lodged by the Treasurer in the Safe of the College, and the key retained by him.

Vouchers to be lodged in Safe.

10. After the Treasurer's Accounts have been approved of, he shall see that the Report be regularly transcribed by the Clerk into the Minute-Book of the College.

Report of Accounts to be entered in Minutes.

11. He shall, previously to the last Meeting of Council before the Quarterly Meeting in November of each year, give to the Clerk a list of the Trustees who may have been absent from any of the Meetings, in order that the penalties exigible from them may be collected and included in the Annual Statement of the contributions and fines.

To keep a List of Trustees absent from the Meetings.

To manage
College, Hall,
and Servants.

12. He shall, subject to the control of the Council, act as General Manager of the College Hall, the servants, and the contained property, with the exception of the Books in the Library and the Specimens in the Museum.

To be Manager
of Ceremonies.

13. He shall also, subject to the control of the Council, act as Manager of all entertainments given by the College, as well as of all ceremonies in which the Fellows may take part.

Proceedings
consequent on
a change of
Treasurer.

14. On the resignation or retirement of the Treasurer, his books and relative vouchers shall be examined by a Committee appointed for the purpose, and if found correct, he shall be exonerated from his intromissions with the funds of the College. He shall also hand over all documents and papers in his custody, with a proper inventory thereof, to his successor in office, whose receipt for the same shall free him from all further responsibility regarding them.

To have a Clerk.

15. The Treasurer shall be authorized to employ a Clerk for the necessary clerical work connected with his office.

§ 5. The Auditor.

To examine
and report on
Treasurer's
Accounts.

1. The Auditor, who shall be a Chartered Accountant, shall examine the Treasurer's Annual Account s and frame an Abstract thereof, to be printed and submitted to the College at the Quarterly Meeting in February.

To report on
state of Funds.

2. He shall also prepare a Statement of the funds and property of the College, to be printed and circulated with the Abstract.

Salary.

3. For these services he shall receive such Fee as the Council may from time to time fix.

§ 6. The Trustees.

1. The Trustees shall consist of the Treasurer, and four Fellows to be selected by the Council, subject to the approval of the College. *How appointed.*

2. They shall invest all property belonging to the College, in the name of the College, in its corporate capacity, with the exception of the amount allowed to be retained in the Bank and in the Treasurer's hands (see Chap. IX., Sect. 4, Law 6). *All Property to be vested in name of the College.*

3. They shall hold two stated Meetings in the year, viz.—on the second Tuesday of May and November, and shall also meet at such other times as the duties imposed upon them in regard to the property of the College may require (Chap. XIV., Laws 3 to 5). *Stated and occasional Meetings.*

4. On a vacancy occurring in the office of Trustee by death, resignation, or otherwise, the Council shall, within a month, nominate a successor, subject to the approval of the College at its next Meeting. *Vacancies how to be filled up.*

§ 7. The Examiners.

1. The Council shall choose from time to time Examiners in Preliminary Education. *The Examiners in Preliminary Education.*

2. The President or Vice-President, or one of the Examiners of the College, or, failing them, some Fellow of the College appointed by the Council, shall from time to time inspect the Examination. *Some Fellow of College to be present at Preliminary Examination.*

3. The Examiners of the College, annually chosen at the Election Meeting, or who may be appointed by the Council to fill the vacancies which may occur between the Election Meetings, shall conduct the Professional Examination of Candidates. *The Examiners of the College.*

4. The Examiners shall have power to conduct the Examinations at such times as the Council may select, and to adjourn them as often as may seem advisable.

§ 8. The Secretary.

1. The Secretary shall take charge of all the correspondence of the College, and cause copies of all his important letters to be entered by the Clerk, or otherwise, in the Letter-Book of the College.

2. He shall, at all Meetings of the College or Council, take himself, or cause to be taken by the Clerk, Minutes of the Proceedings, and shall see that they are properly extended, and, after approval, engrossed in the respective Minute-Books.

3. He shall submit to the College the Opinion of the Council on all motions or other matters of business which have been considered by them, and shall give such explanations to the College as the Council may direct.

4. He shall, in conjunction with the President, sign all Diplomas issued by the College.

5. He shall keep under his custody all the copperplates on which are engraved the forms of Diplomas, and also the lithographed or printed forms of Petition for the Fellowship and Membership.

6. He shall keep under his custody, in the Safe of the College, the various Minute-Books, Letters, and Papers belonging to the College. The Current Letter-Book and Minutes of Council he may keep in his own house, but the Minute-Book of the College is, on no account whatever, to be removed from the building.

7. He shall allow access to these Minutes at all times to the Fellows of the College; but it shall be in

(margin notes:) Examiners to arrange time and place of Examinations. To manage Correspondence. To keep Minutes of Meetings of College. To submit the Opinion of the Council to the College. To sign all Diplomas. To keep the Diploma Plates. To keep the College Minute-Books, Letters, and Papers. To allow access to the Minutes to Fellows.

the power of the Council to authorize the Secretary to withhold the Minutes of the Council as to any particular business still in dependence. Other parties shall only be permitted to inspect them on making written application to the Council and receiving its sanction.

8. He shall arrange for summoning all Meetings of the College and Council, and shall take care that the programme of the business to be transacted at each Meeting is duly entered in the Billet by which the Meeting is called. He shall also, previously to each Quarterly or Extraordinary Meeting of the College, cause a programme of the business to be suspended in the Reading-Room.

To arrange for summoning Meetings of College or Council.

9. He shall, previously to the Meeting of Council before the Quarterly Meeting of the College in November of each year, give to the Clerk a list of Members of the Council who may have been absent from any of the Meetings, in order that the fines exigible from them may be collected and included in the Annual Statement of the contributions and fines.

To report absentees from Meetings of Council.

§ 9. THE REGISTRAR.

1. The Registrar shall have charge of the whole correspondence regarding applications for the Licence and other qualifications granted by the College.

Duties of Registrar.

2. The Registrar shall make the necessary arrangements for Candidates appearing before the several Examining Boards.

To arrange for Examinations.

3. The same Fellow may hold the office of Secretary and Registrar.

May also be Secretary.

4. The Registrar shall receive for his services such salary as the Council may from time to time determine.

Remuneration.

§ 10. THE LIBRARIAN.

1. The Librarian, who shall be Convener of the Library Committee, shall have the general control of the Library, and superintend the ordering of Books, and the performance of the duties of the Library by the Sub-Librarian.

2. He shall, previously to the Meeting of Council before the Quarterly Meeting of the College in November of each year, give to the Clerk a list of Members of the Library Committee who may have been absent from any of the Meetings of the Committee, and also of those Fellows who may have committed any breach of the Regulations of the Library, in order that the fines exigible from them may be included in the Annual Statement of the contributions and fines, and collected.

§ 11. THE SUB-LIBRARIAN.

1. The Sub-Librarian shall have sole charge of the Library, under the Librarian and the Library Committee. The Sub-Librarian alone shall remove Books from the shelves, give them out, take them in, and replace them on the shelves. For these purposes he shall have the assistance of the Porter.

2. The Sub-Librarian's hours of attendance at the Library shall be from 10 A.M. to 1 P.M., and from 4 to 6 P.M., and on Saturday from 10 A.M. to 12 noon ; and no Books shall be given out except at these hours. He shall have every Sunday free, and also all public holidays. He shall have the month of September for his annual holiday ; but for this period, as well as for

any time of sickness, he shall provide a substitute to be approved by the Library Committee.

3. He shall regularly enter all Books, purchased or presented to the College, in the Library Journal kept for that purpose, and in the Alphabetical Catalogue.

4. He shall receive and execute the instructions of the Librarian and Library Committee regarding the concerns of the Library; and shall also attend all Meetings of the Library Committee.

§ 12. THE CURATOR OF MUSEUM.

1. The Curator of Museum, who shall be Convener of the Museum Committee, shall have the general control of the Museum, and the superintendence of the duties connected therewith.

2. He shall, previously to the Meeting of Council before the Quarterly Meeting of the College in November of each year, give to the Clerk a list of Members of the Museum Committee who may have been absent from any of the Meetings of the Committee, in order that the fines exigible from them may be included in the Annual Statement of the contributions and fines, and collected.

§ 13. THE CURATOR OF LABORATORY.

1. The Curator of Laboratory, who shall be Convener of the Laboratory Committee, shall have the general control of the Laboratory, and shall exercise a general supervision over the performance of the duties of the Laboratory by the Superintendent.

2. Every year, previously to the Meeting of Council before the Quarterly Meeting of the College in February,

the Curator shall submit to the Council a written Report regarding the year's work done in the Laboratory, and the expenditure incurred. This Report, along with the Report of the Council upon it, shall thereafter be submitted to the College at the Quarterly Meeting in February.

3. He shall, previously to the Meeting of Council before the Quarterly Meeting of the College in November of each year, give to the Clerk a list of Members of the Laboratory Committee who may have been absent from any of the Meetings of Committee, in order that the fines exigible from them may be included in the Annual Statement of the contributions and fines, and collected.

§ 14. THE SUPERINTENDENT OF LABORATORY.

1. The Superintendent of Laboratory shall be held responsible for the maintenance of order in the Laboratory, and for the safe keeping of all instruments and apparatus.

2. He shall devote such portion of his time as may be determined by the Council to the work of the Laboratory, where, under the supervision of the Curator and Committee, he shall himself undertake the prosecution of Original Research, and be prepared to assist, if required to do so, in the work of other investigators. He shall also be prepared to furnish Fellows of the College with Reports on such matters as the histology of morbid specimens, and the chemical and microscopical characters of urines.

3. For the performance of these duties he shall receive such salary as the Council may from time to time determine.

§ 15. THE CLERK.

1. The Clerk shall attend all the Meetings of the College, the Quarterly Meetings of the Council, and any other Meetings of the Council, or of any of the Committees at which his assistance may be required.

To attend Meeting of College or Council.

2. In the event of the Clerk being unavoidably prevented from attending a Meeting, some competent person deputed by him may attend in his place. But the Clerk shall in no case be absent without such properly qualified substitute, for whom he shall be considered responsible; and he shall in each case furnish a sufficient excuse to the College for his own absence.

When absent, shall provide a Substitute.

3. He shall call the Roll at the commencement and close of each Meeting of the College, and register the fines against those who are late, or absent.

To call Roll.

4. He shall read the Minutes of the College, and any Petitions of Candidates for admission as Fellows or Members.

To read Minutes and Petitions.

5. He shall, at each Meeting of the College, minute the proceedings, and shall subsequently extend them under the direction of the Secretary.

To keep Minutes.

6. He shall submit the draft of the Minute so prepared to the Quarterly Meeting of Council previously to its being read at the next Quarterly Meeting of the College. He shall, within four days after each Minute has received the sanction of the College, cause it to be engrossed in the Minute-Book, and enter the separate items in the Index.

To submit Minutes to Council.

To engross Minutes in the Minute-Book.

7. He shall, when directed by the Secretary, copy all letters or other documents which the interests of the College may require.

To copy all Documents required by College.

8. He shall, on or before the Quarterly Meeting in November, annually collect all the fines incurred by Fellows, and shall keep a regular statement of them and of the contributions, which he shall annually submit to the Auditor of the Accounts.'

9. He shall engross all Financial Statements that have been approved of by the College, in the Account and Minute-Book of the College.

10. He shall issue the Billets summoning the Meetings of the College, with such list of the business to be transacted as shall be furnished him by the Secretary.

11. He shall intimate to every Fellow on the Roll of Attendance, the names of Candidates for the Fellowship and Membership, within one week after the Meeting at which the motion for their election has been made.

12. He shall intimate to Fellows and Members their election, and to Fellows the time when they are expected to take their seats in the College.

13. He shall, within three days of the proposal of any motion, for the censure, suspension, or expulsion of a Fellow, Member, or Licentiate, transmit a copy of the motion to the Fellow, Member, or Licentiate accused.

14. He shall, before the 31st of January of each year, arrange the papers and vouchers of the College for the past year, and shall prepare an Index of the same, to be given to the Secretary for custody.

15. For these services he shall receive an annual salary, the amount of which shall be determined by the Council; and a further sum of two guineas for attendance at and engrossing the Minutes of each Extraordinary Meeting at which his presence may be required.

§ 16. THE OFFICER.

1. He shall be elected by the Council, and hold his office during their pleasure.

2. He shall reside in the apartments provided for him in the College; and shall give his whole time to the performance of the business of the College.

3. He shall be subject to such bye-laws as may be from time to time enacted by the Council.

4. Besides coal, gas, and apartments, he shall receive such salary as the Council may appoint.

CHAPTER X.

Of the Meetings of the College.

1. A Meeting of the Fellows of the College on the Roll of Attendance shall be held annually, at four o'clock in the afternoon, on St. Andrew's Day, if it shall happen to fall on a Thursday; and if not, on the first Thursday thereafter, — for the sole purpose of electing Office-Bearers for the year ensuing.

2. The Ordinary Quarterly Meetings shall be held on the first Tuesday of February, of May, of August, and of November, at four o'clock in the afternoon.

3. On the Tuesday preceding each Quarterly Meeting, the Council shall meet in the Hall at such hour as they may from time to time determine, to consider the business which is to be brought before the Fellows on the Tuesday following, and to instruct the Secretary or

Marginal notes: How to be chosen. — To reside in College. — To deliver Ballots and other Papers. — Salary. — Election Meeting. — Quarterly Meetings of Fellows. — Arrangement of Business for Quarterly Meetings.

Clerk as to the notices to be circulated in the Billets, which shall be issued on the same evening.

4. The business of the College shall be managed solely by the Fellows on the Roll of Attendance, twelve of whom shall be a quorum.

5. The President or Council may call Extraordinary Meetings of the Fellows when deemed necessary; the business for these Meetings shall be arranged by the Council, and printed in the Billets summoning the Meeting.

6. The President shall be bound to call an Extraordinary Meeting of the Fellows, on a requisition to that effect, specifying the purpose of such Meeting, and signed by any five of the Fellows, being delivered to him or to the Secretary of the College.

7. The President, Secretary, or Treasurer may severally call a Meeting of the Council when they think it necessary.

8. Every Fellow of the College resident in Great Britain and Ireland, whose name is on the Roll of Attendance, shall be summoned to the Meetings of the College. The summons shall be by a Billet specifying the day and hour, and the business to be transacted at the Meeting.

9. The Billets summoning the Meetings, and, generally, all intimations required by the laws of the College, may be sent by post; and, in this case, the fact of such Billets having been posted to the address in Great Britain or Ireland last furnished to the Clerk by any Fellow, shall be held to be sufficient evidence of legal delivery. The Billets for Fellows resident in Edinburgh, or in the Extended Royalty thereof, may be delivered by the officer; and, in this case, proof of a Billet being delivered at the last address furnished to the Clerk shall be held to be sufficient evidence of legal delivery.

CHAPTER XI.

Of the Order of Business.

§ 1. OF ELECTION MEETINGS.

The business shall be transacted in the form prescribed in Chapter VIII. Election Meetings.

§ 2. OF THE QUARTERLY MEETINGS OF FELLOWS.

1. The Clerk shall read the Minutes of the last Quarterly Meeting, and of all subsequent Meetings of the Fellows. These Minutes, when approved of, shall be signed by the President, or by the Chairman for the time being. Minutes of former Meetings.

2. Newly elected Fellows shall be introduced.

3. Petitions of Candidates for admission as Fellows shall be considered. Petitions.

4. Ballots for admission to the Fellowship shall take place. Ballots for Fellowship.

5. Petitions of Candidates for admission as Members shall be considered. Petitions.

6. Ballots for admission to the Membership shall take place. Ballots for Membership.

7. The names of those who have received the Licence and Diploma in Public Health of the College since the previous Quarterly Meeting shall be announced. Announcement of Licences granted.

8. Reports of Committees shall be received and discussed. Reports.

9. Any other business, according to the Laws, shall then be brought forward. (*Vide* Chap. XII.) Other business.

§ 3. OF EXTRAORDINARY MEETINGS OF FELLOWS.

Extraordinary Meetings.

The order of business shall be the same as in Sec. 2, except that no Minutes shall be read, and that no business shall be transacted except that for which the Meeting has been summoned.

§ 4. FORMS APPLICABLE TO ALL MEETINGS.

President to be in Chair.

1. All Meetings shall be constituted by the President taking the chair, at the hour appointed ; and all Meetings shall be dissolved or adjourned by the President leaving the chair.

2. The President shall be addressed by those who speak in the Meetings.

Chairman in absence of President.

3. In the event of the President being absent, the Vice-President shall take the chair ; and in the absence of both, the chair shall be taken by the Senior member of Council present.

Roll-call.

4. At the commencement and close of all Meetings, the Clerk shall call the Roll of Attendance, and he shall fine those who are absent.

Notice of all Business to be given in the Billets.

5. Notice of all business to be transacted at the Meetings of the College shall be circulated with the Billets ; and in the case of Billets for the election of Fellows and Members, or for the forfeiture of Fellowships, Memberships, and Licences, or in the case of motions affecting the Property and Laws of the College, the Billets must be issued at least one week before the day of Meeting, and must be otherwise in accordance with the Bye-Laws.

No Business without Notice.

6. No business shall be transacted of which notice has not been given in the Billet.

CHAPTER XII.

Of Motions, Laws, and Protests.

1. No business can be taken up at any Meeting of the College, other than that specially provided for in the Laws, unless it has been first considered and reported on by the Council, or by a Committee appointed by the College for the purpose.

Business to be first submitted to the Council.

2. All business shall be brought before the College, either in the form of a Report by the Council or a Committee, or of a Motion by a Fellow of the College.

Form in which Business shall be brought before the College.

3. When business is to be brought before the College by a Report, it shall either be circulated with the Billets summoning the Meeting, or be laid on the Library table for the consideration of the Fellows, at least six clear days before the Meeting ; and of this due notice shall be given in the Billets.

Reports to be circulated among the Fellows.

4. No Report, or recommendation contained in a Report, shall be approved, disapproved, or otherwise dealt with by the College, unless by a motion or amendment duly proposed and seconded.

Approval or disapproval of Reports.

5. When business is to be brought before the College by a motion, a copy thereof shall be sent to the Secretary at least ten clear days before the Meeting of the College at which it is proposed to be disscused.

Motions to be sent to Secretary.

6. The Secretary shall submit any motion so received by him to a Meeting of the Council, to be held at least six clear days before the Meeting of the College at which the said motion is to be considered ; and the Council shall report their opinion of the expediency of passing

To be, by him, laid before the Council.

the motion to the said Meeting of the College, or refer it *simpliciter* to the College.

7. The Secretary shall cause a copy of the proposed motion, or an abstract thereof, to be circulated with the Billets summoning the Meeting at which it is to be brought forward, and the motion itself to be suspended in that part of the College where notices are usually posted. No motion which has appeared in the Billet shall be withdrawn without the consent of the College.

8. It shall be lawful for any Fellow, at any Meeting of the College, to move the approval or disapproval of any Report and of any recommendation contained in such Report, or to propose, either in the way of motion or amendment, any modification of any such recommendation.

9. It shall not be lawful under the foregoing Law for any Fellow, while a Report is under consideration, to table any motion or amendment relating to matters not brought before the College in the Report.

10. All motions shall be determined by the votes of a majority, except in cases otherwise provided for in the Laws.

11. Motions for the abrogation or alteration of a Law shall be approved of by three several Meetings of the College before they are adopted, a vote being taken for or against at each Meeting. Should such a motion, however, at its first or second reading, be approved of by five-sixths of the Fellows present, it may be immediately adopted and acted on as a temporary regulation.

12. No Fellow shall speak oftener than once on a motion, except the mover, who shall have a right to reply, after which the debate shall be concluded.

13. Any Fellow present at a Meeting may protest in his own name, and in the name of those present who

may adhere to him, against any decision come to by the College. The reasons for such protest shall be assigned either at the time, or shall be given in at the next Meeting of the College.

14. It shall not be lawful to take any exception to the Minutes, except on the ground that their narrative of the *res gestæ* is inaccurate, or that the Meeting in question had not been properly summoned.

Protest cannot be entered against Minutes, unless inaccurate, or Meeting not properly summoned.

15. The College may reject any document, protest, or instrument, the language of which may be considered objectionable, until amended to the satisfaction of the College.

College may reject protests of which language is objectionable.

16. The Standing Orders may be suspended on the motion of any Fellow, on his submitting to the President or Chairman a motion in writing setting forth the subject proposed to be discussed, and the reasons for regarding it as urgent The proposer shall not speak in support of the proposal to suspend the Standing Orders. The President or Chairman shall read the motion from the Chair, and the College shall, without debate, proceed to vote whether or not the Standing Orders shall be suspended. A majority of two-thirds of the Fellows present shall be required to carry the motion.

Standing Orders may be suspended.

CHAPTER XIII.

Of the Contributions and Fines.

1. Every Fellow who shall be absent during the Meeting for Election, or during any of the Quarterly Meetings, shall pay a fine of 2s. 6d.

For absence at Election or Quarterly Meeting.

2. Every Fellow who shall be absent during an Extraordinary Meeting shall be fined 1s.

3. Every Fellow who shall not answer to his name when the Roll is called at the beginning or end of any Meeting, shall be fined 6d.

4. If the Clerk be absent without an excuse satisfactory to the Fellows, and without sending a properly qualified substitute, he shall pay a fine of 5s.

5. At the Quarterly Meetings of Council, any Member of Council absent during the whole Meeting shall be fined 2s. 6d., and at all other Meetings of Council, 1s.

6. All Members of Committee absent from a Meeting of the Library, Museum, or Laboratory Committee shall be fined 1s. for every such absence.

7. Trustees absent from a Meeting of Trustees shall be fined 2s. 6d. for every such absence.

8. No excuse shall be sustained for absence from the Meetings, except confinement to the house by illness.

9. Each Fellow on the Roll of Attendance shall pay annually, at the Quarterly Meeting held in November, one guinea of contribution, and such fines as he may have incurred, whether his domicile be in Scotland or not.

10. The Clerk shall annually make up, and lay before the Quarterly Meeting of the Council previous to the Quarterly Meeting of the College in November, a list of the fines incurred by Fellows during the past year.

11. The gross amount of fines due by each Fellow shall be appended to the Billet summoning him to the Quarterly Meeting of the Fellows in November.

12. The Clerk shall be bound, on application, to show to any Fellow a list of the separate occasions on which he has been fined.

13. The Council shall meet within ten days after the November meeting of the Fellows, for the purpose of considering appeals against fines.

14. All appeals shall be sent to the Clerk in writing, and signed by the appellant; and the Council shall have power to adjourn, if necessary, and to request the appellant to attend, for the purpose of giving such explanation as may be desired.

15. No appeal shall be received after the lapse of one year from the Quarterly Meeting of the College in November.

16. Any Fellow who may be in arrear of his annual contributions and fines for a longer period than two years, shall, after due intimation having twice been given to him, at the interval of a month, be deprived of the use of the Library and Reading-Room, and of the privilege of attending the Meetings of the College, and shall have his name struck off the Roll of Attendance. No Fellow who is in arrear of his contribution and fines for two years shall be allowed to vote at the election of Office-Bearers.

CHAPTER XIV.

Of the Property of the College.

1. No motion tending to alienate any part of the property of the College, or apply it to other than the ordinary purposes of the College, shall be discussed except at Extraordinary Meetings called for the purpose. No such alienation shall take place unless

Marginal notes: Council shall consider Appeals against Fines. — Appeals to be given in to the Clerk in writing. — No Appeal to be received after a year. — Penalties for being in arrears. — Motions tending to alienate the Property of the College.

approved of by a majority of three - fourths of the Fellows present, at three several Meetings, eight days at least intervening between each.

2. No sum of money shall be voted in donation, subscription, or otherwise, excepting for the ordinary expenses of the College, till the propriety thereof has been considered at two several Meetings, eight days at least intervening between each. One of these may be a Quarterly Meeting, provided intimation of the proposal has been given in the Billets; and there must be a majority of three - fourths of the Fellows present at each of these two Meetings, to give effect to such a proposal. But if the sum proposed do not exceed twenty-five guineas sterling, it shall be competent for the Fellows, by a majority of three-fourths of the Fellows present, to vote such sum immediately at any Meeting, Quarterly or Extraordinary, provided in either case notice has been given in the Billets summoning the Meeting.

3. The securities for all the sums of money or property that may belong to, or constitute any part or portion of the funds of the College, and all heritable rights connected therewith, shall be conceived and taken to and in favour of the College in its corporate name, or in favour of the persons who may be Trustees for the time being, and to their successors in office.

4. The Trustees shall have power to lend out and invest the monies belonging to the College on heritable or moveable, real or personal securities, in terms of the Charter.

5. No purchase or sale of property or stock shall be made at any time by the said Trustees, without the special consent of four-fifths of the said Trustees

acting for the time being, expressed by a Minute entered in the sederunt-book of the Trustees, and subscribed by the Trustees so consenting and approving.

CHAPTER XV.

Of the Library and Library Committee.

1. The President, Vice-President, Treasurer, and Librarian, together with two other Fellows appointed annually at the Quarterly Meeting in August, shall form a Committee for the purchase of books and superintendence of the Library, and shall meet at least once a month.

Constitution of Committee.

2. The attending Fellows of the College, and Members who have the use of the Library, may borrow any books from the Library, except manuscripts and such other books as, from their value or other cause, the Library Committee think it inexpedient to circulate. A list of books not allowed to be lent shall be hung in the Library for the information of the Fellows.

Books to be, and not to be, lent.

3. No book shall be lent out unless a receipt be given for it. Every Fellow or Member on borrowing a book from the Library shall give a receipt to the Sub-Librarian.

Receipts from Fellows.

4. On returning books each Fellow or Member shall receive from the Sub-Librarian a receipt for the same.

Receipt from Sub-Librarian.

5. No Fellow or Member shall be permitted to have in his possession at one time more than thirty volumes belonging to the Library.

Number of Books allowed out.

6. No Fellow resident beyond ten miles from Edinburgh shall be permitted to borrow books from the Library except by special permission of the Council.

7. The Sub-Librarian shall attend daily at the hours appointed for giving out and receiving books, and the performance of other duties connected with the Library. In his absence the presses shall be kept constantly locked, except those in the Reading-Room which contain the Consultation Library.

8. The Sub-Librarian shall be responsible for all books lost which are entered in the receipt-book, and for which he can show no receipt.

9. Any books which have been less than a year in the Library may be called in after being a fortnight, and all other books after being a month, in the possession of Fellows. Any Fellow neglecting to return a book after intimation to do so has been duly sent him by the Sub-Librarian, shall be fined one shilling for each day that he detains it, and no other book shall be lent to him until he has given notice that the book has been lost, and the matter has been dealt with by the Council.

10. All books and periodicals shall (unless withheld by order of the Library Committee) lie on the table of the Library for a month after their reception. On being withdrawn from the table, the Sub-Librarian shall insert in the Library Catalogues their titles and places on the shelves; after which they shall be permitted to circulate among the Fellows. The numbers of periodicals, after being removed from the table, shall be laid aside until they form a volume, and then bound. In the meantime, they may be given out to Fellows under the ordinary regulations, but liable to be called in when wanted for binding.

11. A list shall be regularly kept by the Sub-Librarian of all books and periodicals laid upon the table, together with the date of their reception and removal. This list it shall be the duty of the Sub-Librarian to compare with the books actually on the table every morning after 10 o'clock, reporting to the Librarian any that he finds missing, in order that they may be traced, and the proper penalty inflicted for their unauthorised removal or detention.

List of new Books and Periodicals to be kept.

12. In the evenings, at 6 P.M., the Sub-Librarian may give out to Fellows, to take home with them, any of the books or periodicals which are laid on the Library table, on condition of their being returned by 10 o'clock the next morning. He shall mark down in a proper book their titles and the names of the Fellows to whom they are delivered, taking a receipt for the same ; and if not returned at the time appointed, shall record against the offender a fine of one shilling for each hour they are detained.

May be removed after 10 P.M., and returned before 10 A.M. next day.

13. Any Fellow removing books from the Hall without informing the Sub-Librarian shall be reported to the Council, who shall take such action as they deem proper. Newspapers shall on no account whatever be removed from the Reading-Room.

Fine for removal of Books without authority.

No Newspaper to be removed.

14. The Catalogues of the Library, with all recent additions inserted, the Library-table book, the Evening Receipt book, the Proposal book, and a List of fines incurred for infringing the regulations of the Library, shall be regularly laid before the Committee at each of their Meetings.

Committee regularly to examine the Books.

15. Fellows whose names have been taken off the Roll of Attendance may avail themselves of the privileges of the Library and Reading-Room, under the regulations contained in Chap. II., Laws 13 and 14.

Non-Resident, and Non-attending Fellows may have the use of Library under certain Regulations.

Strangers wishing to consult books, if unattended by Fellows, must have the permission of the Council in each case, and shall do so in an adjoining apartment.

16. A fortnight before the Quarterly Meeting in August of each year, all books borrowed shall be called in by the Sub-Librarian. This intimation must be responded to within seven days, in order that the Librarian and Committee may institute an examination and comparison with the Press Catalogue of all the books in the Library, which they shall do within a fortnight after the said Quarterly Meeting. Fellows who neglect to comply with this order shall be fined one shilling for each book and each day of detention. The books shall be called in and examined in like manner on a vacancy in the office of Sub-Librarian, before being handed over to the custody of a successor.

17. After such examination of the Library, a list of any books standing in the receipt book against any Fellow as unreturned, shall be sent to him, and he shall be fined six shillings per week for every book retained thereafter, unless he intimate that he has lost the book.

18. In every case where an intimation of loss has been made, and also in every case where a book has remained unreturned for two months after it has been recalled, the Library Committee shall have power to purchase a copy of the missing book at the expense of the Fellow who has failed to return it.

19. The price paid for such book shall absolve the Fellow from all fines for its non-return, and shall be collected along with, and be subject to all the regulations regarding the fines of the College.

Admission of Strangers.

Books to be called in annually:

and when a new Librarian appointed.

Books unreturned.

Books lost:

to be paid for.

20. The Committee may from time to time make temporary regulations in regard to the Library. But such regulations shall not be acted on until approved of by the Council, and the whole or a part of them may be suspended or abolished by a vote of a majority of the Fellows at any Quarterly Meeting of the College. Such temporary regulations, moreover, shall be held to be in force so long only as a copy of them hangs in the Reading-Room or Library.

CHAPTER XVI.

Of the Museum and Museum Committee.

1. The President, the Professor of Materia Medica in the University of Edinburgh (if a Fellow of the College), the Curator of the Museum, and two other Fellows appointed annually at the Quarterly Meeting in August, shall form a Committee for the superintendence of the Museum, and shall meet as occasion requires.

2. The Curator shall keep the keys of the Museum cases, arrange the specimens, and see that they are all properly put up and preserved.

3. The Curator shall enter in a book kept for the purpose a description of every article presented to the Museum of the College, with the name of the donor, and the date of its presentation, and shall exhibit to the College, at the first Quarterly Meeting thereafter, the donations received since its last Meeting.

4. Any Fellow of the College may give a written order for the admission of visitors to the Museum ; but the cases shall not be opened to such visitors without the consent of the Museum Committee previously obtained, and in the presence of the Curator or one of the Members of the Museum Committee appointed for this purpose.

CHAPTER XVII.

Of the Laboratory and Laboratory Committee.

1. The President, Vice-President, Treasurer, Curator of Laboratory, and six other Fellows, appointed annually at the Quarterly Meeting of the College in August, shall form a Committee for the superintendence of the Laboratory and the control of its expenditure. The Committee shall meet at least once a month, except in August and September.

2. The Laboratory shall be opened without fee—

(1.) To Fellows of the College.

(2.) To Members.

(3.) To any Licentiate who shall obtain the sanction of the Curator and Committee to use the Laboratory for purposes of Scientific Research.

(4.) To any Medical man or Investigator who shall obtain the sanction of the Council of the College, as well as of the Curator and Committee, to use the Laboratory for purposes of Scientific Research.

CHAPTER XVIII.

Of Diplomas, etc.

1. All the Diplomas of the College shall be engraved according to a form approved of by the Council. The plates shall be kept in the custody of the Secretary. Every Diploma issued by the College shall be signed by the President, and countersigned by the Secretary.

2. Forms of petition for admission to the Fellowship and Membership shall be kept by the Secretary, and be furnished by him to intending Candidates.

Forms of Diplomas.

Forms of Petitions.

CHAPTER XIX.

Of Certificates of Qualification to Lecture.

1. Any Fellow of the College desirous of being recognised as a Lecturer by the College and other Licensing Boards, shall make written application to the Secretary, who shall lay the same within ten days thereafter before the Council. The Council shall then appoint five well-qualified gentlemen to be a Board of Examiners, three of whom shall be a quorum.

Certificate of ability to Lecture.

Board of Examination.

2. The Board having met and determined on the mode of examination, shall inform the Candidate of the time and place where such examination shall be held. The examination shall consist of—

Nature of Examination.

> 1. Questions to be answered either *viva voce* or in writing.

2. A lecture on some part of the subject which the Candidate proposes to teach, in the course of which he shall give appropriate illustrations or demonstrations.

3. He shall also give proof of possessing available means for illustrating the course.

Certificate to be conferred.

3. In the event of the Board having reported favourably to the Council, the President shall, at the first Meeting of the College after the Report of the Board has been received, confer on the Candidate a Certificate of Qualification to Lecture.

Terms of Certificate.

4. The Certificate of Qualification to Lecture shall be in the form given in the Appendix No. IX.

Joint Examination of proposed Lecturers not Fellows of the College.

5. For the examination of Lecturers not Fellows either of this College or of the College of Surgeons (which examination is to be conducted by a Joint Board of the two Colleges), the Council shall nominate an equal number of gentlemen with those appointed by the sister College.

Attestation as to character.

6. Previously, however, to any such Candidate being taken on trial, a petition shall be presented to the President of either College, with a testimonial as to general character, signed by at least three Fellows of either College.

Number of Joint Board.

7. The number composing the Joint Board shall be left to the decision of the Councils of the two Colleges.

Fees for Licence.

8. The sum of ten guineas shall in each case be paid to the Board of Examiners, one-half by the Candidate, and the other half, in the case of a Fellow, out of the College funds. The Candidate when not a Fellow shall pay the whole sum required.

APPENDIX.

No. I.

FORM OF PROMISSORY OBLIGATION to be signed by every FELLOW before taking his seat in the College.

Promissory
Obligation by
Fellows.

I _____'__, one of the Fellows of the Royal College of Physicians of Edinburgh, do, by subscribing these presents, solemnly declare and surely promise, *First*, That I shall all my life, according to my power, preserve and maintain the privileges, liberties, jurisdiction, and authority granted to the said College by Her sacred Majesty's gracious Charter, dated 25th August, and sealed 31st October 1861, for the good and necessary ends and uses therein mentioned. *Secondly*, That I shall avail myself of all occasions to promote the welfare, prosperity, and utility of the said College, and shall always give my Vote, when it is asked, as I conscientiously think may be most conducive to these purposes. *Thirdly*, That I shall, as far as I am able, promote and preserve unity, concord, amity, and good order among all the Fellows, Members, Licentiates, and Candidates thereof; and shall heartily wish and endeavour to promote the prosperity of them all. *Fourthly*, That so long as I continue a Fellow of the said College, I shall at all times be subject to the due order and government of the College, according to the foresaid Charter, and shall

conform and be obedient to the Laws and Regulations
of the College, as the same are and shall be from time
to time enacted. *Fifthly,* That I shall never divulge
or publish anything that is acted or spoken, or proposed
to be transacted, in any Meeting of the said College,
or Council or Court thereof, without leave asked and
obtained, according to the laws prescribed by the
College. All the aforesaid articles I hereby promise
to observe, and never wittingly and willingly to break
any one of them, as I desire to be held and respected
an honest man.

No. II.

FORM OF PETITION for admission as FELLOWS.

Form of Petition
for Fellowship.

Unto the Much Honoured the PRESIDENT *and Remanent*
FELLOWS *of the Royal College of Physicians in
Edinburgh.*

THE

PETITION of___ _____

HUMBLY SHEWETH,

THAT, for several years, I applied
myself to the study of Medicine, and have obtained the
Membership of the Royal College of Physicians of Edinburgh, conform to my Diploma, dated_____
and being willing to observe the whole Laws and
Regulations of the College,

May it therefore please the Royal College to
admit me as a Fellow of the College, with
power to enjoy all rights, liberties, and privileges which any other Fellow does or may
enjoy.

No. III.

A DIPLOMA in the following terms shall be granted to every FELLOW of the College :—

"COLLEGIUM Regium Medicorum Edinburgense, rogante Præside, Sociisque annuentibus, decrevit ornatissimum virum A. B. in Societatem suam co-optare, et Collegam adsciscere. Ipsum ideo in societatem co-optat, Socium adsciscit, omniumque honorum atque privilegiorum quibus Socii ejusdem Collegii fruuntur, participem facit. In cujus rei fidem, hoc diploma, sigillo suo, Præsidis Secretariique chirographis munitum, expediri jussit.

"Actum Edinburgi, in Conventu Sociorum, die," etc.

No. IV.

FORM OF PETITION for admission as MEMBERS.

Unto the Much Honoured the PRESIDENT *and* FELLOWS *of the Royal College of Physicians of Edinburgh.*

THE

PETITION of __

HUMBLY SHEWETH,

THAT, for several years, I applied myself to the study of Medicine, and obtained ____ , conform to my Diploma, dated ____ ____ , that I herewith transmit Testimonials, and am willing to present myself for Examination before the Examiners

of the College, and that, in the event of my being
elected, I bind myself to observe the whole Laws and
Regulations of the College,

> May it therefore please the Royal College, on
> the Council of the College and the Board of
> Examiners being satisfied, to admit me a
> Member of the College, with power to enjoy
> all the Rights, Liberties, and Privileges which
> any other Member does or may enjoy.

No. V.

A DIPLOMA in the following terms shall be granted
to every MEMBER of the College :—

"COLLEGIUM Regium Medicorum Edinburgense,
rogante Præside, Sociisque annuentibus, decrevit virum
ornatissimum A. B. in ordinem Membrorum co-optare, et Membrum adsciscere. Ipsum ideo in ordinem
Membrorum co-optat, Membrum adscisit, omniumque
honorum atque privilegiorum, quibus Membra ejusdem
Collegii fruuntur, participem facit.

"In cujus Rei fidem, hoc Diploma, sigillo suo, Præsidis Secretariique chirographis munitum, expediri jussit.

"Actum Edinburgi, in Conventu Sociorum, die," etc.

No. VI.

FORM OF OBLIGATION to be signed by LICENTIATES.

I HEREBY promise faithfully to maintain and defend
all the rights and privileges of the Royal College of
Physicians of Edinburgh ; to promote its interests to

the utmost of my power; to refrain from advertising, or employing any unbecoming mode of acquiring practice; and I shall not allow my name to appear in connection with any one who so acts, or who is engaged in any discreditable kind of Medical work. I also promise to obey all the Laws of the said Royal College of Physicians, made or to be made, and to submit to the penalties therein imposed.

No. VII.

A DIPLOMA in the following terms shall be granted to every LICENTIATE of the College :—

Diploma of Licentiate.

"COLLEGIUM Regium Medicorum Edinburgense, rogante Præside, Sociisque annuentibus decrevit ornatum virum A. B. in numerum Permissorum co-optare. Ipsum ideo in numerum Permissorum co-optat, omniumque privilegiorum quibus Permissi ejusdem Collegii fruuntur, participem facit. In cujus rei fidem, hoc diploma, sigillo suo, Præsidis Secretariique chirographis munitum expediri jussit.

" Actum Edinburgi, in Conventu Sociorum," etc.

No. VIII.

A DIPLOMA in the following terms shall be granted to every DIPLOMATE in Public Health of the College :—

Diploma in Public Health.

IT is hereby certified that_____, a duly qualified Practitioner, has presented himself before this Royal College for Special Examination in subjects relating to Public Health, and has satisfied the Examiners that he possesses a competent knowledge of the theoretical and practical branches of Sanitary Science.

No. IX.

FORM OF A CERTIFICATE to be presented by the
College to FELLOWS who have been examined and
found qualified to Lecture on any Branch of Medical
Science required by the Examining Boards.

"COLLEGIUM Regium Medicorum Edinburgense,
de _____ peracto examine, audita prælectione, inspecto-
que apparatu inter prælegendum adhibendo, his literis
testatur docendo hanc Medicinæ partem virum ingenuum,
consocium A. B. se parem comprobasse. In cujus rei
fidem hanc chartam sigillo suo, Præsidis, Secretariique
chirographo munitam, expediri jussit.

"Actum Edinburgi, in Conventu Sociorum, die," etc.

Charta Erectionis

REGII MEDICORUM COLLEGII

APUD EDINBURGUM.

CAROLUS, Dei gratia, Magnæ Britanniæ Franciæ, et
Hiberniæ Rex, Fideique Defensor, Omnibus probis
hominibus suis ad quos præsentes Literæ pervenerint,
salutem. SCIATIS, Quandoquidem nos, ex innata
nostra bonitate, et erga populum nostrum paterna in-
dulgentia, cum simus scilicet pater patriæ, et omnium
legiorum et subditorum nostrorum parens nutritius,
necnon maxime cupidi et provide curantes, ut non
solum jura, proprietates, et possessiones, aliaque quævis
subditorum nostrorum commoda rata, provisa, et con-
firmata sint, verum etiam (quæ maximi sunt pretii, et
illorum maxime intersunt) ipsorum scilicet vita et
sanitas, omnium aliorum externorum emolumentorum
fundamentum et subjectum, Dei benedictione, media
ordinaria, et honestorum, fidelium, et approbatorum
medicorum diligentiam, et fideles conatus ad morbos
tot et tam periculosos humanæ fragilitati contingentes
curandos et præveniendos comitante, conservetur ; necnon animo revolventes, quod legum aliarumque scien-
tiarum praxis et artium, artificiorum et mechanicarum
technarum exercitium, legibus cura et prudentia nostra,
et Regiorum nostrorum prædecessorum tam commode
regulata et disposita sit, ut nulli liceat aut permissum

Preamble and
reasons of
foundation.

Importance of
Life and Health.

Importance of
good Physicians.

Examination
of Candidates
required in every
other Profession.

sit prius in lege tanquam jurisperitus, vel advocatus, vel
in quovis alio munere aut officio eo spectante, vel in
qualibet scientia, professione, aut arte practicare, quam
per probatum examen capax et aptus inveniatur, perque
viros sufficienti potestate et authoritate in hunc effectum
instructos legitime admittatur: præ nimia tamen et
ingenua nimis medicorum id temporis modestia (ne suo
merito minus tribuere aut diffidere, aliorumve restric-

Medicine been
long practised
without
qualification or
authority;

tionem in commodum et emolumentum suum intendere
et designare videantur), physices et medicinæ praxis per
longum tempus in maxima ataxia et confusione exstitit,
et sine ullo warranto, authoritate, invasa, usurpata, proprioque impetu arrepta, exercita, magnaque in audacia
et impunitate, sine ullo obstaculo aut impedimento, a

and by more
unworthy
Persons;

mulierculis, alliisque non solum ignaris, sed et vilibus et
sordidis personis, sine eruditione et liberali cultu, vel
minima cujusvis literaturæ, ipsorumve medicinæ princi-
piorum et elementorum notitia et tinctura, usa (potius
abusa) fuit. Et non solum hortulani, aliique rudes et

and by Quacks
and Impostors
of every kind.

illiterati, in medicina practicare, et subditis nostris abuti,
illudere, et imponere, ausi sunt; verum etiam ad notitiam
et famam prædictæ tolerationis et abusus peregrini
impostores, agyrtæ, et empirici, nulla prævisa prohibi-
tione, advenerunt, et in hoc regno diu commorati, et
medicinam professi sunt et practicarunt, suaque medicamenta et pharmaca vendiderunt, et sine quovis vel
ipsorum vel pharmacorum suorum conditionis et aptitu-

Some have
assumed the
title of Doctor
who could
neither read nor
write.

dinis examine, populo distribuerunt. Quæquidem tolera-
tio et abusus eo provecta est, ut quidam veneficii rei
habiti et reputati professionem et praxin cum Doctoris
Medicinæ nomine sibi assumere ausi sint; et quamvis
ita plane rudes et ignari ut nec legere nec scribere
queant, dictitare tamen audeant, et præscriptiones et
receptas suas pro morborum maxime desperatorum cura

describendas curent, cum magnis impensis, extortione, periculo, et destructione legiorum nostrorum, et in maximum dictæ professionis et scientiæ, tam antiquæ et necessariæ, tantique, per omnia tempora, et apud omnes nationes, usus et pretii, scandalum et opprobrium.

And all this to the manifest injury of the Public.

Cumque, ab exemplo et aliorum nostrorum regno- rum, aliarumque bene constitutarum et gubernatarum nationum experientia, luculenter constet, quod Medi- corum Societatis et Collegii ex personis gravibus, doctis, integris, et dictæ professioni congruentibus consistentis, erectio, maxime proprium et efficax foret medium, et ad tales abusus reformandos et præveniendos, ne in posterum irrepant, remedium ; cumque nos benignum habeamus affectum erga antiquam civitatem nostram Edinburgum, quæ non solum civium, sed et omnium subditorum nostrorum tantopere interest, cum, nempe, supremarum curiarum nostrarum juridicarum, in quibus authoritas et justitia nostra eminentissime repræsen- tantur et administrantur, sedes sit ordinaria, adeo ut nobilitas, ordoque esquestris, aliique nostri subditi sæpe occasionem habeant, eoque ab omnibus regni angulis proficisci, inque dicta civitate, per tempora et tempes- tates morbis et intemperiebus maxime obnoxia per- manere teneantur, et considerationibus quibus supra Societatum et Collegium Medicorum modo, et cum potestatibus, facultatibus, et privilegiis infra script., Edinburgi erigere apud nos statuentes : Igitur nos dedimus et concessimus, tenoreque præsentium, ex certa nostra scientia, proprioque motu, prærogativa, et potestate nostra regali, damus et concedimus Davidi Hay, Thomæ Burnet, Matheo Brisbaine, Archibaldo Stevensone, Andreæ Balfoure, Roberto Sibbald, Jacobo Livingstone, Roberto Crawfurd, Roberto Trotter, Matheo Sinclare, Jacobo Stewart, Gulielmo Stevensone,

The erection of a College of Physicians is the most appropriate means of reforming such abuses.

Peculiarly necessary in Edinburgh as the Metropolis and seat of the Courts of Law.

College of Physicians to be erected.

First Fellows named in Charter.

Alexandro Cranstone, Joanni Hutton, Joanni M'Gill, Gulielmo Lauder, Joanni Lermonth, Jacobo Halket, Gulielmo Wright, Patricio Halyburton, et Archibaldo Pitcairne, artium magistris, et medicinæ doctoribus, omnibusque aliis qui posthac ab illis in ipsorum societatem co-optati fuerint, et ab illis tanquam collegæ et sodales eorum societatis intra dictam nostram urbem Edinburgi, suburbia et privilegia ejusdem, admissi fuerint, ut in unum corpus, communitatem, et Collegium uniantur et conjungantur omni tempore futuro.

Et creximus, instituimus, et incorporavimus, tenoreque præsentium erigimus, instituimus, et incorporamus viros supra mentionatos eorumque successores, Collegium, societatem, et incorporationem fieri omni tempore futuro, omnibusque, potestatibus, facultatibus, et privilegiis ad liberum Collegium, societatem, et incorporationem requisitis et spectantibus, frui et habere, et absque præjudicio generalitatis prædictæ, quocunque loco et tempore, et quoties sibi visum fuerit, convenire ; cumque potestate illis, eorumque successoribus, commune gazophylacium seu thesaurarium et patrimonium habendi, et voluntaria munera, contributiones, legata, et donationes, in commodum et usum dicti Collegii, et ad medicinæ professionem et physices praxin et exercitium proferendum et promovendum impendendi, inter se erogandi, et ab aliis benevolis accipiendi. Inque hunc effectum, iisdem potestatem tradimus, eosque capaces reddimus, acquirendi, procurandi, habendi, et terras, tenementa, annuos-reditus, possessiones, decimas, aliaque in usum dicti Collegii, ejusque collegarum successorum, cum intra tum extra burgum, possidendi, et commune sigillum habendi, commune Sigillum Regii Medicorum Collegii apud Edinburgum designandum, et habendi, agendi, et exercendi omnes alias libertates,

Power to choose Colleagues and Fellows.

Jurisdiction to extend over Edinburgh, its Suburbs, and Liberties.

Powers and Privileges.

Power to hold Funds.

Power to acquire and hold Property.

A Common Seal.

potestates, et facultates, cuilibet alii libero collegio et incorporationi competentes, quasve ipsi tanquam corpora incorporata debent, seu habere, agere, aut exercere poterint.

All the ordinary privileges of Corporate Bodies.

Et pro meliori dicti collegii regimine, et thesauri et patrimonii eidem spectaturi administratione, dedimus, tenoreque præsentium dictæ societati et Collegio potestatem damus, ejusdemque collegis mandamus, annuatim, omni tempore futuro, Concilium, ex septem dictæ societatis collegarum doctissimis, sapientissimis, et in facultate medicinæ maxime peritis, consistens, eligere : Quod quidem concilium unum ex eorum numero, pro illo anno Præsidem fore est electurum ; cum potestate etiam dicto Præsidi et Concilio, Clericum, Thesaurarium aliosque Ministros in commodum dictæ societatis necessarios et requisitos, eligendi et constituendi. Et declaramus dictum Præsidem, Collegium, et communitatem, sub nomine *Præsidis Regii Medicorum Collegii apud Edinburgum* capacem fore causas coram omnibus et quibuscunque judicibus in quibuscunque curiis et actionibus agere, prosequi, et tueri. Ac ulterius dicto Præsidi et Collegio, corumque successoribus, potestatem tradimus, canones, præcepta, acta, et statuta sanciendi ad medicinæ scientiam promovendam, ejusdem praxin rite disponendam, inque bonam gubernationem, ordinem, regimen, et correctionem dicti Collegii et communitatis, omniumque dictam facultatem exercentium intra dictam civitatem Edinburgenam, ejusque suburbia, solummodo, viz., Letham, Vicum Canonicorum, Portam Occidentalem, Vicum Sancti Leonardi, et Vicum Figulinum, quando, et quotiescunque necesse fuerit. Proviso omnino, sicuti per præsentes providetur et declaratur, quod præsentibus non obstantibus Pharmaco-chirurgi Edinburgenses potestatem habituri sunt, omne genus vulnerum, con-

Government of College.

Council of Seven.

President.

Secretary, Treasurer, and other Officers.

College may be a party in actions at law.

College may make Bye-Laws for promoting the Sciences and regulating Practice of Medicine :

also for its own regulation and that of all Practitioners within its jurisdiction.

Fellows not to practise Surgery, and Surgeon-Apothecaries not to practise Medicine.

tusionum, fracturarum, dislocationum, tumorum, ulcerum, et id genus alia quæ sunt chirurgicarum operationum subjecta, et accidentia exinde orientia duntaxat curandi; curam autem morborum originaliter internorum, ex medicorum dicti Collegii præscripto et directione unice præstandam, minime habebunt.

No unlicensed Person to practise Medicine.

Et similiter concessimus, tenoreque præsentium concedimus, præfato Præsidi et Collegio, eorumque successoribus quod nulli intra dictam civitatem, ejusque suburbia et privilegia, antedictam facultatem prius prac-

College to grant Licence by Diplomas.

ticare et exercere licebit, quam ad eandem per dictum Præsidem et Collegium, eorumque pro tempore successores, warranto et diplomate in hunc effectum per dictum Præsidem et Collegium, eorumque pro tempore successores concesso, eorumque communi sigillo signato fuerit

Penalties.

admissus; idque sub pœna sexaginta libarum monetæ Scotiæ, quovis mense quo quicunque, modo prædicto nondum licentiatus, et admissus, dicta facultate et praxi utetur et exercebit. Quarum quidem mulctarum alterum dimidium pauperum, alterum dicti Collegii usui et commodo applicandum volumus. Si quivis tamen, post censuram modo prædicto, dictam facultatem nihilominus absque licentia exercere persistet prædictam mulctam, quovis mense, quo practicare persistent, duplicandam ordinamus.

Censors

Et pariter volumus, concedimus, et ordinamus, quod annuatim duo ex dicta Societate et Collegio per dictum concilium tanquam Censores eligantur, qui cum Præside

may, with the President, hold courts for trial and punishment of delinquents.

pro tempore, vice et nomine dicti Collegii, potestatem, authoritatem, et jurisdictionem habebunt, omnes dictam medicinæ facultatem absque licentia, ut prædicitur, intra prædictam civitatem, libertates, et suburbia prædicta practicantes et exercentes, coram sese convocandi, illisque mulctas supra specificatas imponendi; dicto tamen medicorum Collegio, ejusve Præside, curias ad delinquentes puniendos tenturo, præpositum civitatis Edinburgi, vel unum aliquem ex ejusdem magistratibus, de curiæ suæ loco et tempore omni modo certiorem faciente, adeo ut (si ipsis visum fuerit) unum ex balivis suis illis in jurisdictione cumulativa assidere constituent: Proviso omnimodo, sicuti per præsentes providetur et declaratur, quod medicorum Collegio nondum licebit quemvis pharmaco - chirurgum Edinburgi burgensem mulctare, sine consensu præpositi, aut cujusvis unius ex balivis Edinburgi, qui assidebit, et talibus actis judicialibus intererit. Et si venire et adesse abnuerint, hoc secreto nostro concilio notum faciendum est, ut hi quod idoneum et justum sit, perficiant, absque præjudicio dicto Collegio, in casu recusationis et moræ procedendi, et similiter invigilandi, gubernandi, et coram se convocandi, et, si necesse fuerit, corrigendi et puniendi omnes medicos, et medicinæ doctores associatos, seu licentiatos, dictam facultatem intra dictam civitatem, et limites prædictos, exercentes, ob quæcunque crimina et delicta ab illis in eorum praxi contra statuta et acta dicti Collegii commissa; idque ab illis talia amerciamenta et mulctas exigendo, ut dicto Præsidi, Censoribus, et supervisoribus visum fuerit, utque delictum promerebitur; dictis tamen mulctis summam quadraginta librarum nondum excedentibus: quæ quidem amerciamenta et mulctæ usibus prædictis applicanda volumus et ordinamus. Et pro iisdem namando, et omni alia executione legali utendo et incarcerando, et ad sententias et mandata de tempore in tempus per dictos supervisores, virtute potestatis et authoritatis illis per nos commissæ, emittenda, magistratus intra dictam civitatem, suburbia et libertates ejusdem prædictas, aliosque nostros legis ministros, per præsentes, authoritate nostra mandamus et requirimus, ad prædictas sententias exequendas assis-

Must give notice that a City Magistrate may be appointed an Assessor.

Surgeon-Apothecaries, Burgesses, not to be fined without concurrence of Provost or Magistrate.

Procedure in the event of the Summons being disregarded.

Magistrates and Officers to assist in carrying these sentences into effect.

tere ; inque hunc effectum, præcepta namationis, aliasque executiones necessarias dirigere, eodem modo quo super propriis suis decretis et sententiis agere solent ; cum potestate etiam dictis Præsidi et Censoribus, quoties

Power of inspecting Shops of Apothecaries and Druggists.

opus fuerit, scrutandi, considerandi, et inspiciendi pharmaca, et medicamenta simplicia et composita nunc aut in posterum vendenda intra dictam civitatem, suburbia, et libertates prædictas, si recentia, bona, et proba sint, et quæ secure ad morbos et infirmitates legiorum nostrorum curandos usurpari et applicari poterint. Proviso omnimodo, sicuti per præsentes specialiter providetur, quod ubi talis inspectio et scrutinium faciendum est, unus ex magistratibus intra dictam civitatem, cum uno pharmacopœo et chirurgo-pharmacopœo, visitoribus pro tempore constituendis, qui assistere requirantur, ut eadem bene, et secundum regulas, pro populi commodo composita et præparata esse videant ; et ubi pharmaca insufficientia et corrupta invenientur, cum potestate illis eadem in publicas plateas ejiciendi, vel destruendi.

No President or Fellow to be cited to proceed on Assize or Circuit ;

Et ulterius, pro nobis et successoribus nostris volumus et concedimus, quod neque Præses, neque quivis alius dicti Medicorum Collegii, neve eorum successores, super assisam aut inquisitionem in urbe aut rure procedere citentur aut summoniantur. Cumque eorum in

nor to watch or ward ;

ægrotos et valetudinarios observantia sit semper adeo necessaria, ut sine maximo præjudicio et ægrotorum

nor on any pretext to be withdrawn from his Patients.

periculo ab eadem quovis pretextu et occasione abstrahi non debeant ; igitur nos, pro nobis et successoribus nostris, dictum Præsidem, omnesque dicti Collegii socios et collegas eorumque successores, ab omnibus excubiis in futurum liberamus et absolvimus.

Powers of the Magistrates and of Surgeon-Apothecaries specially reserved.

Et per præsentes declaramus, quodvis jus, protestatem, et jurisdictionem ad magistratus civitatis Edinburgi, et quævis jura et privilegia ad chirurgo-pharmacopœos pertinentia, illis et singulis eorum respective, prout de jure competit, specialiter reservari.

Per præsentes etiam specialiter providetur, jurium et privilegiorum supra scriptorum dicto Medicorum Collegio concessionem, ad scholarum pro dicta arte medica, aut qualibet ejusdem parte docenda erectionem, seu gradus alicui eatenus conferendos et concedendos, nullo modo extendendam ; eadem per præsentes specialiter declaratur absque præjudicio fore jurium et privilegiorum in favorem Universitatis seu Collegii Andreapolitani, Glasguensis, Aberdonensis, et Edinburgensis concessorum; et præsentibus, et clausulis quibuscunque inibi contentis non obstantibus, licitum et legitimum erit cuivis in dictis universitatibus laurea doctorandis, libertatem et potestatem habere in dicta civitate aliisque locis supra scriptis practicandi, ipsis tamen prædictis mulctis aliisque pœnis supra scriptis nondum obnoxiis, nisi intra dictos limites, vel quamlibet earundem partem, actu commorati fuerint ; in quo casu, dictæ incorporationis et societatis præceptis et regulis, sicut alii in eadem incorporati, solummodo subjicientur : et dictum Medicorum Collegium, more prædicto erigendum, per præsentes obligatur quemvis hominem seu homines in dictis Universitatibus laurea doctorandos, absque quovis prævio seu antecendente examine, sed solummodo ad ipsorum diplomatis, seu ad gradus admissionis Præsidi dicti Medicorum Collegii productionem licentiare.

Per præsentes omnimodo specialiter providetur, quod jurium et privilegiorum supra scriptorum dicto Medicorum Collegio concessio nullo modo præjudicabit quemvis artium magistri gradum in qualibet dicti regni universitate nactum, et statim medicinæ praxin exercentem, vel ad doctoris gradum in quavis ex prædictis

College has no power to erect a Medical School or to confer Degrees.

Graduates of the Scotch Universities may practise in Edinburgh without Fine.

Must be subject to the Bye-Laws of the College.

Not to prejudice Masters of Art ;

or Graduates of celebrated Foreign Universities.

universitatibus, seu qualibet celebri universitate extera admissum, quo minus viri hisce qualitatibus instructi, ad literarum suarum patentium a dictis universitatibus domi aut peregre Præsidi dicti Collegii productionem, intra limites præscriptos practicare licentientur, nullo præeunte examine.

Specialiter itidem providetur, quod publici medicinæ professores respectivarum universitatum hujus regni, ad eorum Præsidi Collegii supplicationem, tanquam socii honorarii ejusdem societatis admittentur.

Et postremo, fideliter promittimus in verbo Principis, hoc præsens diploma in hoc currenti Parliamento ratificatum iri, et per præsentes status Parliamenti idem conformiter ratificari requirimus. In cujus rei testimonium,

præsentibus magnum Sigillum nostrum appendi mandavimus, apud aulam nostram de Whitehall, vigesimo nono die mensis Novembris, anno Domini millesimo sexcentesimo octogesimo primo, et anno regni nostri trigesimo tertio.

Per signaturam manu S. D. N. Regis suprascriptam.

Charter of Ratification

IN FAVOUR OF THE

ROYAL COLLEGE OF PHYSICIANS,

EDINBURGH,

Dated June 16, 1685.

*At Edinburgh, the Sixteenth day of June, One Thousand
Six Hundred eighty and five years.*

OUR SOVEREIGN LORD, with advice and consent of the
Estates of this present Parliament, ratifies and approves,
and for His Majesty and his successors perpetually con-
firms, the Letters Patent granted by His Majesty's
dearest brother, King CHARLES the Second, of ever
blessed memory, whereof the tenor follows.

*Ratification
and approval
of Charter.*

[*Here the Letters-Patent are engrossed* verbatim.]

Together with all acts, decrees, and sentences of His
Majesty's Privy Council, or of the Lords of Session, or
of any other judicatory within this kingdom, conceived
in favour of the Royal College of Physicians, for making
the Patent above written, and privileges therein contained, effectual: And specially, but prejudice of the
generality, an Act of His Majesty's Privy Council, of the
date the twenty-first day of November, one thousand
six hundred eighty and four years, ordaining the
said Royal College, at least twice a year, to visit all

*Ratification of
Act of Privy
Council, 1684,
ordaining the
College to visit
all Apothecaries'
Shops twice a
year.*

apothecaries' shops and chambers within Edinburgh, suburbs and liberties thereof, calling to their assistance one or two of the eldest or ablest of the brotherhood of the apothecaries; as also, that they desire one of the Bailies of Edinburgh, or respective Magistrates of the place where the shops to be visited do lie, to grant their

Magistrates to grant their effectual concurrence.

concurrence in the said visitation; and these Bailies or Magistrates are, by the said Act, ordained, upon any such desire, to grant their effectual concurrence for ejecting and destroying all corrupt and insufficient drugs: and also ordaining, that the apothecaries, when required,

Apothecaries to receive Visitors with respect.

shall attend and assist the said physicians; and that all masters of apothecaries' shops or chambers, or their servants, receive these visitors of the shops with all respect, and expose to their view all the drugs that shall be called for; and that upon oath, to be administered both to themselves and servants; and shall quietly and peaceably suffer the drugs that shall be found insufficient by the said physicians to be ejected and destroyed, as they will be answerable; And sicklike, ordaining that no persons who have not already been examined and admitted by the fraternity of apothecaries, be suffered in any time coming, by the Magistrates aforesaid, to

None to open Apothecaries' Shops who have not been examined by the Fraternity of Apothecaries, or by President and Censors of the College.

keep any apothecaries' shops or chambers, except such allenarly as shall be tried and approven by the President and Censors of the said Royal College: And in like manner, ane act of the Lords of Session, dated the twenty-first day of March last bypast, proceeding upon suspension, at the instance of an chirurgeon-apothecary,

Ratification of Act of Lords of Session, dated 21st March 1824.

of a sentence pronounced by the President and Censors of the said Royal College, for unwarrantable practice of Medicine: whereby it was found by the said Lords of Session, that where the Magistrates of Edinburgh refuse or delay or give concurrence to punish delinquents, that

the College, in that case, have both the judicative and
executive power, in all and sundry heads, points, articles,
circumstances, and conditions, contained in the said
Letters Patent, and Act above mentioned, and after the
terms and tenor thereof, in all points : And His Majesty,
with advice and consent foresaid, wills and grants, and
for His Majesty and his successors, decerns and ordains,
That this present ratification is, and shall be, as valid,
sufficient and effectual, to the said Royal College, and
their successors, as if the acts above mentioned were
herein at length *de verbo in verbum* specially insert and
engrossed : Whereanent our said Sovereign Lord, with
advice and consent foresaid, for His Majesty and his
successors, hath dispensed, and by their presents
dispenses for ever.—Extracted forth of the Records of
Parliament, by George Viscount of Tarbat, Lord M'Leod
and Castlehaven, Clerk to His Majesty's Parliament,
Council Registers and Rolls, &c.

TARBAT, CLER. REG.

ROYAL WARRANT

FOR

Charter of Incorporation

IN FAVOUR OF THE

ROYAL COLLEGE OF PHYSICIANS

OF EDINBURGH,

16th August 1861.

VICTORIA R.

VICTORIA, by the Grace of God, of the United King-dom of Great Britain and Ireland, Queen; Defender of the Faith:

Whereas the Royal College of Physicians of Edin-burgh have, by their Petition, humbly represented unto Us that our Royal Predecessor Charles the Second was pleased to erect and incorporate the said College by Charter or Letters Patent, bearing date at Whitehall, the twenty-ninth day of November, one thousand six hundred and eighty-one, in the thirty-third year of his reign, which Charter was afterwards ratified, approved, and confirmed by an Act of the Scottish Parliament, bearing date the sixteenth day of June, one thousand six hundred and eighty-five; and that the establish-ment of the said College has fulfilled the high purposes

Preamble and History of Foundation.

Success of
College in
advancing
Medical science.
of consolidating the medical profession, elevating its
character and dignity, and encouraging and advancing
medical learning and science: And whereas the said
College have also represented unto Us, that by an Act
passed in the twenty-first and twenty-second year of
our reign, intituled "An Act to regulate the Qualifications of Practitioners in Medicine and Surgery," it
was enacted that it should be lawful for Us to grant to
the Corporation of the Royal College of Physicians of
Edinburgh a new Charter, and thereby to give to the
said College of Physicians the name of "The Royal
College of Physicians of Scotland," and that it should
be lawful for the said Royal College of Physicians,
under their Common Seal, to accept such new Charter,
and that such acceptance should operate as a surrender
of all Charters heretofore granted to the said Corporation; and that by another Act, passed in the twenty-
Medical Act of
1858.
second year of our reign, intituled "An Act to amend
the Medical Act (1858)," it was enacted that the term
"Member" should be added to the Qualifications de-
scribed in the schedule to the first-mentioned Act, in
reference to the said College; and further, that by
another Act, passed in the twenty-third and twenty-
fourth year of our reign, intituled "An Act to amend
the Medical Act (1858)," it was enacted that any new
Charter to be granted to the said College may be
granted either by and in its present name, or, as provided by the Medical Act, by and in the name of the
Changes
required in
Original Charter.
Royal College of Physicians of Scotland: And whereas
the said College have further represented to Us that the
said Charter granted by our Royal Predecessor contains
various provisions, which, by reason of the great changes
that have taken place in the practice of medicine, have
altogether gone into desuetude, and that it is expedient,

and would be for the benefit of the said College, and of the medical profession, that a new Charter should be granted to the said College, by and in its present name, in pursuance of the provisions of the said Acts: Now know ye, that We, taking the premises into our Royal consideration of our especial grace, certain knowledge, and mere motion, have given, granted, and ordained, and by these presents, for Us, our heirs and successors, do give, grant, and ordain, as follows (that is to say) :—

New Charter to be given to the College in its present name.

I. Alexander Wood, Doctor of Medicine, President; James Young Simpson, Doctor of Medicine, Vice-President; and Peter Fairbairn, William Seller, Charles Bell, William Henry Lowe, Alexander Keiller, and William Tennant Gairdner, Members of the Council of the said College, and their successors in office, and the other existing Fellows of the said College, and all other persons who shall hereafter be admitted or elected Fellows and Members of the said College, as hereinafter provided, shall be and are hereby united and incorporated into one body politic and corporate, by the name of "The Royal College of Physicians of Edinburgh," and shall by that name have perpetual succession, and a Common Seal, with power to break, alter, and renew the same from time to time, and may by that name sue and be sued; and the College shall at all times hereafter be capable in law to take, purchase, possess, hold, and enjoy, for the uses and purposes of the College, any lands, tenements, or other heritages, and personal estate not exceeding in the whole the yearly value of Ten Thousand Pounds, and, if necessary, to sell, dispone, and convey the same, and to lend money on heritable or moveable, real or personal securities, and to hold goods and chattels for the uses and purposes of the

First Fellows named in Charter.

Power of College to have Common Seal:

to hold Lands, etc.

College; and all charters, dispositions, securities, and other deeds or instruments affecting heritable or moveable, real or personal property, to be granted in favour of the College, may be taken in their corporate name, or to Trustees, on behalf of the College; and all charters, dispositions, or other deeds or instruments to be granted by the College, shall be under the Common Seal, and shall be subscribed by three of the Trustees, and by the President, or Treasurer, or Secretary of the College, for the time being.

II. All property, heritable and moveable, real and personal, wheresoever situated, and all feu-charters, dispositions, bonds, instruments of sasine, leases, agreements, and other deeds and instruments, and vouchers of such property, or relating thereto, which have been already acquired by, or taken, granted, or executed in favour of the said Royal College of Physicians of Edinburgh, or any person or persons, as Trustee or Trustees, or otherwise, for the use or on behalf of the said College, whether the same be held absolutely or in security, and in general all estate and effects, and all debts, obligations, rights, interests, liberties, privileges, and immunities of and belonging to the said College, or vested in any person or persons for the benefit of the said College at the time of the granting of these presents, shall be, and the same are hereby transferred to and vested in the Royal College of Physicians of Edinburgh hereby incorporated, as fully as if the same had been acquired by, or taken, granted, or executed in favour of the College after the granting of these presents; and the same shall in future be held, managed, sold, conveyed, assigned, leased, discharged, or otherwise disposed of by the College, under their corporate name of "The Royal College of Physicians of Edinburgh," without the necessity of any connecting or continuing title, or separate investiture, or writing, or procedure, other than these presents.

III. The existing Fellows of the Royal College of Physicians of Edinburgh, at the time of the granting of these presents, shall be the first Fellows of the College hereby incorporated.

Existing Fellows to be first Fellows of the College.

IV. The Fellows may, from time to time, elect and admit to be Fellows and Members of the College such persons as they shall think fit and qualified, in such manner, at such times, under such regulations, and on payment of such fees, as may, from time to time, be directed by the Bye-Laws.

Fellows to have power to elect Fellows and Members.

V. The Fellows may, from time to time, admit to be Licentiates of the College, any persons who shall have gone through such course of studies, and passed such examinations, or submitted to such other regulations, and paid such fees, as may, from time to time, be directed by the Bye-Laws; and the existing Licentiates of the Royal College of Physicians of Edinburgh, at the time of the granting of these presents, shall be Licentiates of the College hereby incorporated.

Fellows to have power to admit Licentiates.

VI. If it shall at any time hereafter appear that any Fellow, Member, or Licentiate of the College has obtained admission to or licence from the College, or the Royal College of Physicians of Edinburgh, by any fraud, false statement, or imposition, or that he has violated any bye-law, rule, or regulation of the College, then, and in every such case, and after such previous notice to, and such hearing of, such Fellow, Member, or Licentiate, as under the circumstances the Council shall think proper, it shall be lawful for the Fellows, with the concurrence of not less than three-fourths of their number, present at a Meeting, specially summoned for the purpose, to pass such censure or sentence of suspension against the Fellow,

Fellows to have power of suspension or expulsion of Fellows, Members, or Licentiates.

Procedure for suspension or expulsion.

Member, or Licentiate so offending, as shall be determined at such Meeting, or to expel such Fellow, Member,
or Licentiate from the College; and upon any such
sentence of suspension or expulsion being passed, such
Fellow, Member, or Licentiate shall cease to be a Fellow,
Member, or Licentiate of the College, and to have any
right or interest in or to the property or funds of the
College, either absolutely, or for such time as shall be
specified in the sentence of suspension; and all the
rights and privileges granted to such Fellow, Member,
or Licentiate, as the case may be, shall cease and determine upon such expulsion or during such suspension.

VII. Ordinary Meetings of the Fellows, for the
transaction of the business of the College, shall be held
at such times as shall, from time to time, be fixed by
the Bye-Laws.

VIII. Extraordinary Meetings of the Fellows, for the
consideration and disposal of any special business of the
College, may be called by the President or the Council
at any time when the same shall be deemed necessary;
and it shall be incumbent on the President to call an
Extraordinary Meeting of the fellows on a requisition to
that effect, specifying the purpose of such Meeting, and
signed by any five of the Fellows, being delivered to
him or to the Secretary of the College; and notice of all
Extraordinary Meetings of the Fellows shall be given in
such manner as shall be directed by the Bye-Laws.

IX. Ordinary Meetings of the Fellows and Members
for the consideration of matters affecting the general
interests of the medical profession and the public, shall
be held at such times as shall from time to time be
fixed by the Bye-Laws.

X. Extraordinary Meetings of the Fellows and
Members may be called by the President or the Council

Ordinary Meetings of Fellows.

Extraordinary Meetings of Fellows.

Ordinary Meetings of Fellows and Members.

Extraordinary Meetings of Fellows and Members.

at any time when the same shall be deemed necessary ; and it shall be incumbent on the President to call an Extraordinary Meeting of the Fellows and Members on a requisition to that effect, specifying the purpose of such Meeting, and signed by any five of the Fellows or Members, being delivered to him or to the Secretary of the College; and notice of all Extraordinary Meetings of the Fellows and Members shall be given in such manner as shall be directed by the Bye-Laws ; and any matters affecting the general interests of the medical profession and the public, which shall be specified in such requisition and notice, may be considered at any such Extraordinary Meeting of Fellows and Members.

XI. The Council of the College shall consist of the President and six of the Fellows resident in Edinburgh, or within seven miles of the General Post-Office in Edinburgh, by the nearest public highway. *Council of College.*

XII. A meeting of the Fellows shall be held annually, on such day and at such hour as may, from time to time, be fixed by the Bye-Laws, for the election of the President and the Members of the Council. *Meeting for election of President and Council.*

XIII. The Council shall elect the Examiners of the College, and shall also elect a Treasurer, Secretary, Clerk, and such other officers as may be deemed necessary, annually, and as often as occasion may require, or vacancies occur, by death, resignation, or otherwise. *Council to elect Office-Bearers.*

XIV. The Council shall, with the approval of the Fellows, nominate four Fellows, who, along with the Treasurer, shall be Trustees for the College ; and as often as a vacancy shall arise by death, resignation, or otherwise, the Council shall fill up the same ; and the existing Trustees of the said College at the time of the granting of these presents, shall be the first Trustees under these presents. *Trustees.*

Existing Office-Bearers shall continue in Office till next Election Meeting.

XV. The existing Members of the Council of the said College at the time of the granting of these presents shall continue in office, and be the first Council of the College under these presents; and the existing President shall continue in office, and be the first President of the College under these presents; and the existing Treasurer, Secretary, Clerk, and other officers of the said College shall continue to hold their several offices until the first Annual Meeting of the Fellows for the election of the Members of the Council and the President, to be held after the granting of these presents.

Vacancies in the Presidentship or Council may be filled up by Fellows.

XVI. If it shall happen that any election of the President or of the Members of the Council, or any of them, shall not be made on the day appointed for that purpose, or if any Fellow elected to any such office shall not accept thereof, the person or persons then filling such office or offices shall continue to fill the same until another person or persons shall be appointed thereto; and the Fellows present at any Ordinary Meeting, or at an Extraordinary Meeting, to be called as herein provided, may elect out of the Fellows a person or persons to fill the said office or offices, or such of them as shall not have been filled up, or shall be vacant by reason of non-acceptance as aforesaid, for such part of the year of office as shall be then unexpired.

Filling of Vacancies caused by Death or Resignation.

XVII. If the President or any Member of the Council shall die or resign before the expiration of the year, or other time for which he shall have been elected, the Fellows present at any Ordinary Meeting, or at an Extraordinary Meeting to be called as herein provided, may elect out of the Fellows a President or Member of the Council, as the case may be, in the place or stead of the President or Member of the Council so dying or resigning; and the Fellow or Fellows so elected shall serve for the remainder of the year of office, or other time, for which the President or Member of the Council so dying or resigning was elected.

XVIII. The property and affairs of the College shall be managed and administered by the Fellows and the Council, in such manner, and under such regulations, as may from time to time be directed by the Bye-Laws.

Management of Property and Affairs of College.

XIX. All Acts done by the President, or by any Meeting of the Council, or by any person acting as President or Member of the Council, shall, notwithstanding it may be afterwards discovered that there was any defect or informality in the election or appointment of any such President or Member of the Council acting as aforesaid, or that they, or any of them, were or was disqualified, or that there was any vacancy in the office of President, or in the Council, be as valid as if every such person had been duly elected or appointed and was duly qualified, and as if no such vacancy had existed.

Acts of President or Council not to be invalidated by any Informality in their Election.

XX. It shall be lawful for the Fellows, and We do hereby grant full power and authority to them, from time to time, to make Bye-Laws, Rules, and Regulations, for promoting the Science of Medicine, for duly ordering the practice of the same, and for the good government, order, and direction of the College; for the admission and election of Fellows, Members, and Licentiates, and fixing and defining the qualifications of persons to be so admitted and elected; for the management of the property, funds, and affairs of the College; for the regulation of all meetings, actings, and proceedings of the College, and of the Council and Fellows, and of the Fellows and Members, and of the several Office-Bearers

Fellows to have power to make Bye-Laws.

and Officers of the College, and fixing the times for holding such meetings; and for the division of the persons composing the body corporate of the College into such orders of Resident and Non-resident Fellows or Members, or otherwise; and for giving and assigning to these orders such qualifications, powers, privileges, exemptions, and restrictions, as the Fellows may from time to time determine; and it shall be lawful for the Fellows, from time to time, to repeal, vary, or alter such Bye-Laws, Rules, and Regulations: Provided that every Bye-Law, Rule, and Regulation to be hereafter made, and every repeal, variation, or alteration of any existing Bye-Law, Rule, or Regulation, shall be submitted to and approved by an Ordinary or Extraordinary Meeting of the Fellows, in such form and manner as they shall from time to time direct and appoint.

All new Rules or any change to be approved by a Meeting of the Fellows.

XXI. The Bye-Laws, Rules, and Regulations of the said Royal College of Physicians of Edinburgh existing and in force at the time of the granting of these presents, except in so far as the same may be inconsistent with these presents, shall be and continue to be the Bye-Laws, Rules, and Regulations of the College hereby incorporated, until the same are repealed, altered, or varied, in whole or in part.

Existing Bye-Laws to continue in force unless inconsistent with this Charter.

XXII. The College hereby incorporated, and the Fellows, Members, and Licentiates thereof, shall and may have, exercise, and enjoy all such powers, functions, rights, and privileges, as the said Royal College of Physicians of Edinburgh, or the Fellows, Members, or Licentiates thereof respectively, before the granting of these presents, had or might have had, exercised or enjoyed under and by virtue of the several Acts of our reign hereinbefore recited.

College to have same powers as it possessed before the granting of this Charter.

XXIII. The following words and expressions in these presents shall have the several meanings hereby assigned to them ; that is to say :—

Interpretation Clause.

The expression "the College" shall mean "The Royal College of Physicians of Edinburgh," hereby incorporated ; the words "Council," "Fellows," "Members," and "Licentiates," shall respectively mean the Council, Fellows, Members, and Licentiates of the College for the time being ; and the word "Bye-Laws" shall mean and include the Bye-Laws, Rules, and Regulations of the College, made *or to be made, as herein* provided.

And with the consent of the College, testified by their acceptance of these presents, and by the authority of the Act of our reign first before recited, We do hereby accept the surrender made to Us by the Royal College of Physicians of Edinburgh of the said Charter or Letters Patent granted by our Royal Predecessor King Charles the Second, and do hereby revoke, annul, and make void the same: And We do hereby, for Us, our heirs and successors, further grant to the College, that this our Charter shall be in and by all things valid and effectual in law, according to the true intent and meaning of the same, and shall be held, construed, and adjudged in the most favourable and beneficial sense, and for the best advantage of the College, notwithstanding any misrecital, defect, uncertainty, or imperfections whatsoever : And We do hereby, for Us, our heirs and successors, covenant, grant, and agree to and with the College, that We, our heirs and successors, shall and will, from time to time, and at all times hereafter, upon their humble suit and request, give and grant to the College all such further and other powers, privileges, and authorities for

Old Charter revoked.

rendering more effectual this our grant, according to the true intent and meaning of these presents, as We, our heirs and successors, can or may lawfully grant, and as shall be reasonably advised and devised by the Council learned in the law of the College for the time being.

This Charter to pass the Seal.

And We further will and command that this our Charter do pass the Seal appointed by the Treaty of Union to be kept and used in Scotland in place of the Great Seal thereof *per saltum*, without passing any other Seal or Register : For which these presents shall be, as well to the Director of our Chancery for writing the same, as to the Keeper of the said Seal for causing the said Seal to be appended thereto, a sufficient warrant.

Given, at our Court at Saint James's the sixteenth day of August 1861, in the Twenty-fifth year of our reign.

By Her Majesty's Command,

G. GREY.

𝕮𝖍𝖆𝖗𝖙𝖆 𝕴𝖓𝖈𝖔𝖗𝖕𝖔𝖗𝖆𝖙𝖎𝖔𝖓𝖎𝖘

IN FAVOREM

COLLEGII REGII MEDICORUM

EDINENSIS.

1861.

VICTORIA, Dei gratia Britanniarum Regina; Fidei Defensor; OMNIBUS probis hominibus ad quos præsentes literæ Nostræ pervenerint salutem:

Quum Nobis Collegium Regium Medicorum Edinense, petitione sua, reverentissime ostendisset, placuisse Regio Nostro Antecessori Carolo Secundo, Charta sive Literis Patentibus, in Aula apud Whitehall datis, vigesimo nono die mensis Novembris anno Domini millesimo sexcentesimo octogesimo primo, anno regni illius trigesimo tertio, dictum Collegium constituere et incorporare: et eandem chartam postea, per Actum Parliamenti Scotiæ latum, die decimo sexto mensis Junii, anno Domini millesimo sexcentesimo octogesimo quinto, sancitam, approbatam, et confirmatam fuisse: necnon ejusdem Collegii institutionem, medicinæ professionem consolidando, gratiam dignitatemque ejus attollendo,

Preamble and History of Foundation.

doctrinam scientiamque medicam suscitando atque pro-
movendo, gravia implevisse consilia. ET QUUM Nobis
dictum Collegium quoque ostendisset, decretum esse
per actum latum, vigesimo primo et vigesimo secundo
annis Nostri regni, cui titulus est, vernaculo sermone, "An
Act to regulate the Qualifications of Practitioners in
Medicine and Surgery," ut Nobis liceat novam concedere
Chartam Collegio Regio Medicorum Edinensi, in qua
charta, dicto Collegio nomen, vernaculo sermone, "The
Royal College of Physicians of Scotland," daretur, utque
dicto Collegio liceat novam hanc Chartam sub sigillo suo
communi accipere, qua quidem accepta, id ipsum pro
deditione omnium Chartarum catenus dicto Collegio concessarum haberetur : porro decretum esse per aliud actum
latum, anno Nostri regni vigesimo secundo, cui, vernaculo

sermone, titulus est, "An Act to amend the Medical Act
(1858)," ut verbum, vernaculo sermone, "Member,"
qualificationibus enumeratis in schedula acti primum
recitati quatenus ad dictum Collegium attinet, adjicere-
tur : deinde autem decretum esse per aliud actum latum,
vigesimo tertio et vigesimo quarto annis Nostri regni,
cui titulus est, vernaculo sermone, "An Act to amend
the Medical Act (1858)," ut quæcunque nova Charta
dicto Collegio concederetur, concedi possit, vel ex et
sub præsenti ejus nomine, vel, sicuti provisum est in
Acto cui, vernaculo sermone, titulus est, "The Medical
Act," ex et sub nomine, "The Royal College of Physicians of Scotland."

ET QUUM præterea Nobis dictum Collegium ostendisset dictam Chartam a Regio Nostro Antecessore
concessam quædam in se habere provisa, quæ, propter
ingentes in medicinæ arte mutationes, prorsus obsole-
verint ; necnon et convenire et beneficio fore dicto
Collegio et medicinæ professioni, novam dicto Collegio

Chartam concedere, ex et sub præsenti ejus nomine, quatenus licet per recitatorum Actorum decreta. NUNC SCIATIS: Nos hæc præmissa animo Nostro Nobiscum versantes, singulari ex gratia, vera opinione, meroque motu, DEDIMUS CONCESSIMUS et ORDINAVIMUS et his præsentibus literis pro Nobis, pro Nostris heredibus, et pro Nostris successoribus, DAMUS CONCEDIMUS et ORDINAMUS, quæ sequuntur, scilicet:

1. Alexandrum Wood, Medicinæ Doctorem, Præsidem; Jacobum Young Simpson, Medicinæ Doctorem, Vicepræsidis; et Petrum Fairbairn, Gulielmum Seller, Carolum Bell, Gulielmum Henricum Lowe, Alexandrum Keiller, et Gulielmum Tennant Gairdner, qui Concilii dicti Collegii sunt, et illorum successores in eo munere; necnon ceteros dicti Collegii exsistentes Socios, aliosque omnes, quicunque posthac dicti Collegii Socii, et Membra admissi aut electi fuerint, ut postea provisum sit, conjunctum iri et in unum corpus politicum et incorporatum constitutum iri, et hac charta revera conjungi et in unum corpus politicum et incorporatum constitui sub nomine, "The Royal College of Physicians of Edinburgh;" eosque, eo nomine, perpetuam habituros successionem, et sigillum commune cum potestate idem frangendi mutandi et renovandi identidem, et eosdem, sub eo nomine, in jus vocare et in jus vocari posse. Et, omni futuro tempore, jure licitum iri huic Collegio capere, emere, possidere, tenere et in usufructu habere pro usibus et commodis Collegii terras, tenementa, aut alias hereditates et bona personalia, quorum totus annuus reditus decem millia librarum non excedat, ac, si necesse fuerit, eadem vendere, disponere et alienare: necnon pecuniam fœnorare sub satisdatione heritabili aut mobili, reali aut personali, et pro usibus inceptisque Collegii bona resque tenere: præterea omnes chartas, dispositiones, vadimonia aliaque

New Charter to be given to the College in its present name.

First Fellows named in Charter.

Power of College to have Common Seal;

to hold Lands, etc.

documenta aut instrumenta quæ attineant ad res heritabiles aut mobiles, reales aut personales, quæ in Collegii beneficium data sint, vel in nomine ejus incorporato, vel a Fiduciariis pro Collegio, teneri posse : omnesque chartas, dispositiones aut alia documenta aut instrumenta a Collegio concedenda, datum iri sub communi sigillo ; atque a tribus ex Fiduciariis et vel a Præside vel a Thesaurense vel a Secretario, quicunque his Collegii muneribus pro tempore perfungantur, iri subscriptum.

2. Omnes res heritabiles et mobiles, reales et personales, ubicunque positæ sint, et omnes feudæ chartas, dispositiones, obligationes, instrumenta sasinæ, codicillos locationis, pacta aliaque documenta et instrumenta, et vernaculo sermone "vouchers" earum rerum, aut ad eas

spectantia, quæ jam acquisita fuerint a Collegio, aut capta, aut concessa, aut peracta in commodum dicti Collegii Regii Medicorum Edinensis, aut in commodum cujusvis hominis aut quorumvis hominum ut Fiduciarii aut Fiduciariorum, vel aliter, in usum aut in partem dicti Collegii, sive eadem absolute, sive in securitatem, retenta fuerint : et, in universum, omnes res et bona, omnemque pecuniam debitam, obligationes, jura, commoda, libertates, privilegia, et immunitates dicti Collegii et quæ dicto Collegio possidentur, vel quæ a quolibet homine aut quibuslibet hominibus tenentur pro dicti Collegii beneficio, quo tempore hæ literæ conceduntur, transferenda esse, et eadem revera transferri et dari possidenda Collegio Regio Medicorum Edinensi his literis constituto, tam plene quam si eadem acquisita fuissent ab eo Collegio, aut capta, aut concessa, aut peracta in ejus Collegii commodum post hasce literas concessas, eademque omni tempore futuro esse tenenda, dirigenda, vendenda, alienanda, assignanda, locitanda, liberanda aut alio modo disponenda ab eo Collegio sub nomine incorporato "The

Royal College of Physicians of Edinburgh ;" atque nihil opus futurum esse titulo connectente aut continuante aut separato infeofamento aut alio scripto aut processu præter has præsentes literas.

3. Illos qui exsistunt Socii Collegii Regii Medicorum Edinensis tempore, quo hæ literæ conceduntur, Collegii sic constituti primos Socios futuros esse.

Existing Fellows to be first Fellows of the College.

4. Sociis licitum iri identidem eligere et in Societatem ejus Collegii Sociorum et Membrorum ascribere illos viros quos habiles idoneosque censeant, eo modo, iis temporibus, sub iis regulis, et eo soluto præmio, sicut leges propriæ Collegii, alio atque alio tempore latæ, jusserint.

Fellows to have power to elect Fellows and Members.

5. Sociis licitum iri identidem in numerum ejus Collegii Permissorum ascribere illos qui eum studiorum curriculum peregerint, et eas probationes subierint, aut sese aliis regulis conformarint, et ea præmia solverint, sicut propriæ Collegii leges, alio atque alio tempore latæ, jusserint : et illos qui Permissi exsistunt Collegii Regii Medicorum Edinensis tempore, quo hæ literæ conceduntur, Collegii sic constituti fore Permissos.

Fellow to have power to admit Licentiates.

6. Si aliquo futuro tempore pateret quemvis Collegii Socium aut Membrum in Societatem Collegii Regii Medicorum Edinensis ascriptum fuisse, aut quemvis Permissum in numerum Collegii Permissorum ascriptum fuisse, ex dolo aut fraude aut mendacio, aut alterutrum quamlibet Collegii legem propriam, quamlibet regulam, aut quodlibet præceptum perfregisse, tunc et in omni hujusmodi exemplo, quum is, sive Socius, sive Membrum, sive Permissus, de ea re certior factus et postea auditus fuisset, ea modo, quo, cunctis rebus consideratis, concilio visum fuerit, sociis iri licitum, dummodo tres partes sociorum ex quatuor in toto conventu ad hanc rem convocato concurrant, cum sive Socium, sive Membrum sive Permissum aut censura reprehendere, aut in

Fellows to have power of suspension or expulsion of Fellows, Members, or Licentiates.

Procedure for suspension or expulsion.

cum suspensionis sententiam dicere, prout ei conventui
placuerit; aut eum sive Socium, sive Membrum, sive
Permissum e Collegio expellere; et tali suspensionis aut
expulsionis sententia decreta, istum, sive Socium, sive
Membrum, sive Permissum, non amplius fore Socium,
Membrum, aut Permissum Collegii; nec habiturum esse
aliquod jus nec aliquod beneficium in Collegii bonis et
pecunia, aut omnino, aut per temporis spatium quod
in suspensionis sententia edictum sit, et omnia jura et
privilegia huic, sive Socio, sive Membro, sive Permisso,
concessa, prout res se habeat, ex hujusmodi expulsione
finitum iri, aut durante hujusmodi suspensione vacatura
esse.

7. Ordinarios Sociorum conventus ad transigenda
Collegii negotia iis temporibus advocandos esse quæ,
alio atque alio tempore, legibus propriis præscripta
fuerint.

8. Extraordinarios Sociorum conventus ad consider-
andum et judicandum quodvis speciale Collegii negotium
advocari posse a Præside aut Concilio iis temporibus, ubi
opus esse visum fuerit, et extraordinarium Sociorum
conventum a Præside advocandum esse, quoties requisitio
talem conventum postulans et ejusdem propositum indicans, et a quinque ex Sociis subscripta illi vel Secretario
Collegii tradita fuerit, et de omnibus extraordinariis
sociorum conventibus præmonendum esse, eo modo, quo
leges propriæ jusserint.

9. Ordinarios Sociorum et Membrorum conventus ad
res considerandas quæ ad universæ professionis Medicinæ
commodum, commodumque publicum spectent, advocandos esse, iis temporibus, quæ alio atque alio tempore, a
legibus propriis præscripta fuerint.

10. Extraordinarios Sociorum et Membrorum conventus advocari posse a Præside aut Concilio iis tem-

poribus, quibus opus esse visum fuerit; et extraordinarium Sociorum et Membrorum conventum a Præside
advocandum esse quoties requisitio talem conventum
postulans et ejusdem propositum indicans, et a quinque
ex Sociis aut Membris subscripta illi vel Secretario Collegii tradita fuerit; et de omnibus his extraordinariis
Sociorum et Membrorum conventibus præmonendum
esse eo modo quo leges propriæ jusserint ; et omnes res
quæ ad universæ professionis medicinæ commodum commodumque publicum spectent, in aliquo tali Sociorum
et Membrorum extraordinario conventu, quatenus in ea
requisitione et præmonitione indicatæ fuerint, considerari
posse.

11. Concilium Collegii constituendum esse ex Præside
et sex Sociis Edinburgi habitantibus aut intra septem
millia passuum a domo, vernaculo sermone, "the General
Post Office of Edinburgh," appellata, per proximam viam
publicam.

12. Conventum Sociorum quotannis habendum esse,
eo die, et ea hora, sicut, alio atque alio tempore, leges
propriæ jusserint, ad Præsidem eligendum, et ad eos, qui
in Concilio futuri sint, eligendos.

13. Eligendos esse a Concilio Collegii Examinatores,
etiamque Thesaurensem, Secretarium, vernaculo sermone
"Clerk," omnesque alios administros quibus opus fuerit,
quotannis et quoties res postulet, si morte, resignatione
aut aliter, vacat officium.

14. Eligendos esse a Concilio, annuentibus Sociis,
quatuor Socios qui simul cum Thesaurense Fiduciarii
futuri sint Collegii ; et quoties, vel morte vel resignatione,
vel aliter, officium vacat, Concilio sufficiendum esse alium
Socium in prioris Fiduciarii locum ; et dicti Collegii
Fiduciarios, tempore quo hæ literæ conceduntur, futuros
esse primos, sub his literis, Fiduciarios.

15. Socios, qui ex Concilio dicti Collegii sunt, tempore quo conceduntur hæ literæ, in eo munere permansuros esse, et futuros esse, sub his literis, primum Concilium ; et illum, qui Præses est, eodem tempore, usque in eo munere mansurum esse, et primum sub his literis Collegii Præsidem futurum esse ; et illos qui, eodem tempore Thesaurensis, Secretarius, vernaculo sermone "Clerk," ceterique dicti Collegii administri sunt, quemque suum munus retenturum esse, usque ad primum Sociorum annuum conventum ad membra Concilii eligenda, et ad Præsidem eligendum, post has literas concessas, advocandum.

16. Si acciderit ut ulla electio Præsidis, aut membrorum Concilii, aut aliquorum ex his, die statuto non facta fuerit, sive ut aliquis Socius, ad alterutrum officium electus, id non acceperit, illum aut illos, qui tunc hoc munere, aut his muneribus perfunguntur, in eodem aut iisdem permansuros esse, donec alius aut alii in eum locum singuli suffecti fuerint ; et Socios qui adfuerint in aliquo ordinario conventu, aut in extraordinario conventu, ut in his literis provisum est, advocando, posse eligere aliquem aut aliquos ex Sociis qui eo munere aut iis muneribus fungantur, aut ea eorum munerum parte, quæ nondum impleta fuerit, aut quæ vacaverit quia munus non acceptum fuisset, ut dictum est, pro ea portione unius anni post annuam electionem quæ nondum finita est.

17. Si Præses, aut quivis eorum qui Concilio sunt, mortuus fuerit, aut a munere abdicaverit, ante annum completum aut ante aliud aliquod temporis spatium completum, pro quo electus fuisset, Socios qui adsint in aliquo ordinario conventu aut aliquo extraordinario conventu, ut in his literis provisum est advocando, aut Præsidem, aut membrum Concilii, prout res se habeat, ex

Sociis posse eligere, vice et loco Præsidis aut membri
Concilii, qui mortuus fuerit, aut qui a munere abdicaverit : et Socio aut Sociis ita electo aut electis perfun-
gendum esse eo munere aut iis muneribus, per reliquam
partem anni post annuam electionem, aut per aliud
aliquod temporis spatium, pro quo Præses aut membrum
Concilii qui mortuus fuerit, aut qui a munere abdicaverit
electus fuisset.

18. Omnes res, quæ Collegio possidentur, omniaque
Collegii negotia gerenda esse atque administranda Sociis
et Concilio, eo modo et sub iis regulis, sicut, alio atque
alio tempore, leges propriæ jusserint.

19. Omnia acta facta a Præside, aut ab aliquo Concilii conventu, aut ab aliquo fungente Præsidis munere,
aut munere eorum qui sunt in Concilio, etsi postea
patuerit aliquod vitium fuisse aut aliquid solennis usus
prætermissum fuisse, sive in ejus Præsidis, sive in membri
vel membrorum Concilii, electione aut designatione, dum
munere fungebantur ut dictum est, aut eos, aut aliquem
ex iis, jura ad id munus exercendum non habuisse, aut
munus sive Præsidis, sive membri vel membrorum Concilii, eo tempore, vacavisse, habenda esse æque valida,
ac si talis Socius jure electus aut designatus fuisset et
satis lege polleret et nullum munus vacaret.

20. Sociis licitum iri, et Nos his literis concedimus
illis potestatem et auctoritatem, alio atque alio tempore,
decernendi leges proprias (bye-laws), regulas, et præcepta,
quæ medicinæ scientiam promoveant, artemque medendi
rite dirigant ; quæ decus, ordinem, observantiam Collegio
suadeant ; quæ, quomodo eligendi sint Socii, Membra,
Permissi, jubeant ; et quæ conditiones qualificationes,
sub quibus horum singuli sunt admittendi, describant et
proferant ; quæ, quomodo res, pecunia, et negotia Collegii
sint administranda, moneant ; quæ omnium conventuum

Fellows to have power to make Bye-Laws.

et agendi rationum, sive Collegii, sive Concilii et sociorum, sive sociorum et membrorum, sive administrorum
Collegii, omniumque muneribus Collegii fungentium
ordinem ac leges confirment ; et quæ tempora his conventibus advocandis instituant ; quæ illorum, ex quibus
constat corpus societatis, divisionem in ordines, resi-
dentium et non-residentium Sociorum et Membrorum,
aut aliter, regant ; et quæ his ordinibus assignent eas
qualificationes, potestates, privilegia, immunitates et re-
strictiones quæ Sociis placuerit, alio atque alio tempore,
jubere : porro Sociis licitum iri, alio atque alio tempore,
abrogare, variare et mutare hasce leges proprias, regulas,

All new Rules, or any changes, to be approved by a Meeting of the Fellows.

præcepta ; dummodo omnis lex propria, regula aut
præceptum posthac decernendum, et omnis abrogatio,
variatio, aut mutatio, quæ ad aliquam exsistentem legem
propriam, regulam aut præceptum attinet, submissa
Sociis approbata fuerit in conventu Sociorum ordinario
aut extraordinario sub ea forma atque in eo modo, sicut
illi identidem constituerint et jusserint.

Existing Bye-Laws to continue in force unless inconsistent with this Charter.

21. Leges proprias, regulas, præcepta dicti Collegii
Regii Medicorum Edinensis quæ existunt sancita, tempore, quo hæ literæ conceduntur, nisi quatenus his literis
contradixerint esse et futura esse leges proprias, regulas,
et præcepta Collegii his literis constituti, donec aut
omnino, aut ex parte abrogata, variata aut mutata
fuerint.

College to have same power as it possessed before the granting of this Charter.

22. Collegium ita constitutum et ejusdem Socios,
Membra et Permissos, et retinere posse et retenturos,
exercituros, et in usufructu habituros esse omnes potestates, munera, jura, et privilegia quæ Collegium Regium
Medicorum Edinense aut Socii, Membra, aut permissi
ejusdem, antequam hæ literæ concessæ sunt, retinerent
aut retinuissent, exercerent aut exercuissent, in usufructu
haberent aut habuissent, ex decreto Actorum Parliamenti

in Nostro regno, de quibus supra in his literis mentio facta est.

23 Sequentia verba et verborum formulas in his literis has significationes habitura esse quæ iis infra assignantur; scilicet, "Collegium" significare "Collegium Regium Medicorum Edinense" his literis constitutum; verba "Concilium, Socii, Membra et Permissi" significare singulatim Concilium, Socios, Membra et Permissos Collegii pro eo tempore de quo agatur; verba "leges propriæ" significare et includere leges proprias, regulas, et præcepta Collegii lata aut ferenda, sicut in his literis provisum est.

Interpretation Clause.

Et cum Collegii consensu, his literis acceptis significato, et acti Nostri regni primum supra recitati auctoritate, NOS revera, ACCIPIMUS deditionem Nobis factam a Collegio Regio Medicorum Edinensi Chartæ aut Literarum Patentium a Regio Nostro Antecessore Carolo Secundo concessarum, et his literis easdem REVOCAMUS, ABROGAMUS, VACUASQUE REDDIMUS. Et Nos his literis pro Nobis, pro Nostris heredibus, et pro Nostris successoribus, Collegio CONCEDIMUS hanc Nostram Chartam in omnibus rebus et per omnes res futuram esse validam et in lege efficacem secundum verum propositum et ejusdem significationem tenendam, interpretandam et judicandam sensu gratiosiore et utiliore et ad maximum Collegii commodum, non obstante imperfecta qaucunque recitatione, aut defectu aut menda aut errore.

Old Charter revoked.

Et Nos his literis pro Nobis, pro Nostris heredibus, et pro Nostris successoribus, SPONDEMUS et CONCEDIMUS Collegio, et cum illo CONVENIMUS, Nos, Nostros heredes, et Nostros successores, aliis temporibus et semper posthac, quoties a Nobis Collegium reverenter petiverit atque rogaverit DATUROS et CONCESSUROS ESSE

Collegio omnes alias et ulteriores potestates privilegia et auctoritates, ut efficacior hæc nostra CONCESSIO reddatur, secundum verum harum literarum propositum et significationem, quantum Nos, Nostri heredes, et Nostri successores QUEAMUS et POSSIMUS et quatenus ex rei ratione Jurisconsulti docti legibus Collegii moneant et suadeant.

This Charter to pass the Seal.

IN CUJUS REI TESTIMONIUM HUIC PRÆSENTI CHARTÆ NOSTRÆ SIGILLUM NOSTRUM PER UNIONIS TRACTATUM CUSTODIENDUM ET IN SCOTIA VICE ET LOCO MAGNI SIGILLI EJUSDEM UTEND. ORDINAT. APPENDI MANDAVIMUS APUD AULAM NOSTRAM APUD ST. JAMES DECIMO SEXTO DIE MENSIS AUGUSTI ANNO DOMINI MILLESIMO OCTINGENTESIMO SEXAGESIMO PRIMO ET NOSTRI REGNI VIGESIMO QUINTO ANNI.

Per signaturam manu,
S. D. N. Reginæ suprascriptam.

Sealed at Edinburgh, the thirty-first day of October, in the year one thousand eight hundred and sixty-one.

Written to the Seal, and Registered the thirty-first day of October 1861.

JAS. HAY MACKENZIE,
Depute Keeper of the Seal.
£80 Scots.

JAMES P. HALLEY,
Depute Director of Chancery.

MORRISON AND GIBB, PRINTERS, EDINBURGH.